Sunday, June 27, 2010

Dear Miriam עליה,

Happy Birthday!

I read this book and thought of you — of all the good deeds you do — large and small. It is a זכות to be your friend.

May הקב"ה bench you for all of your מעשים טובים with נחת and בריאות and gezunt and everything wonderful עד"ק

Love,
Corinne

1 SMALL DEED

A SHAAR PRESS PUBLICATION

CAN CHANGE THE WORLD

True stories of
everyday encounters
with extraordinary results

Compiled by **NACHMAN SELTZER**

Edited by **Miriam Lea Rosenberg**
and **Sara Chava Mizrahi**

© Copyright 2010 by Shaar Press

First edition – First impression / June 2010

ALL RIGHTS RESERVED
No part of this book may be reproduced in any form, *photocopy, electronic media, or otherwise without* written *permission from the copyright holder, except by a reviewer who wishes to quote brief passages in connection with a review written for inclusion in magazines or newspapers.*
THE RIGHTS OF THE COPYRIGHT HOLDER WILL BE STRICTLY ENFORCED.

Published by **SHAAR PRESS**
Distributed by MESORAH PUBLICATIONS, LTD.
4401 Second Avenue / Brooklyn, N.Y 11232 / (718) 921-9000

Distributed in Israel by SIFRIATI / A. GITLER
6 Hayarkon Street / Bnei Brak 51127

Distributed in Europe by LEHMANNS
Unit E, Viking Business Park, Rolling Mill Road / Jarrow, Tyne and Wear, NE32 3DP/ England

Distributed in Australia and New Zealand by GOLDS WORLD OF JUDAICA
3-13 William Street / Balaclava, Melbourne 3183 / Victoria Australia

Distributed in South Africa by KOLLEL BOOKSHOP
Ivy Common / 105 William Road / Norwood 2192, Johannesburg, South Africa

ISBN 10: 1-4226-0989-8 / ISBN 13: 978-1-4226-0989-7

Custom bound by Sefercraft, Inc. / 4401 Second Avenue / Brooklyn N.Y. 11232

In loving memory of
REB ARYEH YEHUDAH BEN YITZCHAK

and his dear wife
ADEL BAS REUVEN

*Who were paradigms of love for
the fulfillment of mitzvos
between man and his fellow man.
They were beloved by Heaven
and admired by all who knew them.
May their memory be blessed.*

TABLE OF CONTENTS

A Few Words of Thanks 11
Introduction 13

1. THE SECRET OF SHALOM

Welcome Dividends 21
Ilana's "Hello" 25
Four Lives for a Greeting 28
The Taxi Driver Saves the Day 31
The Woman Who Didn't Say Hello 34
"The Hand of the Tongue" 37
The Gracious Power of a Greeting 39
A Shul With a Mission 42
Just One Hello 44
Rise to the Occasion 48
Greetings 50
A Gift of Life 54
My Brother 57
"She's a Human Being" 59
Homemade Yerushalmi Kiruv 60

2. CAN I HELP?

What the Banker Saw 65
A Chain of Events 70

Speak Now, or Forever Know No Peace	75
Eliezer's Grin	86
Thanking Mrs. Schwartz	88
An Enduring Light	93
Seeds of Comfort	97
South of Lebanon	102
A Welcoming Word	108
Just Say Yes	116
A Fifty-Dollar Blessing	120
A Beggar's Past…and Future	122
Tears of Caring	126
"You Saved His Life!"	128
One Small Act	130

3. BE A MENTSCH

A Mighty Powerful Weapon	137
Open the Door and Let Me In!	144
Just a Clap on the Back	148
Mrs. Happy's Nickel	150
Yossi's Bar Mitzvah	157
The Gypsy Woman	160
An Infusion of Shabbos	162
A Most Unusual Shabbos Guest	165
An Expression of Thanks	169
The Perfect Girl for My Son	171
The Potential in Each Moment	176
Just a Smile and a Wave	183
Just One Brief Question	186
A Story of Kindness and Kiddush Hashem	188
The Real Kaddish	193

4. LIFESAVERS AND LIFE CHANGERS

The Doctor	203
The Inscription	208
The Giver	214
The Right Words at the Right Time	222

A Proud Legacy 226
Fringe Benefits 231
One Kind Word 234
The Magic Words 236
All the Way Home 241
Just a Few Lines 247
With Faith Back Into Life 249
Embracing a Street Kid 252

5. FATEFUL ENCOUNTERS

A Natural Choice 259
Shab*bus* *268*
The Names in the Flap 270
A Few Words That Built a Life 278
The Candle Lady 280
Accept Me as I Am 286
Overcoming Painful Feelings 289
Penetrating Warmth 294
Tear-stained Pages 301

6. FROM OUR GEDOLIM

Thirty Days to Divorce 315
One Greeting for 5,000 Souls 317
Turn Right for Life 320
Once-in-a-Lifetime Opportunity 322
Six Smiles 324
Remembering When Others Have Forgotten 326
This Is How to Greet a Jew 328
Discovering the Gem Among the Rubble 330
A Healing Visit 333
A Matter of Priorities 334

About the Contributors 335
Glossary 339

A FEW WORDS OF THANKS

I would like to express my thanks, first and foremost, to former Knesset Member, chairman of the Degel Hatorah party, Rabbi Avraham Ravitz, *z"l*. When I told him what I would like to achieve with this project, he responded to the concept with such enthusiasm and positive energy that he filled me with the courage and determination to see this through to fruition. He gave generously of his time, coming out several times to meet me in order to advance the project, never standing on ceremony. It was he who put me in touch with those he felt could help bring my vision to fruition. I am deeply indebted to him, and only wish he were here to see this beautiful product of his caring concern. *Yehi zichro baruch.*

Dovid Herskowitz worked tirelessly, putting together an amazing team to bring excellence to every aspect of this book.

The C-Nachas Foundation (info@cnachas.com), that stood behind this book, has assisted numerous organizations and been involved in a multitude of different national and international projects of Jewish interest around the world.

To the ArtScroll staff, particularly Miriam Zakon and Shmuel Blitz, I wish to express my sincere appreciation. Your interest in this book, your strong professional advice, and your practical guidance along the way were more helpful than you can imagine. I would also like to thank Mrs. Judi Dick for the final editing; Mrs. Mindy Stern for proofreading; Mrs. Reizy Ganz for layout; and Mrs. Tzini Fruchthandler for the beautiful cover.

I cannot overlook the wonderful blessing of my dear family, every one of whom gives me great *nachas* and joy. Your warm support brings out the best in each other and in me, enabling me to find within myself the strength and creativity to pursue my goals.

My greatest thanks go to the *Ribono shel Olam*. I feel His Presence constantly with me. Without His support, moment by moment, I could achieve nothing. May He bless all of *Klal Yisrael* with happiness, success, and relief from all pain, illness, and difficulty, and may He bring the ultimate Redemption to all our people. Amen.

Miriam Lea Rosenberg

INTRODUCTION
*Repairing Our World,
One Greeting at a Time*

The Second Lebanon War took place in the summertime — which was a terrible time for compassion and an even worse time for worry.

It was vacation time. People really needed their well-earned summer rest. They had been saving up for it; they were looking forward to it. In just a few short weeks autumn would arrive and life would go back to normal. In the meantime, one wanted to just unwind and enjoy.

I don't blame anyone. Maybe I just have a more fertile imagination, which was working overtime that summer. Whatever the reason, I seemed to be taking the war more to heart, really feeling the tragedy of it. I was a bundle of nerves.

My insides were crying, screaming. It was particularly hard for me when I would imagine our boys at the front. *Our boys*; ***my*** boys! Are they not all *my boys, our boys*?

What about the parents, the wives, the sisters, the children of those who were on the battlefront defending our nation? What about the citizens in Israel's north, under fire? How could I *not* be on edge? How could I even think of anything else?

Even when I tried to go out and relax, I would see the headlines. I would be confronted constantly with what I was trying, for just a moment, to forget. The war was everywhere and it was around the clock — in the newspapers, on the radio, floating along on rumors. I felt it ripping away at me. I even saw it — or imagined that I saw it — in the accusing looks on the faces of non-Jews.

What can I do? I thought. *What can **we** do? We must do…something.*

I was davening with special *kavannah*, with great concentration, and wondering incessantly: *What can we do?!*

I was begging Hashem, in His infinite mercy, to give me, to give us all, the recipe (I am a woman, after all!). How could we achieve this?

One day as I was davening I was struck by how often the word *shalom* is mentioned in our *tefillos*. As far as I know there is no other religion, no other language, and no other nation in which this theme is so central. In our *tefillos*, in our songs, and in our yearnings since time immemorial, *shalom* has been *the* theme.

Okay, now I realized this; I understood that what a Jew always needs most is this elusive *shalom*. But the burning question remained — *How to achieve it?*

All of a sudden, during davening, the simple, bold solution to this Gordian knot — or at least a sign on the road pointing us in that direction — struck me with dizzying force. Simple, obvious, easy, right there in the prayers that we say many times over every day — we speak of *shalom* again and again throughout our davening. How could it be overlooked?

We all know that Hashem repays a person *middah k'neged middah* — measure for measure. If we will just focus on "giving *shalom*," on greeting and acknowledging our fellow Jews, would that not evoke Hashem's blessing of *shalom*, for which we plead constantly? If we intensify our efforts to greet and bless one another, to acknowledge one another, couldn't we expect Hashem to give us all *shalom* in return? "Giving *shalom*" to one another would show *Hakadosh Baruch Hu* that we care for one another, and that would serve as a powerful prayer and *segulah* for *shalom* in our lives. The very thought was overwhelming. Could this really be possible?

I began looking through the *tefillos* more carefully to find where and in what contexts the word *shalom* is used.

In *Shemoneh Esrei*, for example, in the *berachah* of *Sim shalom*, we ask Hashem to *establish peace*, and at the same time we ask for general goodness, blessing, life, grace, kindness, and compassion, upon *us* and upon all of Yisrael, *Your* nation. In that *berachah* we place ourselves among our brethren, and in this way we can ask for *peace* and for the multitude of other *berachos* mentioned there.

When we recite *Kaddish* and other *tefillos*, we say, "*Oseh shalom bimromav, Hu ya'aseh shalom aleinu ve'al kol Yisrael* — May the One Who creates *shalom* in His upper spheres create *shalom* among us and among all *Yisrael....*" I would like to interpret these words, giving them a *kavannah* of my own: For anyone who creates *shalom* in his circles, Hashem *Yisbarach* will *give us and all Yisrael shalom — ve'imru Amen*!

Similarly, in *Birkas HaChodesh*, the blessing over the new month, we say "*chaveirim kol Yisrael*" — we implore Hashem that in the *zechus* of our nation's being *chaveirim* — treating one another as friends — He will shower us with all the most beautiful *berachos*. How can we show that we are all *chaveirim*? We can do it by blessing one another with *shalom*. Hashem even allows us to use His Name for this purpose!

This is one of the simpler keys to our survival. Although the world may be spinning out of control, we have the ability to "hit the brakes" — by banding together and showing that we truly care about one another.

Many of us have heard the story of an elderly father and his seven sons. The man sent one of his sons to gather seven small sticks, and he tied them together in a bundle. Then he asked each of his sons to try to break the sticks. They were all exceptionally strong, hardworking fellows, but none of them was able to break the bundle. Then their father, who was quite weak in his old age, untied the bundle and broke each stick.

"You see," he told his sons, "when the sticks are bound together no one can break them. But each stick alone is easy to destroy."

It is clear that if we as a nation will only learn this lesson and act accordingly, binding ourselves together through *shalom*, then our "neighbors" — all our enemies, wherever they may be — will never be able to harm us. All that is needed is a small effort on our part, with dividends so great as to be able to alter the course of history.

Does this seem like too much to hope for? *Chazal* tell us (see *Maseches Derech Eretz Zuta* Ch. 9 and *Bereishis Rabbah* 38) that as long as we are at peace with one another, Hashem will not afflict us with any punishment whatsoever, no matter what other sins we have committed! A simple *shalom aleichem*, a well-placed *hello*, merely acknowledging someone's presence — can make a person's day, can give him the encouragement he needs to achieve success, can reshape his world, can even save his life. We are not always aware of just how much we have accomplished by one small act of *mentchlichkeit* — sometimes we don't find out until much later; sometimes we never find out — but there is no doubt that reaching out to others is what Hashem wants us to do. A small act of kindness can take a thousand forms; all of them bring joy and, often enough, salvation, to oneself and to others, and they give more pleasure to Hashem than we can possibly know.

❖❖❖

Rabbi W. is one of the friendliest men I know; and, apparently, I'm not the only one who feels that way. In many circles I've heard him called "the smiling rabbi." He's so friendly, I remember thinking, that others would certainly respond in kind. *He'd* never be overlooked or experience those lonely feelings so many of us have known.

Still, I thought he would be able to identify with others who have experienced the desolate feeling of being ignored. Yet when I told him of my plan to launch a campaign encouraging people to acknowledge and greet those with whom they come in contact, his response was lukewarm. Basically, he brushed the idea off; he thought it was trite. Perhaps with his charming nature, acknowledging others simply comes naturally and it never occurred to him that others do not experience life the same way he does.

Some time after our conversation, Rabbi W. traveled to a Midwestern city with a sizeable Jewish population. I must add that I myself have heard wonderful things about that community; the Jews there are known to be quite friendly. Yet when Rabbi W. showed up in shul there, *no one greeted him*!

He thought up many ways to justify their behavior — for example, maybe they were afraid he would approach them for a donation… but whatever their reasons, they all ignored him and walked away. As to their obligation to welcome a stranger — it seemed everyone thought that someone else would greet and invite him.

Later, when Rabbi W. reported this incident to me, his attitude toward my intended project had made a complete turnabout. He realized now, he told me, that I was addressing an area of genuine concern.

● ● ●

This book is chock-full of carefully chosen stories and anecdotes — some by writers whose names may be quite familiar to you, some by first-time writers. Each story you will read here demonstrates the power of a greeting, just a few words or a simple gesture, that shows others that *we care*, that *we value them*, that their existence matters to us. These stories are true, though in many cases names and identifying details have been changed. They are stories of the extraordinary blessings that ordinary people acting in ordinary ways can bring about.

We can all bless others and, in the process, bless the world, with the simplest of actions. With just a little thought and effort, every one of us will have a story — or many stories — to share, and we would love to hear them.

Send in your own stories to: LemaanHashalom@gmail.com

Wishing you *shalom* and every blessing that accompanies it!

Miriam Lea Rosenberg

1

THE SECRET OF SHALOM

(Just Say Hello)!

WELCOME DIVIDENDS

Yitzchak Kornblau

It's so simple to break through someone's loneliness.

The heat was making Motty a little lethargic, but he kept on plugging away at his Gemara. There was nothing like the serenity of the *beis medrash* during *bein hasedarim*, and it had a way of luring him into its tempting embrace.

Suddenly, a cool wisp of air brushed his shoulders. Taking a brief look toward the doors behind him he saw a new face. Wait…wasn't that guy here earlier on in the day too? Motty surveyed the boy carefully. He didn't appear to be looking for someone or waiting for something. Perhaps he had just come to learn? No, that couldn't be…he seemed too out of place. "Ah! A new *bachur*!" Motty confirmed to himself. The look was patented: nervous, yearning…as if he could somehow rebuild, recreate the friendships, comforts, and status he had enjoyed in his former yeshivah.

Usually the first one to greet the fresh arrivals, today Motty felt as if his tired muscles had melted into the hard wooden bench beneath him, and a voice in the back of his brain seemed to be telling him, "Let someone else say hello for a change! Besides, the Gemara says that you shouldn't interrupt your learning when there's someone else available who can do a *chessed* instead of you."

"Well said, Mr. Yitz R. Hara," Motty chided himself. A quick scan around the *beis medrash* discouraged his feeble attempt to acquit himself from this calling — the few *bachurim* who were there were too preoccupied to notice the new boy.

Motty's eyes returned to the new boy. By this time 15 minutes must have elapsed, and the fellow was still standing near the entrance, looking awkward and uncomfortable. "Let's go!" Motty told himself, tackling his *yetzer hara* from behind as he made a beeline toward the new boy.

"*Shalom aleichem!*" Motty pressed the boys' nervous, sweaty hand enthusiastically. "Are you new here?"

"Um…yes…actually, I've been here most of the day…and I really haven't gotten my bearings yet…."

"Well then, *welcome!*" Motty squeezed his hand a little harder, ushering him in to his new yeshivah and offering to help with whatever the new boy might need.

That brief exchange, which transpired almost two decades ago, lasted only a few moments, but it imbued Motty with a beautiful feeling that never left him.

● ● ●

Recently, Motty was laid off from his job as a rebbi in yeshivah. Considering the current financial situation, he felt that chances of his finding another yeshivah willing to hire him were bleak, but with eight children and many debts to pay, he was ready to do whatever it would take — even leave his beloved profession — to support his family.

After a few days of job hunting, he found one yeshivah that still had a position to fill, and not just any yeshivah, but one he was quite familiar with and would have loved to be a part of. Though he had heard through the grapevine that hundreds of applicants were vying for that position, he threw his hat in the ring. "Hashem runs the world," he said to himself. "All I have to do is my *hishtadlus*."

To his shock, Motty landed an interview, which went well. He went home to wait for an answer, figuring it would take weeks to get a response; after all, sifting through hundreds of applications takes time. But it was only a few days later that he received the phone call. "Please come down to our office for a meeting. We're interested in you."

The boss looked him up and down. "I'll be honest; I've heard very good things about you, and to be quite frank, one of my most respected rebbeim, Rabbi Ephraim Kahn, can't stop enthusing about you."

"Rabbi Ephraim Kahn…?" Motty wracked his brain. He knew the name, but he wasn't sure if he had the right picture in his mind.

"Don't you know who he is?" The boss looked confused. "He's a big fan of yours…."

Before Motty could become awkward, the door opened and Rabbi Kahn himself walked in. "MOTTY! How are you?"

"*Effie Kahn…*" Everything rushed back. Two decades had etched their marks on the features of these two old friends, but their countenances remained the same.

After a quick embrace, Rabbi Kahn turned to his boss.

"I have to tell you something. When I came to Israel for the first time, I was so homesick that I regretted ever having decided to come, and to make matters worse, I came in the middle of the *z'man*. People were friendly, but I felt so alien, so out of it. After just one morning I was determined to book my ticket back home, but I told myself, 'I'm going to give it one more chance. If by the time afternoon *seder* ends I still don't feel like I'm a part of the yeshivah, I'm changing my ticket and going home on the next flight' — and to tell you the truth, that would have been devastating for me. Who knows where I'd have wound up, or if I ever could have gotten to where I am today? Then one *bachur* — this man — came up to me and welcomed me so warmly — really making me feel part of the yeshivah — that my homesickness melted away completely, and I decided on the spot that I would stay."

Then Effie turned to Motty and pressed his hand. "Now it's my turn: Welcome to *our* yeshivah!"

The Shulchan Aruch tells us that a person can be repaid for a chessed he does years, even decades, later. In this instance, just one little "welcome" did more than Motty could ever have imagined, and many years later Motty was repaid in kind.

ILANA'S "HELLO"

Miriam Lea Rosenberg and Sara Chava Mizrahi

A simple hug can change your outlook on life in no time at all.

Miriam Lea Rosenberg writes: Everyone talks about what a warm person Ilana is. Whenever she greets someone, her words and actions are bursting with enthusiasm. When she sees a woman she knows, she never fails to say *hello* with a hug and a kiss.

The most remarkable thing about Ilana's by now well-known greetings is that if someone she knows happens to be together with another woman who is a perfect stranger to Ilana, Ilana will approach both women with exactly the same warm, effusive greeting: a hug and a kiss for both of them, as if they were both her best friends.

I've spoken to some of the women who've experienced Ilana's simple magic, and I've learned that a moment with Ilana is transformational. It leaves a person feeling like a multimillionaire. Once you've been in Ilana's presence, the world becomes a happy place again.

● ● ●

Sara Chava Mizrahi adds: Intrigued by Miriam Lea's account of Ilana's high-energy greeting, I decided to conduct a little experiment of my own: Was there something extraordinary about Ilana's personality, or could anyone do this? I was determined to find out.

An opportunity presented itself soon enough. That Friday morning, a friend called asking if I could host a seminary girl for the Friday-night *seudah*. The girl was spending Shabbos with relatives who live nearby, and she needed a place to eat for that meal. I agreed readily.

Shortly before the men arrived home from shul, a lovely almost-20-year-old showed up. I said *good Shabbos* with a big hug (trying my best not to let my actions seem too awkward), as if I'd known her all her life. I asked her name, and we had a few minutes to get acquainted before it was time to eat. We then enjoyed a pleasant meal, and she seemed to feel at home.

The following Friday morning, as I was in the kitchen cooking for Shabbos, one of my older daughters, who was helping me, asked if I remembered Aviva, the girl who had joined us for the *seudah* the week before. Of course I did.

"Well," my daughter went on, "I saw her on the bus this week. She told me how depressed she had been that her relatives couldn't manage to find a place for her at their family Shabbos table and that she had been farmed out to eat with perfect strangers. She didn't even want to come — didn't want to see anyone. She was sure she would spend the entire Shabbos feeling miserable.

"Then," my daughter went on, "she told me, 'But I walked into your house, and your mother gave me such a big hug, it put a smile on my face that stayed on for the whole Shabbos!'"

It is clear to me that Hashem orchestrated the timing such that Aviva just happened to have been one of the first "victims" of my experiment, and her Shabbos was saved.

Needless to say, I'm sold on Ilana's method, and I highly endorse the manner of greeting of this woman whom I've never met.

◆◆◆

I related this incident to Miriam Lea Rosenberg, who had first told me about Ilana's special form of greeting. Shortly thereafter she told me about her own experience:

A very *chashuveh* couple was spending Shabbos in Miriam Lea's home. Miriam Lea is accustomed to hosting many guests, but this special couple was anything but run-of-the-mill, and somehow this time she felt intimidated.

"Then," Miriam Lea told me, "I thought of Ilana's greeting, and of your experience with it, and I decided to give it a try." When the couple walked into her house for the first time, Miriam Lea greeted the rebbetzin with a big hug, and immediately both women felt comfortable with each other. "We hit it off great!" Miriam Lea reported; and the Shabbos was a success.

Why not give Ilana's approach a try? It just may be the catalyst for an amazing experience!

FOUR LIVES FOR A GREETING

Rabbi Shiloh Ben David

A "Good morning" and "Good evening" can move mountains.

Reb Yehudah, an earnest yeshivah student, came to realize how important *Chazal* had considered the act of extending a friendly greeting to every person one meets. They taught (*Berachos* 17a): "One should act in peace with one's brothers, relatives, and all others, even with non-Jews one meets in the marketplace. In this way one will be beloved in Heaven and well-liked on earth." We are told that Rabban Yochanan ben Zakkai was always first to extend a greeting to anyone he met, even to non-Jews.

Reb Yehudah made it a priority to act accordingly. He did his best to emulate this exalted behavior, greeting every person he met warmly, regardless of that person's social status or age, and regardless of whether he was Jewish. He continued practicing this behavior until it became second nature to him.

At one point, Reb Yehudah was hired as a *mashgiach* at a large meat-packing plant in Argentina. Together with a number of men, including another *mashgiach* and several *shochtim*, he flew to Argentina from Israel and was escorted into the plant's giant complex. There were many workers there, most of whom were non-Jews.

In Argentina as well, Reb Yehudah continued to practice his habit of greeting everyone. The first person he met every day was the non-Jewish guard at the plant's gate. Reb Yehudah would always smile and nod his head as he greeted the guard upon entering, and at the end of his workday he would wish the guard a good evening as he left.

At first the guard was astonished at this behavior. In all the thirty years he had held this position no one had ever paid any attention to him in this way. He had no idea why this rabbi was so careful to extend his greetings to a man he did not even know. As time went on, though, he grew accustomed to it and looked forward to Reb Yehudah's greeting each morning and evening.

One day, the two *mashgichim* and two other employees entered the walk-in freezer where thousands of sides of beef were stored. Suddenly there was a blackout in the plant and everything went dark. As a result, the heavy door of the freezer room swung shut automatically, locking the four men inside. They tried banging on the door to get someone's attention but their efforts were futile. The four men realized that in all likelihood no one would open the door until the next day, and by then the four of them would be frozen solid — just like the sides of beef they had been inspecting.

Time passed and the workday came to an end. Other than the four men trapped in the freezer, no one was left in the plant. The four of them were freezing; they knew that only a miracle could save them now.

His strength waning, Reb Yehudah tried to recite *Tehillim*. Tears rolled down his cheeks as he prayed. Certain that death was very near, he began to recite his final *vidui*.

Suddenly, the door swung open and the lights went on. Standing dumbstruck at the freezer's entrance was the guard from the front gate!

After they recovered, they asked the guard why he had opened the freezer. He explained that he had planned to go home much earlier, but he had a strong feeling that there was something wrong. He remembered that Reb Yehudah had greeted him upon entering that morning, but he had not wished him a good evening at the end of the day. Since Reb Yehudah had never missed acknowledging him when he passed, the guard was sure that he would never forget to do so, and he concluded that the rabbi must still be somewhere in the plant. He searched high and low for him until Hashem inspired him to check the freezer, and their lives were saved in the nick of time!

THE TAXI DRIVER SAVES THE DAY

Tzvi David

Taking a taxi in Israel can be fascinating. The driver could be an ex-government official; a former minister; even an expert in economics; or he may have spent his years scuba diving; Israeli taxi drivers are certainly a colorful bunch.

After what seemed like an endless wait, a taxi finally pulled up. The driver and I looked each other over before I sank into the comfortable leather seat. My weighty everyday concerns began to fade as the Mercedes pulled smoothly away from the curb.

I was almost napping when the thought struck me that many drivers enjoy schmoozing with their fares. The least I could do was to acknowledge my driver with a simple hello and a friendly "How're things going?"

Of course one thing led to another, and before I knew it he was telling me his personal history, and it was actually quite fascinating. My taxi driver, Benji, had been a high-ranking member of the Israeli police force for decades before his recent retirement. He was definitely a star. I could see his strength and stability in the way he held the wheel and in the way he sat as he drove.

We spoke for quite a while, and as the conversation meandered along we connected with each other. By the time we reached my destination we were friends.

Before I stepped out we exchanged phone numbers, and he made me promise him that if I ever needed something I felt he could help me with, I wouldn't hesitate to call for assistance. As I watched him drive off into the sunny afternoon I was thinking that I'd probably never see this man again.

●●●

I am the director of a large organization in Israel, and I often arrange various major activities. It is only logical, therefore, that I run into numerous bureaucratic snags. At one point we were planning a huge field trip to the Ben Shemen forest, located 25 miles out of Jerusalem, in the Modiin area, for families participating in our program. We were expecting about 5,000 people in all. In order to eliminate the need for official security escorts, we had stipulated that each child must be accompanied by a father or older brother who would be legally responsible for the child. We would not be needing the army, navy, or air force this time around.

Two days before the trip, just when I thought everything was under control, I received a call from Keren Kayemet L'Yisrael, the government body that oversees much that has to do with Israeli lands, their development, their use, and, most importantly, the people who like to see permits — many, many permits from people who traverse those lands. I was informed that since we were lacking some of those critical pieces of paper, the trip would have to be cancelled.

This was a disaster! How could I inform 5,000 people by the next morning that this long-awaited trip was off? It just wasn't feasible!

I thought and thought. In my mind I ran through every name I could think of, anyone I even vaguely knew, people I hadn't spoken with in ten years. I couldn't think of anyone who could help me out of this mess…until I found the number of that former high-ranking police officer — my friend Benji, the taxi driver. I phoned him and explained the whole situation to him; and wouldn't you know it — he was free the next morning!

He spent his entire day traipsing around to all the necessary offices — the police, the fire department, and Keren Kayemet L'Yisrael, and wherever we met up with authorities who told us they couldn't help us, they changed their minds when they came face-to-face with my friend. His reputation, his charm, and his fortitude were an undefeatable combination.

A catastrophe had been averted; the trip that almost wasn't turned out to be a smashing success because I had decided just to smile and say a few words of thanks to a taxi driver I never expected to see again. In the end, it was I who found myself thanking my taxi driver for saving the day for 5,000 people.

THE WOMAN WHO DIDN'T SAY HELLO

Chava Dumas

*She'd have expected a response...
and she didn't just let it go at that...*

It was Shabbos morning. I was coming home from shul, on the way to the entrance of my building, when I noticed a new neighbor walking by. I smiled and said hello, but she didn't even glance in my direction. We had met recently, and I knew she was a sweet, friendly young woman, so I called out in a loud voice, "Hello, Naomi! Good Shabbos!"

No response.

That's odd. Why wouldn't she answer me? I wondered. *She must have heard me.* I went back up the stairs and followed her; I don't even know why. It wasn't that I was insulted that she had ignored me...I just thought I should keep trying.

"Naomi! Naomi!" I called as I ran to catch up with her. She was walking in a strange, stiff, robot-like manner.

Sidling right up to her, I tried to make eye contact and said again, "Hello! How are you?"

Naomi didn't say a word. She just kept right on going.

Something is definitely wrong. I kept up with her. Usually a bubbly fountain of camaraderie, I didn't know what to say in this uncomfortable one-sided monologue. So I just walked alongside her, babbling with good intentions, trying to make light conversation, as though she were not plodding along in this zombie state, wishing she would speak and give some indication that she was hearing me at all.

Our neighborhood was fairly new. The roads and sidewalks were still under construction, and dirt and dust accompanied our steps. I followed Naomi up and down the paths that led, finally, to the forest. There the *eiruv* ended. I didn't know what she would do. She still hadn't said a word. Her expression was grim, her eyes wide, staring straight ahead.

We reached the end of the road, and there before us stretched an open view of undulating desert hills. Naomi stopped suddenly.

"What's happening, Naomi? Can I help you? Can you tell me what's wrong?" I begged.

She just stood there staring blankly out into space. *Can she hear me?*

"Naomi…um…did something happen? Are you okay?"

There was nowhere to go except back the way we came. Tentatively, gently, I reached out to touch her arm. "Come home with me. You can stay with us. It'll be okay. Whatever it is that's bothering you, you'll be with us and everything will work out," I mumbled quietly, sincerely, hoping she would agree.

Her shoulders drooped and she seemed to sigh. Her eyes glanced down at the rocky road. She turned around slowly, mechanically. She didn't pull away from me, so I grasped her arm gently and we began our walk back.

When we reached home I guided her inside. My husband was sitting at the Shabbos table waiting for me. He looked up in surprise as he watched me usher Naomi past him and into our spare bedroom.

"Here, you can stay right here and lie down if you want. I'll get you some water," I said.

Still no response.

I stepped out of the room and tried to apprise my husband of what was going on, though I really had no idea myself.

"I'm going to get Yocheved. She's a good friend of Naomi's. Maybe she can come over now and talk to her."

When I reached Yocheved's home she welcomed me warmly with a wide smile, which disappeared as soon as I told her about her friend Naomi's baffling behavior.

"Where is she now? At your house?" she asked, suddenly agitated. "You have no idea how worried her husband has been! Can you please go let him know that you found her? I'm just going to tell my husband to watch our kids, and I'm coming right over to you!"

Yocheved arrived quickly, and I showed her into the room where Naomi was still standing exactly where I'd left her...staring blankly out the window at the desert hills in the distance.

I left the two of them together, praying that Yocheved would be able to handle the situation.

●●●

Three hours later Yocheved emerged from our guest room.

"Thank G-d you found her! She's talking a little now. She'll be okay."

She told me that Naomi was suffering from post-partum depression. She was supposed to be taking medication for it but had been negligent lately, claiming she didn't need to be on drugs.

"No one knew where she disappeared to or what she was capable of doing to herself! How did she get to your house?"

"Um...well, it was only because she didn't look at me when I said hello that I noticed something was amiss."

Yocheved began to cry. "I don't know what would have happened *if you hadn't said hello!* Thank G-d you did!"

"THE HAND OF THE TONGUE"

Rabbi Shmuel Yaakov Klein

It was just a hello, literally; but the ripple effects were truly phenomenal!

I have been giving a Thursday-night *shiur* on *Sfas Emes* for a number of years, and in the course of the weekly gathering I have had the privilege of meeting and teaching a broad spectrum of individuals who have one primary thing in common — a love of *Sfas Emes*.

One *yungerman* who attended the *shiur* for several years was a particularly refined individual who was also a *baal teshuvah*. At the time, however, he had been *frum* for years; he was a veteran of yeshivos and had even spent several years studying in *kollel* after his marriage.

One evening, when the two of us happened to arrive early and were waiting for the others attendees of the *shiur*, I asked him what had precipitated his process of becoming Torah-observant.

"As a child," he began, "I used to go with my parents almost every Shabbos to a Conservative shul." When he named the particular synagogue — Adath Israel — I noted with curiosity that it was just around the corner from where I live.

"One Shabbos I was walking with my parents out of the shul — I must have been about 12 at the time — and I noticed a big, burly chassid walking toward us." (I couldn't help but note how this description rather reminded me of myself!) "As he approached us, he looked me straight in the eye and said, 'Gut Shabbos!'"

The young man proceeded to confide that this brief encounter, which lasted no more than a few seconds and encompassed a grand total of two words, infused him with a warm feeling and the sense that "this very religious-looking person acknowledged me...," and reached out to him, if only briefly. The impression that this made on him allowed him to feel — even years later — that he was "somehow attached to those very religious Jews."

It was that deeply embedded memory that gave him the boost, later on, to draw closer to Torah. He must have been reading my thoughts as I pondered the unplanned *zechus* that the *Yid* in his story had achieved with such a painless and simple gesture as saying "*Gut Shabbos*," for he continued, smiling, "That chassid was you!"

How mysterious are the workings of the Creator. On my way home from davening I had uttered a *"Gut Shabbos"* to a boy I would have predicted would forever remain a stranger to Torah, and years later I was spending an hour a week with him — a true *ben Torah* now — delving into the profundities of the *Sfas Emes* — and largely as a result of that salutation, spoken almost two decades earlier.

Shlomo HaMelech may have had this potential in mind when he wrote the famous words (*Mishlei* 18:21), "*Maves vechaim beyad lashon* — death and life are in the hand of the tongue," and this might be why he used the word "*beyad* — in the *hand*." The hand is, very literally, an instrument of "outreach," and Shlomo HaMelech is revealing to us that the tongue possesses the power of the hand. Our ability to speak can be used to reach out and elevate those around us, and this need not necessarily be done by sharing well-developed profundities of Jewish thought. It can also be done, as I discovered, through a strategically positioned "*Gut Shabbos*."

THE GRACIOUS POWER OF A GREETING

B. Schreiber

The first day of school can be the most frightening experience of one's life.

The following incident took place twenty years ago, but it is still as fresh in my mind as the day it happened.

It was the first day of school — a common enough experience, but for my seventh-grade daughter it was an event fraught with apprehension. As we had recently made *aliyah*, she didn't know anyone who might be in her class, and to make matters worse, she was embarrassed to speak her weak, American-accented Hebrew (even though we were renting an apartment in a largely English-speaking neighborhood to make our acclimatization a bit easier). Another sore point was that she realized that most of the girls in her class would have been in the same school since kindergarten. This meant that there were sure to be close bonds of friendship. Could she even hope to be accepted into a group of pleasant girls?

Try as we might, my husband and I were unable to reassure our daughter or make her feel comfortable and more optimistic at this new stage in her life. It did not make things easier that her twin brothers, two years her junior, were looking forward to the experience of entering a new school in a foreign country and regarding it as both a challenge and an exciting adventure. In any case, they had each other, she pointed out, while she was virtually alone. Only her beloved 3-year-old brother would be in close proximity, since his preschool was near her school building, but this was hardly a consolation.

After she davened *Shacharis* on the first day of school, I noticed that her eyes were glistening with unshed tears that threatened to spill at the slightest provocation. Undoubtedly she was imagining how the friends she had left behind were anticipating *their* first day, and her heart must have been filled with longing for the security of her previous environment. (Later, she acknowledged that this had indeed been on her mind.)

Though I was concerned about her likely reaction, I offered to accompany her to school. She hesitated for a moment, as if weighing the lesser of two evils, then agreed. As we walked along we did not see as many girls heading toward the school as I thought we might, and I assumed this was due to the early hour. (Actually, I had hoped that by arriving early she would feel less self-conscious than if she entered the classroom after most of the girls were there.) Seeing that she could not be diverted by small talk, I reminded her about the many times our family had reached out to make newcomers feel welcome in our neighborhood, and told her that I prayed that her own merit in this *chessed* would help her now.

I asked her permission to enter the building with her, explaining that I wanted to meet the teacher briefly before the classroom started filling up. Reluctantly, she nodded in agreement and we headed to the room. To my surprise — and probably her dismay — we noticed that the room was buzzing with activity as groups of girls were chatting excitedly inside. There was, however, no sign of a teacher.

In that endless moment as I stood there trying to figure out what would be the prudent thing to do while glancing at my daughter from the corner of my eye (I read her expression as, "Oh, no, how am I ever going to live through this?"), I noticed a girl with a slight build and a wide smile approaching us from one of the clusters of girls. She introduced herself in English and asked my daughter whether she was new to the neighborhood. "More than that — I'm an *olah chadashah*!" she blurted in relief.

The angel in a Bais Yaakov uniform responded with a compliment and asked whether she preferred to be introduced to the class as a whole or to individual groups. By this time girls had begun to edge toward the doorway where we were standing. Some bore friendly or shy smiles; others stared with frank curiosity. My daughter bravely said that a general introduction would be fine. At this point I discreetly thanked my daughter's new friend and said a relieved good-bye to my daughter. As I turned down the hallway I heard — following the angel's announcement (in Hebrew) that a new student from America was joining their class — exclamations of welcome in English and Hebrew. "*Kol Yisrael chaverim*," I said silently in thanks to Hashem.

A postscript to this story is that, as it turned out, Yocheved (the angel's name) did not become one of my daughter's closest friends, but she will forever have a special place in our hearts and *tefillos*. She was not a star pupil, nor the class queen, nor (not surprisingly!) an angel — just a sweet, considerate person who put herself in another's place and tried to make the situation easier for a fellow human being.

This lovely young girl probably never realized the difference her caring greeting made to an entire family of *olim chadashim*. We had chosen to move to Israel against the conventional "wisdom" that warned of the dire consequences of immigrating with an adolescent, and this thought echoed in my mind on that fateful first day of school. I sensed that the kind of welcome my daughter would receive could make all the difference between her seeing school as an ordeal to be overcome or as a promising new beginning.

The graciousness of a single greeting had a ripple effect that was felt by everyone in my family.

A SHUL WITH A MISSION

Rabbi Nachman Seltzer

Here's one shul where they'll never neglect a newcomer.

The *rav* of the large new shul in a vibrant neighborhood in Eretz Yisrael was known for his oratorical skills. He stood up to speak one Shabbos at a bar mitzvah.

"*Rabbosai*...," he began, smiling as he stroked his beard and looked around the crowded room at all those who had come to celebrate. "Before I take this opportunity to wish our *baal simchah* and his entire *mishpachah* a heartfelt *mazal tov*, I'd like to ask you all a question: Why did we build this shul? What have we to offer that everyone else isn't already providing? There are so many shuls, so many *minyanim* around us! What can we hope to achieve?

"I must tell you the answer, *Rabbosai*. This is the shul of Reb David, our *baal simchah*."

The shul was quiet as all eyes turned in some confusion to Reb David Eisen, a happy man with a good sense of humor, whose bar mitzvah *bachur* sat at his side. What did he have to do with their new shul? they all wondered.

"I can sense your curiosity," the rav went on, "as you ask yourselves what Reb David has to do with our new building." The rav paused dramatically.

"You may remember," he said, speaking softly now, "that Reb David came to daven at our shul very soon after he moved here from America. He seemed to enjoy the davening, and I assumed that he would remain a member of our congregation. Suddenly, though, after a few months, he was gone. He simply stopped attending.

"It bothered me when I remembered to think about it, but as you know, I'm a rather busy man [the congregation laughed at this understatement of the century], and the matter sort of slipped my mind — until we happened to meet one day at a neighborhood *simchah*, and I saw him sitting at one of the tables in the back of the room, tucking in to a generous portion of fudge.

" 'Reb David,' I said, 'what happened to you? We haven't seen you in months. I had the impression that you enjoyed davening with us. Did you find a better shul to daven in?' I continued with a few more half-joking, half-serious lines.

"Reb David's response shocked me. 'Rabbi Lewis,'* he said, totally serious, 'I've been trying out many of the neighborhood shuls since I left your *minyan*, and I still haven't found a place that I can proudly consider my own.'

" 'Why not?' I asked with concern.

" 'Because,' he said, his eyes moist, 'until I find a shul where someone comes over to me and asks me my name, where someone wishes me *Shalom aleichem* and acts like I mean something to him; until I find a shul where I don't feel invisible — until then, I will not have found a shul for me!'

"At that moment," said the *rav*, "I knew that I was going to build a new shul, a beautiful new edifice where everyone would feel welcome, would feel part of our *kehillah*.

"And *baruch Hashem*, we have accomplished that here, and it's all thanks to Reb David!"

---

* *Name has been changed*

JUST ONE HELLO

Tova Younger

You can never know where you'll meet up with someone who will become a best friend.

I hung up the phone, ending my nightly conversation with my dear friend Ahuva. It's hard to believe that a woman with a large family, someone I met by chance — or now I know to say "by *hashgachah*" — has been like a sister to me and opened up so many doors in my life.

My special miracle began over twenty years ago. I was working in Kmart at the time, lonely as could be. My husband had passed away a few years earlier, leaving me a young, childless widow. That description, and many happy memories, were all he actually left; he died suddenly, and there was no insurance, no relatives to help. The small amount of money we did have went to funeral and *Kaddish* expenses; although I was not observant, I had been raised with strong Jewish feelings. I didn't want to take any chances when it came to perhaps causing my dear departed husband any harm. A rabbi came to ensure that everything was done properly.

As I tried to recover and see about starting anew, I realized that I was totally on my own: If I didn't work I wouldn't be able to pay the rent and eat. I was not highly skilled or trained, so all I could find were low-paying jobs. For a number of years I worked two jobs, a total of over 60 hours a week. I ate the simplest of meals, watching every penny. I didn't even have my own apartment — I rented a room from another widow, and managed with that.

So my life continued, full of hard work, without much to break the monotony. Until I met Ahuva.

AHUVA:

It was just another day. Some laundry, straightening up in the house, and then some errands. A routine trip with my children to Kmart.

We wandered around the store, collected the items we needed and waited on line to pay. As we were paying, the cashier metamorphosed into a person.

There I was, checking out Kmart shoppers, occasionally having a bit of conversation with them as I searched for relationships. As I checked out the items for this young lady I heaved a sigh.

"Hello — how are you? What is the matter?" Ahuva greeted me, sensitive to my mood.

I let myself be very honest. "I'm so lonely. I have no friends and no family. It's so hard for me!"

Ahuva quickly took out a piece of paper. "Would you like to give me your phone number? Here's mine. I'll call you! I'll be your friend!"

I'm usually not so quick to give out my number, but here she was offering me hers…I gave her my number, thinking that she might just call. I knew not to get my hopes up. I thought, well, maybe we'll have a conversation or two. She looked pretty busy, with a few young children in tow. "Thank you! Looking forward to speaking with you!"

Just One Hello | 45

was all I said. *I'll see what will be*, I thought...

That evening Ahuva called. We chatted for a while, introducing ourselves to each other. We discussed a few topics, and we hit it off. When our conversation was over I thought, *Will this be the end? Will I hear from her again?*

That was the beginning of a relationship that has continued for over twenty years. Ahuva calls me once or twice a day, and she is such a lifeline for me. At first I felt very awkward in her home, as she is strictly Orthodox. So many things she has introduced me to that at first felt so strange...I knew I could never be like her, and told her so, but she was always kind and open with me, just telling me about all kinds of mitzvahs. I knew — and she knew — that it was up to me. I took on what I could when I could.

AHUVA:

Initially, I was her only contact in the community. I called her regularly, once or twice a day, sharing my life — that of a busy working mom — with her. In turn she regaled me with insights, relaying conversations she'd had with friends and strangers, depending on how she had spent her day. I was fascinated in the role of her confidant, learning about how she had grown up in Europe and survived the war, and of her life as a very independent, self-supporting, intelligent, sensitive widow.

◆◆◆

Unfortunately, a few years later I was diagnosed with cancer. Ahuva put me in touch with all the *bikur cholim* programs in our community. I made so many new friends, as several women took me to appointments and treatments, helped me get various medicines and even a special bed. Students, young mothers, and women of all ages visited me at home and in the hospital.

AHUVA:

Many of my friends knew I had a special acquaintance, and some were amazed at the longevity of our relationship, but none of them were really involved. Until her illness. As word got around, so many joined in the circle of friends, each doing what she could. I was astounded.

People began calling regularly, taking her to the doctor, holding her hand — providing her with emotional support that has carried her through two bouts with cancer, and ongoing medical issues.

As I recovered, I realized my illness had brought me many new friends. Ahuva is still my closest and dearest; I know I can talk with her about anything at all — but so many others call me, take me to lunch, help me when I am feeling down. They invite me to their homes for visits and holidays, include me in their family *simchos*...I truly feel that I have a wonderful extended family...and it all began with a caring stranger's *Hello*.

AHUVA:
As I look back on my life, I feel so grateful to Hashem for having given me the opportunity to share a relationship with such a special friend. She has enriched my life and that of my family in many ways. She ends almost every conversation with, "I am davening for you, Ahuva — you and your family!" and showers me with many berachos. My "Hello" has clearly paid wonderful, incredible dividends.

RISE TO THE OCCASION

Brachah Stern

Physical stature isn't everything.

Wherever Mr. Klein went, his presence was felt. He carried himself with dignity, and there was a nobility about him that could not be denied. You couldn't help but respect him. People were proud to be associated with him.

With the passing years his strength waned, and eventually he found himself in a wheelchair. Essentially, the man was no different, but he was no longer the tall, impressive, independent person everyone had known. Still, people held him in high regard.

When he felt strong enough to begin attending shul again, his friends told him they were thrilled. One group begged him to daven in *their* shul, and he agreed.

It took a lot of courage on his part to be wheeled in to the shul. Mr. Klein had never needed anyone's support in the past. But he came — though sitting in his wheelchair he was no longer like the other men in shul, who could stand and walk around freely.

It seemed that the others in shul were shocked and distraught to see Mr. Klein in his current state. No one greeted him. No one approached him to speak to him. It seemed that, in a sense, they feared him. And Mr. Klein learned the painful truth that being in a wheelchair changes one's image drastically. Physically, he was no longer the same as the others, so people did not know how to deal with him.

The lesson hit home — those people who are in some way different physically from others have no less stature as a human being. Their *neshamos* are endlessly precious, as are the *neshamos* of anyone else, and they deserve full recognition.

For the rest of his life, though Mr. Klein remained wheelchair-bound himself, he would always have a ready, warm greeting for anyone with a physical handicap or limitation. Rather than wait for someone else to take the initiative, he would make sure to be the one to approach and speak to that person directly, giving him his full attention and full respect.

The wonderful result of Mr. Klein's actions was that they had the effect of breaking through the invisible barrier that often seems to surround people who are going through difficulties in life: Other people would naturally follow his lead, and the individual Mr. Klein had approached would experience not discomfort or a feeling of isolation, but rather wide acceptance. Open friendliness is infectious!

GREETINGS

Batya Jacobs

Reflections on the power and potential we all possess ...

I live in a little village that used to be the lone point of civilization on a mountaintop surrounded by empty hillsides. Many of those hillsides are now covered by buildings filled with families bringing Torah to yet another area of Eretz Yisrael. Now we enjoy the convenience of shopping centers within walking distance, and busses that come to our area three or four times an hour instead of only twice a day.

This morning I was strolling up one of the roads in our neighboring town after having walked my daughter to her schoolbus. (These early-morning excursions with my daughter give us a chance to have a close, mother-daughter chat about anything and everything under the sun.) I was on my way back home when I noticed a woman coming toward me — a complete stranger (although I am not quite sure what an incomplete stranger would look like), but someone who was, after all, a fellow human being. She was walking up a road very near my neighborhood, so…I greeted her with a friendly smile and a "Hello." She looked somewhat taken aback and hurried away silently.

Why did she do that, I pondered. Here I was, a hop, skip, and a jump from my little village roads, empty of traffic and full of clear, fumeless air, and this anonymous town dweller did not return my natural, friendly greeting. In my little village we greet each other all the time, giving a friendly good morning, a "Hi," or even an energetic hand wave to a passing car. If anyone should pass a person with stony-faced, unrecognizing silence, it would be understood to mean that something was wrong.

I recalled another time when the whole parent body of a moshav where I once lived had gathered together to deal with and discuss a general lack of *derech eretz* among their children. The fact that the children didn't greet the adults was brought as a worrisome symptom of the problem at hand. Why did they never greet the adults? What could be done? During that meeting one brave parent declared, "How many of us greet one another? How many of us greet the children?"

So why is it that people in towns seem not to automatically greet and/or return a greeting to passersby (women to women and men to men, of course), whereas people in our little village do? My husband, in his calm, objective way, ventured to suggest that it might be a function of the practicalities of town life. "If they greeted everyone they saw, they would never have a chance to stop talking!"

Practicalities of the crowded town life might be part of the answer, but I rather think our lack of willingness to greet people might stem, at least in part, from something else. There is a tendency nowadays to stress the individual: his privacy, his needs, his personal development. That idea is likely to somewhat devalue the importance of others, especially complete strangers. Kindergarten children are taught about the mitzvos *bein adam l'chaveiro*, and it fills my heart to the tippy-top when I enter our kindergarten and am greeted with a chair and a glass of water from the willing children's dimpled hands. Wouldn't it be wonderful if these children could carry that simple caring for the rest of their lives?

The greeting of *shalom* has its own special merits. The word *shalom* is one of *Hakadosh Boruch Hu's* Names; it is one of His attributes. Just think, every time you use that greeting you have an opportunity to reflect on *Hakadosh Boruch Hu* in general and on that attribute in particular, and you are giving the person you are greeting an opportunity to do the same thing.

Greetings can be so powerful. Smile and say good morning to someone who is lonely and you will have made his day. Observe what happens if your greeting reaches its mark, even a fraction of the way. See cross, stern faces softening their lines, see the smile of children, hear the person who is just bursting to be heard as he or she responds to you.

We are told that if (*lo aleinu*) a dead body should be found in the fields, the people from the nearest towns have to beg forgiveness. They are held responsible for the murder, because no one accompanied this person on his way out of the town. Someone who is accompanied for part of his way gains protection, from the very fact of the accompaniment. The caring and concern of another person produces a kind of spiritual "shield" for the person being accompanied. That "piece" of the accompanier, the spiritual power of his caring, gives the traveler extra strength to face the dangers of being alone and lonely. Our "*shaloms*" touch the people we have greeted in just this way. They bestow a piece of our caring and, especially if we use the word *shalom*, a piece of *Hakadosh Boruch Hu's* caring, onto the person we greet. That person is no longer going it alone.

In our rush-rush, crowded, noise-blasted, information-busted world, where people put far too much store in solitude and individuality, a little greeting, a simple, smile-filled, friendly *shalom* is more important than ever.

Today I was walking at a "must get my daily exercise" pace around my moshav's perimeter road, still pondering these greeting thoughts. Then I saw in the distance an exercising pacer like myself coming toward me at full pelt. "Well," I said to myself, "you'd better give a jolly good greeting now. You don't want to be a hypocrite!" I positively beamed at my fellow walker and said, "*Boker tov*," and even though she didn't know me from Adam (or Eve, for that matter) she beamed back and greeted me. I flung out my arms and said "*Eizeh ananim* [look at those clouds]!" and she replied, "*Mashehu* [Isn't that something]!" I have been beaming all day long on the strength, yes, *strength*, of that little interchange. Just a little smile, just a little *shalom* — can you imagine what a difference it makes?

A GIFT OF LIFE

Miriam Lea Rosenberg

𝔍𝔲𝔰𝔱 𝔞 𝔫𝔬𝔡 𝔞𝔫𝔡 𝔞 𝔰𝔪𝔦𝔩𝔢…
𝔞𝔫𝔡 𝔞 𝔩𝔦𝔣𝔢 𝔦𝔰 𝔰𝔞𝔳𝔢𝔡.

It was on an Erev Yom Kippur some twenty years ago that Shimon first met Misha; Shimon was heading down Broadway in New York City when he saw another *frum* Jew. One look told Shimon that this man was a very recent Russian immigrant.

Shimon was, understandably, in a rush, but he did not want to miss the opportunity, especially on Erev Yom Kippur, to greet a fellow Jew, so he made sure to smile and nod to him. The other responded in kind, and, just to be polite, Shimon asked where he was planning to daven on Yom Kippur. The stranger told him that he didn't know yet.

Mildly alarmed, Shimon asked him where he was planning to eat his last meal before the fast. Again, the man replied that he didn't know.

Shimon and his family were scheduled to eat at his parents' house, and he knew how they loved doing *chessed*. He also knew that his mother always prepared a huge abundance of food for any occasion. "She'd never forgive me," Shimon thought, "if she found out that I didn't give her the opportunity to help these people." Without hesitating, Shimon invited his new friend to join him and his family for the *seudah hamafsekes*.

"But I have a wife," the man said.

"No problem," Shimon told him. "We'll be happy to host her."

"But I have a daughter…," the man went on sheepishly.

"That's all right. Just bring her along," Shimon said cheerily.

"But my daughter has a husband…"

"Okay, we'll be happy to have him too…."

By the time they had settled on all the details, Misha's family — a crowd of eight in all — was slated to join Shimon's family for the *seudah hamafsekes*.

And the two families hit if off famously! Erev Yom Kippur was the beginning of an ongoing relationship that both families appreciated, and they kept in touch.

On Chanukah, Misha's family — the whole bunch — was invited to Shimon's house for a festive dinner. When they arrived, Shimon apologized that one of his children, Moshe, wouldn't be there to join the fun — he was in bed with a fever.

Misha's daughter-in-law happened to be a pediatrician, though she was not yet licensed to practice medicine in the United States. At that time the American medical establishment generally did not accept Russian-trained doctors, as it was thought that their qualifications were not up to American standards. She insisted on taking a look at the child before she sat down to eat — as she told them, it was the least she could do for her gracious hosts.

After a brief examination, she instructed Shimon and his wife to take Moshe straight to the hospital. "All right," Shimon said, "but first let's eat the delicious Chanukah dinner my wife prepared. Then we'll go."

"Yes," said his wife. "Come sit down, before the latkes get cold!"

"No!" she insisted. "There's not a moment to lose. Leave right now — his life is in danger!"

Shimon heeded her warning and rushed Moshe to the hospital. As it turned out, that was the right thing to do; the child had meningitis. Shimon's guest's timely advice saved his life.

That was many years ago. Today Moshe is married with children of his own, and Shimon and his wife are, of course, proud grandparents.

Shimon saw fit to acknowledge another Jew one Erev Yom Kippur, when he was "almost too busy" to do so, and the payoff was almost immediate, as he gained the life of his young son Moshe, and all the generations that would follow.

MY BROTHER

As told to Chani Wagschall

Yaakov Avinu knew the universal secret to acceptance.

In Mesivta Torah Vodaath we were taught by our Rosh Yeshivah, Harav Yaakov Kamenetzky, *zt"l*, that *Parashas Vayeitzei* provides us with the model for the correct approach one should take when speaking to strangers.

When Yaakov Avinu came to Charan he encountered a group of shepherds sitting with their flocks around a well. He asked why they were idle and gave them some unsolicited advice and admonishment. As *Chazal* tell us, he told them that they were being either unethical or illogical: If they were hired hands, they should still be out in the fields with the flocks; if the sheep were their own, it wasn't wise economically to bring them in so early when they could still be grazing.

Reb Yaakov asked how it was that Yaakov Avinu concluded his words uninterrupted, and even received a civil response and an explanation. Shepherds are not known to be the most refined of people. What compelled them to relate respectfully to words that would evoke an angry response from most people?

It was Yaakov Avinu's opening word, "*Achai — My brothers*, where are you from?" (*Bereishis* 29:4), that won them over. He approached them as brothers, with warmth, which showed that his remonstrations were rooted in kindness and concern. As his words were in no way condescending, they were met with respect and acceptance.

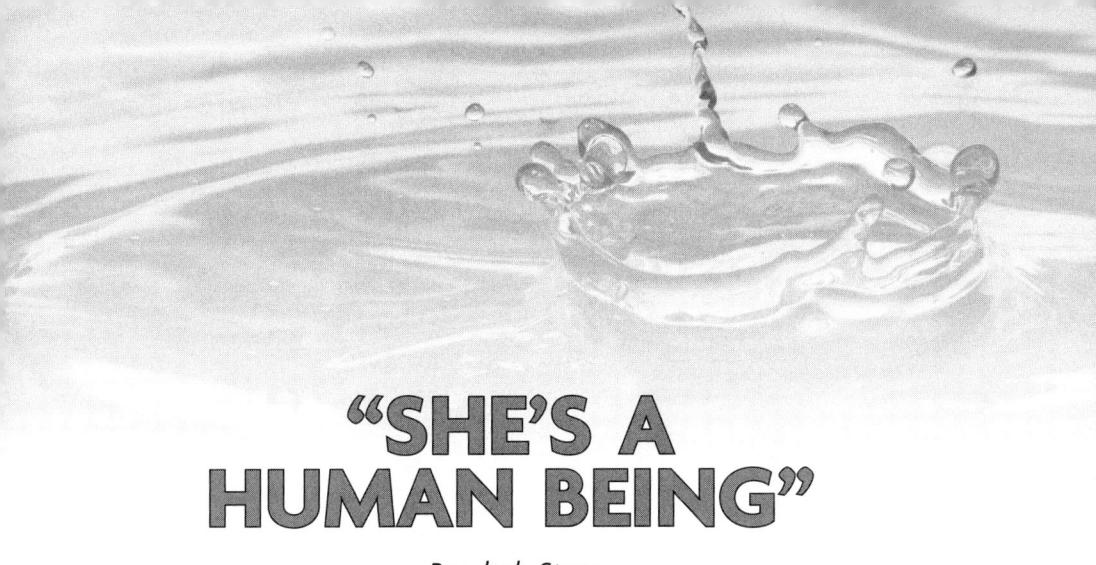

"SHE'S A HUMAN BEING"

Brachah Stern

A kiddush Hashem, day by day...

Rachel's lovely, comfortable home is always tidy and clean, and Rachel has always been proud to give her maid the credit. Her family has grown accustomed to having someone around keeping the place in tip-top shape, but Rachel doesn't let anyone take it for granted. She makes sure that her children greet the maid every day when she comes in, and that they tell her goodbye when she leaves.

"Don't just walk by Melissa when you see her," Rachel says. "Say hello! Never forget that she's a human being. And keep in mind that she does things for you — she helps us all. We have to treat her with respect!"

It's clear how good this makes the maid feel. Melissa is so pleased with everyone in Rachel's family. When they greet her, she responds enthusiastically, "And good morning to *you*! G-d bless you! Have a good day!"

"What fine people the Jews are," Melissa tells her friends.

HOMEMADE YERUSHALMI KIRUV

Rabbi Yitzchok Kornblau

There are those who don't have all the right words, but they care so much that it doesn't matter...in this case, it all began with one small "Halo!"

Chaim Moshe was your run-of-the-mill *Yerushalmi*. Long black jacket, matching *peyos* — so much part of the backdrop of the holy city, he could slip in and out of the Jerusalem stone walls and no one would be the wiser.

Speaking of walls...like any *Yerushalmi* worth his Jerusalem stone, Chaim Moshe was a fixture at the Kosel. Day after day he'd trek there to visit and converse with *der Tatte in Himmel*, never letting the flurry of tourists and other distractions hamper his business. He was never late for his appointment, and neither was *der Tatte*....

Well, he was *almost* never late. There was one part of the scene that always vied for his attention: the polished *kiruv* professionals who canvassed the Wall for stray Jews who, unbeknownst to themselves, were yearning somewhere deep inside to leave the scene that washed them up by the Kosel and schedule a real appointment with *their Tatte*.

Chaim Moshe was entranced each time those rescue workers pulled another spiritual casualty out of the morass, bringing them back to vitality by warming their souls with aish haTorah, the fire of Torah. If only he could help them, jump in alongside them and participate in their holy craft, but alas, he was from a different world. He knew he could never help them — even if he were able to speak their language.

But on that crisp morning as he arrived at the Kosel, a young, assimilated Jew was approaching the Wall next to him. Instinctively, Chaim Moshe scanned the plaza for someone on the beat, but no *kiruv* canvassers could be found. How could this be? Here's a Jew who needs help. *Where are they?!*

As the precious minutes passed Chaim Moshe realized that if someone didn't do something soon, this Jew would get swallowed up again by the currents of society, and he would be lost forever.

NU! What about you?! A voice from deep inside egged him on.

Ach, meshugas! He deflected the voice — he barely knew enough English to get himself out of a paper bag, much less converse with this American Jew. But before the argument became heated, the voice inside let off its final salvo: *He's leaving!*

Chaim Moshe snapped out of his reverie and realized that, indeed, his charge was leaving. *Nu*, Chaim Moshe thought to himself, *it might not work, but could it hurt?*

"Halo!"

Sonny paused for a moment. Was someone talking to him? A quick survey revealed that, indeed, one of the strangely dressed natives was smiling widely at him. His curiosity piqued, Sonny smiled back with a warm, Southern Californian "Hi" and waited to see where this was going.

Now what?! Chaim Moshe's mind raced. "Ah...du yu like Yizrael?"

Viewed from the fence, the two of them grappling in awkward

conversation might have made an interesting postcard shot. From up close it must have been even more entertaining. But somehow, some way, Chaim Moshe got the ball rolling, and soon he had Sonny following him up the stairs to an Old City building.

If you're imagining that Sonny was the happy-go-lucky hippie type, you're wrong. Sonny was intelligent. Ruthlessly intelligent. Chaim Moshe's only opportunity lay in the fact that Sonny was interested in a bit of diversion, and this fellow, who looked as if he had landed from Mars, definitely offered that today as he shlepped him up into the entrance of Aish HaTorah, earnestly telling him that if he would like to learn "gud tings about Judishkite — deese peeple speek Inglesh."

And English they spoke, with a quality and content Sonny had never heard before. Clarity, truth, honesty…and other simple words that seemed recently to have slipped out of contemporary English… and soon enough Sonny had scheduled his own appointment with his *Tatte*.

Now, you might be thinking, *Aw…that's such a nice kiruv story*. But the story didn't end there — because Chaim Moshe *didn't* let it end.

He was there for Sonny when Sonny decided that *this* was the way it was meant to be.

He was there for Sonny as he moved up the ranks of the program.

He was there for him when he was accepted to one of the most prestigious American yeshivos in Israel.

He was there for him when he married a wonderful young *bas Yisrael*. He came to *all* their *simchos*, and he remained there for them to watch as they raised a family of *ehrlicheh kinderlach*, steeped in *Yiddisheh* values.

And now, twenty years later, he's still there to *shep nachas* from "Sonny," who is now one of the most respected *avreichim* in a prestigious *kollel* in Eretz Yisrael.

And it all started with one little *"Halo."*

2
CAN I HELP?

WHAT THE BANKER SAW

Rabbi Nachman Seltzer

*Small actions can change the world —
and that is just what they do, all the time.*

One Friday night in my neighborhood shul, a wonderfully warm *kehillah* in Ramat Beit Shemesh, there was guest in the crowd. Rabbi Shmuel Bloom was in town for his grandson's bar mitzvah, and the *rav* had asked him to say a few words between *Kabbalas Shabbos* and *Maariv*. In the course of his talk he told a most moving story....

●●●

When Rabbi Shaya Greenberg moved to a small town in Ontario, Canada, he realized almost immediately how much work he faced. This particular town boasted a large cross-section of Jewish activity. Socially it was a fantastic place to be, but from a religious standpoint it wasn't that great. Rabbi Greenberg took a good, long look at his place of worship on that first Friday night and tried to see it from an outsider's point of view. What he saw was far from encouraging. The building was on the smallish side, and there was nothing in the way of ceramic tiles, marble pillars, or a deep-pile carpeted *kiddush* hall equipped with gleaming, state-of-the-art equipment to accommodate three hundred.

Au contraire, the building's paint was flaking and peeling, the air conditioning was in desperate need of an overhaul, and the entire shul from top to bottom had the ambience of a history-scarred Catskill hotel that had seen better days. It would never be able to compete with the Reform edifice that had been constructed on six acres across town, or the Conservative place of worship with its heated pool and sauna rooms available to all paying members. The best the Orthodox shul could offer was Sunday morning "Coffee with the Rabbi," and the coffee there was often lukewarm by the time it arrived. It was obvious to the new rabbinical leader that something needed to be done. The question was simply what that something was and how they were to achieve it as economically as possible.

So he called a board meeting to discuss the issue of growth, of change, of modernizing and slicking up the shul's look, so that the Jews of this small Canadian place of residence would be interested in coming to check out the new show in town. After a few hours of deliberation the board agreed unanimously with Rabbi Greenberg's desire to bring their shul up to speed. But when it was time for the members to shell out the cash, the board members found that the shul's account was nowhere near their goal. To construct the type of building they needed, complete with stainless-steel stoves in the industrial-sized kitchen, and acoustics that ensured that the *chazzan's* voice would be heard all over the sanctuary, Rabbi Greenberg was going to need big money. Everyone knew that it was worth it, because that would entice Jews to come; but how could they raise the necessary funds?

The rabbi could already hear the jackhammers pounding away, the breaking of the ground, the sound of shovel striking dirt at that very auspicious moment, but how to translate this vision into reality?

They were going to need a loan. He hated loans; the board hated loans; but what other choice did they have? So a loan it was to be.

●●●

The First National Bank of Canada* was an imposing fortress of a place on Main Street. It occupied the most desirable corner lot in town and maximized its image of solidity with a spate of glossy advertisements in the windows offering everything good in the world to those folks who chose to take a mortgage from First National. Rabbi Greenberg entered the shiny edifice, his heart beating at three times its normal rate. He had no idea whether the man he was scheduled to meet would be sympathetic to his plans or whether he would inform the rabbi that the bank was not interested in assisting him at all.

He took a seat in a plush room and waited his turn. Pulling a *sefer* from his briefcase he relaxed in the pleasant surroundings as classical music played in the background and phones and computers beeped endlessly. Eventually he was called in to his meeting with one of the managers.

The nameplate on the door read Jack O'Brien, and Rabbi Greenberg wondered what kind of man he was. He found O'Brien sitting comfortably behind a glass-topped desk, an affable expression on his face. He motioned to Rabbi Greenberg to sit on one of the armchairs in front of his desk and asked him if he wanted a cup of coffee or water. The rabbi declined graciously, and O'Brien sat back to hear what he had to say.

"I am the rabbi of one of the neighborhood synagogues," he began. "Since I've undertaken this job our membership has been growing, and we're looking to construct a much larger building that will better serve our needs. It will include a hall that can be rented out for affairs — weddings and such — and used for the synagogue's social events." The rabbi went on to explain all the relevant information and provide the banker with all the pertinent facts.

---

* *Name has been changed*

The banker listened carefully, occasionally jotting down some salient points on a legal pad as he took everything in.

"Rabbi Greenberg," O'Brien said when the rabbi had finished, "tell me something, please. With what denomination of Jews is your place of worship affiliated?"

The rabbi wasn't sure where this was going, but he had no choice in the matter. He was going to tell O'brien the truth, even though he didn't know what the banker would do with this information. He swallowed nervously and replied, "Orthodox, sir, Orthodox."

"I see," the banker said. "Then allow me to inform you that I am approving a loan for as much money as your board feels you need!"

Rabbi Greenberg was shocked and stunned. He was expecting to have to beg a little, to play on the man's conscience. He had been prepared to do whatever it might take — but the banker was ready to approve a loan without any heroic efforts on Rabbi Greenberg's part.

Together they went through the documentation, filling out the details on every page and signing or initialing the bottom, until a hefty pile of paperwork lay on the desk between them. When they had finally finished all the forms and the loan was fully approved, the rabbi looked the banker in the eye and asked him why he had been willing to go out on a limb for the synagogue without even knowing him.

O'Brien leaned back in his seat and stared into the past for a few moments. Locking his hands behind his head, his gaze shifted to the ceiling as he waited that extra second before he felt ready to begin.

"You have no idea what it means to be an orphan," he finally said, delivering the line in a quiet tone. "It's a tough role to play. We had no money, and my mother was constantly searching for ways to pull together the funds for our month-to-month expenses. But there were times when we just didn't have enough money.

"Those were the worst times, because then we had to subsist on stale bread, cereal, and noodles for days on end, and sometimes there wasn't even enough money for that. My mother was beside herself. How could she watch her growing son march off to school each day knowing that he was still hungry because he hadn't eaten a good breakfast? She just didn't know what to do. She was working as hard as she could, but try as she might, she couldn't see a way out for us.

"And then one day we were walking through the isles of our local grocery store when the owner called us over to his little office at the back of the shop.

"'Mrs. O'Brien,' he said to her in a voice that was almost a whisper, 'I happen to know that your financial situation is not the greatest right now. I also know,' he went on, 'that you always pay for what you buy up front and that you're a very honest person. So I'd like to make you an offer.' My mother waited silently for the man to go on," O'Brien said, "and I stood there by her side, curious to hear what this man was going to do.

"'Mrs. O'Brien,' he said, 'I would consider it a personal favor if you would continue shopping in my store, and on those days when you just don't have the money and you need the food, please, please, feel free to take whatever you feel is necessary for your son's health and well-being. I know that you'll pay me back when you can and that you'll only take what you really need. I trust you implicitly.'

"It was that offer of help, that wonderfully kind and sincere offer of assistance to a woman and child who didn't even share his religion, that showed me what kind of people you Orthodox Jews are. And even though my mother didn't often avail herself of his kindness, just knowing that his offer was there was enough. Just knowing that someone cared enough to offer help pulled us through."

The rabbi nodded and shook the banker's hand, knowing that the small actions we take, the kind offers, the warm words, the beautiful smile, the care that we show, can impact the world even many years later.

A CHAIN OF EVENTS

By Yossi

Often enough, it takes no more than a few words to open the door to a future that is amazing beyond imagining.

My story begins about four years ago. I had just completed my army service and gotten married, and I was broke. I had been doing a little work at my cousin's store, making barely enough to get by, when there was a huge misunderstanding between us and my cousin fired me.

Needless to say, I was in a pretty bad state of mind. I had a wife, and bills to pay, and no way to make the money I needed. Being a high-school dropout, I didn't find many doors open to me.

I had spent about three days moping in bed when my wife told me to go out and learn some Torah with her father. I told her I didn't want to face anyone. Still, I was a good husband, and so I listened and went off to learn with him.

While we were learning, a certain Rosh Yeshivah approached us and began speaking with my father-in-law, who is a well-respected *rav* and *rosh kollel*. Over the years my father-in-law has taught and guided thousands of people, many of whom have young families to support and would appreciate some extra income. The Rosh Yeshivah apologized for interrupting us, gave me a warm, friendly smile, and asked my father-in-law if he knew of anyone who would be willing to tutor a boy who needed extra help in Gemara.

My father-in-law looked at me. I said, "No way!" You see, I had told myself that I never wanted to go back to yeshivah, having had some painful experiences there. He explained that if I was getting paid it really wasn't considered being in yeshivah. In the end I agreed.

It went really well with that boy, and soon the yeshivah had me learning with another boy. Within two months I was teaching a small class of three boys and making four times the amount I had been earning working for my cousin — in half the time!

Over the next several years I grew as a person and as a teacher. Today, *baruch Hashem*, there are many boys who consider me their "rebbi" and who seek my advice on a daily basis. I look back at the day I was fired — which at the time seemed like the worst day of my life — and recognize that sometimes things work out in the most unexpected ways.

● ● ●

At one point I invited a prestigious speaker to give a lecture to my students at the school. As it turned out, though, he ended up coming to my home to speak instead. About forty guys packed into my living room, and he really spoke well.

A few days later the speaker called me to say that he had forgotten something at my house. He wanted my address again and I gave it to him. All of a sudden he said, "One second — where did you say you live?"

He told me that there was a young, newly-married couple living in my building, and they were trying to become more observant. He asked me if I would mind having them over sometime.

I discussed the matter with my wife, and she told me to invite them for a Shabbos meal. As it happened, that Friday night we were having fifteen boys over for the *seudah*. So I called the neighbor, gave her (it was she who answered) my friendliest hello, introduced myself and invited them, asking if they'd prefer to come for a loud evening meal or a quiet lunch. She told me that it would be her husband's first real Shabbos experience, and they'd like to come Friday night.

That Shabbos meal was the first of many. My students gave this young couple a warm welcome, and the meal was delightful. Our new friends were intrigued by this group of *frum* American yeshivah boys, not all of whom had come from *frum* backgrounds. We shared beautiful *divrei Torah*, and the *zemiros* were uplifting. There were some songs the couple enjoyed so much that they asked us to sing them again and again.

Over the next eight months they ate at our home almost every week, and it was truly inspiring to watch them grow and to feel a part of that growth. The thought hit me that had the speaker spoken at school instead of at my home, or had he not forgotten something at my house, this would never have happened. We and this couple would have been living side by side without ever knowing how much potential was there.

●●●

That couple invited us to their house for meals many times. My wife and I usually made some excuse for why we couldn't go, since we didn't know what their level of kashrus was. Eventually, though, when they invited us for a cookout one fine Adar evening, we decided to attend. At least we could join them for some drinks.

We arrived at about 10 p.m. Needless to say, the crowd was not our type; there were a bunch of young people there who had just returned from Thailand. When the twenty bottles of beer and three bottles of vodka were empty, my wife and I decided it was really time to leave. *Kiruv* was one thing; a drunken party was something else altogether.

At about midnight my wife left and I planned to follow, when all of a sudden one of the guys, who was already pretty drunk, grabbed me and said, "Rabbi, I have a question for you. If you can answer it, I'll be yours forever."

Not taking him too seriously but intrigued by the possibility of an interesting question, I sat down. He said that while in Thailand a friend of his had wanted to go out to eat shark head. He told his friend that he shouldn't, since it wasn't kosher. His friend said, "So what?" He tried to explain it to his friend and convince him that he shouldn't do it, but he wasn't able to. If I could give him a good answer, he told me, he would do whatever I wanted.

My answer impressed him.

The next question came from someone who had witnessed a terrorist attack firsthand and saw a baby get blown up. He told me that after that experience he no longer believed in G-d and wanted me to explain it to him.

Before I knew it three hours had passed with these people. They asked me all sorts of questions. I realized that, deep down, even in their drunken state, they really wanted someone to just listen to them. I left with promises to stay in touch and get together again soon.

I didn't expect anything to happen so fast.

It was Sunday of a three-day Purim in Jerusalem. As there was no *Megillah* reading that day (we had read it on Friday), I started celebrating pretty early in the morning. My phone rang; it was the neighbor from downstairs. She told me that one of the boys who had been at the barbecue the previous week had a friend whose brother was in from Germany and was looking for a rabbi he could speak to. She wanted to know if she could give him my number. I told her that I wasn't the best "rabbi" for the job but that I would be happy to meet him sometime. I hung up and went back to my learning and wine. Fifteen minutes later my phone rang. It was David from Germany. He wanted to know if he could come over right away. I told him he could.

He showed up around 11. I offered him a drink. He took water.

He told me that for the past seven years he had been dating a girl who wasn't Jewish. I was thinking that explaining why to marry Jewish while not completely sober wasn't exactly what I needed at that moment. But David told me that wasn't the reason he had come, since they had broken up. So I asked him what I could do for him.

He told me that since his breakup everyone had been telling him to find a nice Jewish girl, and he didn't understand what the big deal was. I told him that the reason he didn't understand was that he himself had no idea what it means to be Jewish. I asked him how long he would be in town. He told me he was leaving the next day. I said there wasn't much I could do for him in such a short time, but I promised to find him someone in Germany who would help him out.

I walked him to the door. On his way out he noticed my *tefillin* and asked me if he could put them on. He said he hadn't donned *tefillin* since his bar mitzvah. He was 30 years old.

After he put them on I invited him to return to my house later that day for the Purim meal. Surprisingly, he showed up.

Today David lives in Israel and learns in yeshivah.

I've learned that there's a reason for everything that happens in your life. Sometimes it may appear to be bad, while in reality it is the best thing that has ever happened to you. Sometimes it's from some unexpected source, while at other times it can be from a word or story that touched you. The main thing is to seize those moments, analyze them and grow from them. And, of course, tune in to all the people who touch your life; acknowledge their presence and allow yourself to be part of Hashem's ongoing Plan.

SPEAK NOW, OR FOREVER KNOW NO PEACE

Barbara Bensoussan

You could be anywhere, anywhere at all when that chance arrives, and your job is always to serve as Hashem's ambassador.

He was standing in the menswear section of a department store in Manhattan, fingering the ties lackadaisically. He wanted a new tie for Shabbat, and it was the designer silk tie with the pewter and silver stripes that caught his eye. It was what his yeshivah friends would call a *"chassan* tie." Eliyahu paused reflectively. Maybe he should speak to the Rosh Yeshivah about whether he ought to start putting his name onto some *shidduch* lists. He was, after all, almost 23...

Then again, it was already August, and maybe he'd be better off waiting until he went home to Paris for Succos to start thinking about *sidduchim*. After all, what were the chances that he would find common ground with an American girl? Americans seemed to live in a different universe, a world in which people wove their way in and out of fleeting friendships, where food and clothing were abundant but lacking spice, where strangers bonded by telling each other their life stories at bus stops. Eliyahu was more used to his own milieu in Paris, where people shut their apartment doors firmly in the evenings and never spoke to strangers, where anti-Semites and Arabs rendered the Jews wary.

Then there was the food; he was sure he could never adapt to the bland, monochromatic Ashkenazi cooking he suffered through when well-meaning rebbis and *avreichim* invited him to their Shabbos tables. Maybe he didn't look especially Sephardi — Eliyahu had red hair and light-brown eyes, just like his mother — but his parents were Moroccan from way back.

Suddenly, as if his musings had somehow conjured forth Gallic hallucinations, his ears picked up sounds of people speaking French. Wheeling around in surprise, he spotted a couple over at the next rack of ties.

They were so sure that no one around them could understand what they were saying that they weren't paying attention to the volume of their voices. The man was husky, fair-haired, and red-complexioned, wearing modish glasses; she was short and thin in a high-strung kind of way, with wavy black hair. Both of them looked to be in their late 20's.

"Come on, Philippe. You have to hurry up!" the woman said impatiently. "Just pick two ties and let's get out of here! It's Friday morning, remember?"

"It's so hard to choose," the husband protested. "Look at how gorgeous these ties are! They're all brand names! And so cheap compared to Europe — I'm tempted to buy a couple dozen of them!" His eyes lit up. "Hey, maybe we should," he said. "We could give them as gifts when we go back."

"So buy them all, but we need to move on," the wife said through gritted teeth. Then, to Eliyahu's surprise, she continued, "Philippe,

I have no idea where I can find a store that sells kosher food. How am I supposed to organize a Shabbat for us when I don't even know where to get hold of a piece of chicken?"

Oh, wow, Eliyahu thought with a start. *They're not just French. They're Jewish.*

"Why are you worried about finding chicken?" Philippe said. "Listen, Orly, there's nowhere in the hotel where you can cook it anyway. I thought we agreed to just buy some tuna and bread and fruit for Shabbat."

Eliyahu stood there listening, having moved from the ties to a bank of button-down shirts, wondering if he should do something. He was by nature a reserved person, even shy; it grated against his upbringing to approach strangers in a department store. *But these people are Jews*, his conscience prodded him. *Are you going to let them suffer through a Shabbat of tuna fish and bananas?*

But if he offered to find them a place, would they accept it? Or would they brush him off with chilly, forced smiles? They didn't look all that religious — the woman was wearing jeans — and not everyone likes to be pushed into a "religious experience" by a guy wearing a white shirt and black pants. They'd probably think he was some fanatic *chareidi* guy out to do *kiruv* on them — and get offended; after all, it was obvious they already observed Shabbat at some level.

Then again, the wife did seem to attach considerable importance to Shabbat, given the way she was pushing her husband to make tracks out of the store. So maybe they would appreciate a Shabbat option that would beat packaged rolls and tuna fish hands down?

Eliyahu's yeshivah training kicked in as he weighed the options. If he said nothing, he knew he would feel guilty forever for not having tried to help; maybe the blame for the couple's failure to keep Shabbat properly would fall squarely on his head. *What's the worst-case scenario?* he asked himself. If he said something and got rebuffed, well, at least he would have tried to do his duty as a Jew. Eliyahu decided to risk making the leap and approaching them.

"*Excusez-moi*," he said politely, clearing his throat as he made his way around the banks of plastic-wrapped dress shirts. "Did I overhear you saying that you need to find things for Shabbat? I'm sorry for eavesdropping, but you were speaking loudly enough for me to hear, and I'm also French. And Jewish."

They stared at him in surprise. Then, to his vast relief, they broke into broad smiles and began to laugh. "Oh, my!" said the wife. "We had no idea! What a relief — finally somebody who speaks our language! Where are you from?"

"From Paris — from the Jewish section," he answered. "Nineteenth *arrondissement* [district]." Based on the way the two of them were dressed, Eliyahu could tell that normally they would never have spoken to a yeshivah guy like him. But now they were just glad to find a fellow French speaker, and his friendliness disarmed any suspicion they might have felt. He had to admit, that was one thing he had learned from the Americans: a big smile and friendly manner take you a lot further than remaining fretfully in your corner. "Where are you guys from?" he asked.

They named a town he'd never heard of. "It's on the French-Swiss border," the husband explained. "It's tiny. Almost everybody there works in Geneva, including my whole family — our name is Levy, by the way.

"I work for a Swiss bank myself," the husband continued, "a bank that mostly invests for a large group of private clients. I was sent to the U.S. this summer to visit our branches here, get to know the American staff and learn how the U.S. operations work. So far we've been to Miami, Boston, Philadelphia and Chicago. The New York office is big; we're going to be here for a month and a half."

"Where are you staying?" Eliyahu asked, as if he hadn't already overheard.

"Well, we took a hotel room," Philippe said. "Of course, the company is paying."

"Hmm…," Eliyahu said, pretending to mull over the idea. "Doesn't sound like the best of options for Shabbat, especially if you don't know anybody. It seems to me that maybe you two could use a better place to go. Would you like me to find you a place in Brooklyn?"

He saw them hesitating. Eliyahu had the distinct impression that perhaps they had been planning to spend their Shabbat taking a walking tour of Manhattan and hadn't given much thought to finding a shul. On top of that, a well-brought-up French person doesn't just barge into a stranger's home on Erev Shabbat. "I know a Moroccan family — French-speaking — that always has people over," he persisted. "Why don't you try? They're friends of mine. The wife makes very good Moroccan food."

The mention of a hot Moroccan Shabbat meal seemed to soften Philippe immediately; a smile crept over his face, and unconsciously he put one hand over his broad stomach. The wife seemed more hesitant. Finally she ventured, "But would they have room for us? And isn't it awfully late to be inviting ourselves?"

"Hey, why don't we find out?" Eliyahu said. He took his cell phone from his pocket, hoping against hope the Adahans would be able to take them in. He didn't see why not, since he and his friends sometimes called them two hours before Shabbat asking for an emergency placement, and they'd never said no before. Somehow Ilana Adahan was able to magically produce enough last-minute food to handle the overflow; he didn't know how. Maybe it was like all those folk tales where the jug magically refills with wine, and the *cholent* meant for two feeds fifteen.

Eliyahu couldn't find the Adahans' number in his phone, so he called his friend Gavriel. "Gaby," he said, "I just met a couple who needs a place for Shabbat. Their name is Levy and they live near Geneva. Can you call Adahan for me and see if they can take two people, a married couple?" He hung up his phone. "Want me to help you find some more ties? There are more racks further down. In fact, I just saw a silver one that's really sharp."

●●●

When Gaby reached Ilana Adahan, she was ensconced in her kitchen, deep in culinary inspiration. She sounded breathless, and Gaby could hear sounds of water running in the sink, pots clanging, and a toddler singing to herself. Ilana was a bit behind schedule because the baby had refused to nap yet and had already made a mess on the kitchen floor with a leaky bottle and Cheerios. Would she ever pull this kitchen and this house together in time for Shabbat? And now the phone was ringing…

"Madame Adahan," Gaby began respectfully, "I hate to bother you, but my friend Eliyahu — you know, the one who comes with me on Shabbat — just met a couple of French people in Manhattan who need a place for Shabbat, otherwise they'll be eating in a hotel room. It sounds like they're not super-religious, but apparently they keep kosher and more or less keep Shabbat. Could you and your husband possibly put them up? Maybe you guys could be a good influence on them!"

Ilana took a deep breath. She wasn't even sure she would finish on time, let alone have her house in any shape for guests. She was tired and had kind of been looking forward to rolling into bed early, which would certainly not happen on a June Friday night if there were extras at the table. *You're allowed to say no*, her petulant Inner Egotist chimed in. But then the voice of her conscience and soft heart won out. "Okay," she said, pulling reflexively at her headscarf and grabbing a glass mug away from her toddler just in the nick of time. "Tell them what time Shabbat begins and make sure they have enough time to get to us."

Philippe and Orly weren't sure what to expect; the idea of going to perfect strangers for Shabbat was very foreign to a couple accustomed to spending every Friday night comfortably with family. They had heard of Brooklyn but had never been there; someone had once described it to them as the Bnei Brak of America, only bigger, which sounded awfully intimidating.

They rattled across the East River in a Q train, passing through dark and ominous-looking subway stations before emerging into the fading light of day, eventually disembarking onto a commercial avenue in Flatbush. Orly insisted on buying a bouquet of flowers spray-dyed in raucous colors from a Mexican vendor waiting hopefully underneath the train, while Philippe peered around for street signs to help him get his bearings.

They hadn't anticipated that the train from Manhattan would take so long; it was just a few minutes before candle-lighting time. The streets were hushed except for a few trucks lumbering home for the weekend and the occasional Jewish car careening past, daring itself to make it home before the siren. As they followed Eliyahu's directions down the avenue and onto a side street, Orly and Philippe saw they were in a residential neighborhood of two- and three-story homes, some well-appointed, others ramshackle. Turning onto the Adahans' block — they had made one wrong turn and had to stop a Jew hurrying to shul to get it right — they saw little children already suited up in Shabbat outfits and robes playing in driveways and pocket-sized front yards.

Back at the Adahan household, Ilana and Danny were getting nervous. "Do you think they backed out?" Danny said, pacing the living room. "Got cold feet? I'm already late for shul; I can't wait too much longer for them."

Ilana was thinking: *I made two extra salads and three desserts because Gaby said they were coming, not to mention changing the linens in the little kids' room, and I won't be pleased if they don't show up after putting me to all that trouble.*

Then the doorbell rang, and there they were: two sweating, disheveled, apologetic French people toting flowers and a couple of overnight bags. Ilana and Danny disregarded the lateness and did their best to welcome them graciously, installing them in one of the children's bedrooms; Philippe ran to do a 5-minute washup and change of clothing before rushing out to shul with Danny.

Despite the flustered beginning, the two couples got on famously. Ilana's warmth and Danny's sense of humor put everyone at ease, despite Danny's formidable black beard and his wife's terribly religious-looking headscarf, which only brought out her pretty features. The couple's seven children were sweet and lively — Orly was entranced by the chubby, smiling baby — and the house, while not huge or fancy, was roomy enough (not to mention neat enough, thanks to a lot of last-minute rushing). A couple of French yeshivah boys joined the family for supper; the meal did justice to Ilana's culinary prowess, and the Levys were treated to a lengthy introduction to what Jewish life in Brooklyn is all about.

Shabbos day went equally well; Danny took Philippe to a Moroccan shul where everyone spoke French, and after lunch he took the couple on a walking tour of the neighborhood, pointing out shuls, yeshivahs, stores, and organizations. "Everything is Jewish!" Orly marveled. "I feel like I'm in Israel!"

It was something of a revelation to Philippe and Orly — who came from a small village where very few people were seriously religious and most Jews did their best to keep a low profile — to see that Jews in New York practiced their religion with the sort of naturalness and nonchalance more characteristic of their counterparts in Israel. Orly's family, which had come from Casablanca, had always remained highly traditional; Philippe's family, from Algeria, was much less so, though he'd had a bar mitzvah and could follow the *tefillah* in a shul. The fact that the couple's home merited at least some level of kashrut and Shabbat was largely due to Orly's insistence.

When Shabbat came to a close and the *Havdalah* candle sputtered out, Danny decided to get right down to business. Determined to keep Philippe and Orly in a neighborhood where the spiritual accomplishments of their first Shabbat could be maintained, he confronted his guests: "Okay, the two of you are going to be in New York for six weeks. Why would you stay in a non-Jewish neighborhood in Manhattan, where it will cost a fortune, when we could help you find a place in *our* neighborhood? We're only a short commute from Manhattan."

The Levys were flabbergasted; this hadn't even occurred to them. But Danny was resolute. He pulled out a newspaper, turned to the classifieds and began calling for furnished rentals. "It's the summer," he said confidently. "Lots of people go away. There must be somewhere you could rent."

After half an hour of calling, they had gotten nowhere. Suddenly, the Adahans' 12-year-old daughter piped up: "Papa, what about the house across the street, with the furnished basement? Didn't their tenant move out not so long ago?"

Danny whooped with delight. "You're right!" he shouted. "You're absolutely right!" He strode out the door, rang the neighbors' bell, and before you knew it Philippe and Orly were being introduced, and an agreement was promptly struck.

●●●

The next day, Sunday, the Levys piled their suitcases into their little white rental car and drove themselves to their new home. They spent the rest of that summer in Brooklyn and, to their own surprise, for the first time in their lives found themselves living in a truly religious neighborhood. Orly stopped wearing her jeans, because she no longer felt comfortable wearing them around the neighborhood, and every Shabbat the couple ate with the Adahans, becoming steadily more exposed to Torah ways of thinking. Eliyahu met up with them there several times when he came with his friend Gaby for Shabbat meals. Orly picked up Ilana's recipes for *matbucha* and chicken with olives; in turn she taught Ilana how to make a real French chocolate mousse.

It was on one of their walks home from shul that Philippe spoke admiringly to Danny about the Adahans' brood of children. "They're great kids," he said. "I'm looking forward to raising kids myself one day, when the time is right."

Danny stopped in his tracks. "What do you mean, when the time is right?" he asked anxiously.

"Well, you know…," Philippe said lightly. "Orly and I have been married for only two years. We aren't really prepared to have children yet; we want to enjoy ourselves for a while. We were hoping to wait a few years before we have to settle into family life."

He was surprised to see the appalled look that came over his friend's face. Danny, usually amiable and light-hearted, had to struggle not to blow up with the full force of a North African sandstorm. "You can't think like that!" he exclaimed incredulously. "Having children is the first mitzvah in the Torah! You should never want to put off things like that! One day you'll be too old to have children!"

"G-d forbid!" Philippe retorted in shock.

"It really hurts me when people tell me they'd rather not have a family right away because they want to 'live a little first,'" Danny railed. "What is *living*? What is life all about? Is there any greater pleasure, anything more meaningful than having children?"

Philippe looked cowed. "Maybe you're right," he conceded. "But Orly has to feel that way too, you know. The wives are the ones who take on most of the burden."

"So discuss it with her," Danny said shortly, and he kept uncharacteristically silent the rest of the way home just to prove his point.

●●●

The summer drew to a close, and it was time for the Levys to return to France. The Adahans hosted them for a final farewell barbecue and accompanied them the next afternoon to the airport to see them off. The two women were teary as they hugged each other. "I don't know when we'll see you next," Ilana said.

"Come see us in France," Orly urged. "Can't you leave the kids with your parents and take a little vacation?" But she knew the chances of that happening were close to nil.

"Don't forget what I told you," Danny hissed in Philippe's ear as he gave him a hug.

But the two men actually did get to see each other again, sooner than expected. Around Chanukah time Philippe's firm sent him on business to New York again for a week, and where else would he spend that Shabbat but with the Adahans?

And then, several months later, shortly after Shavuos, Danny found himself suddenly obliged to board a plane bound for *la belle France*. After all, there was no way he was going to miss out on being the guest of honor at the *brit milah* of the Levys' first child.

●●●

A few weeks after that Eliyahu and Gaby were seated once again around the Adahan Shabbat table, and Danny was showing off pictures of the Levys' new baby, a tiny bundle with a crinkled face and full head of black hair sticking out in all directions. *Well, I guess all's well that ends well*, Eliyahu thought. He puffed up a little as he tucked into his plate of couscous and lamb, imagining that he deserved just a bit of the credit for all this. After all, if he hadn't opened his big mouth that day at the department store in Manhattan and made the connection, Philippe and Orly Levy would have spent a touristy but spiritually empty summer in Manhattan and would never have made any significant changes in their lives. Now Orly was working part-time for an important rabbi in Geneva and was even covering her hair. Philippe had found himself a *chavruta*, and both of them were attending regular *shiurim*.

"What did they name the baby?" Eliyahu asked Danny, as he handed back the small stack of photos. "Do they name for living relatives in Philippe's family? I guess if they did, then they'd name him for Philippe's father."

"You're right, that's what they did," Danny said. He paused. "You know what Philippe's father's name is?"

Eliyahu shrugged; how was he supposed to know?

"Well, in French they call him Etienne," Danny said. "But in Hebrew his name is…"

Suddenly he tipped his head back and gave a roar of laughter. "In Hebrew," he said, "his name is Eliyahu!"

ELIEZER'S GRIN

By Judy Gruenfeld

*We can all succeed, each in our own way,
in bringing love and light to others.
Just look at Eliezer.*

I know a boy who is pure joy…
When he smiles, the sky lights up for miles;
When he laughs, you're drawn right in
To all that's pure and free from sin.
His voice is heard, though not with words,
By those who hear, though not with ears;
When looking into his big brown eyes,
I see all that's important and all that is wise.
One day while perched on tippy-toes,
He made an attempt to kiss my nose;
He couldn't get it just quite right,
And so the kiss became a bite.

The sweetest kiss I've ever had
Was given to me by you, my lad;
You're the bestest hugger in the world...
You give of yourself, with a love that's unfurled.
We look for life's meaning when we are down,
But I just have to turn around,
And take a look at where I've been,
And remember Eliezer's grin.

●●●

EDITOR'S NOTE:

A dear friend of ours reported that she was staying in a hotel for Pesach and was feeling rather alone, as there were few people she knew or with whom she felt comfortable. "But there was one handicapped young child there," she relates, "sitting in his wheelchair, who stretched out his hands to greet me with a longing smile whenever he saw me. So I would stop and smile to him, and our smiles became hugs. He was so pleased!

"This made me feel so happy that I began to have a much easier time making contact with the other people there.

"In his own way, the little boy was trying to build a friendship with me, and I responded by giving him that friendship he sought, but in the process I gained so much! Who, I pondered, was giving to whom?"

THANKING MRS. SCHWARTZ

By Hannah Kafree

With a few sincere words, a teacher can move mountains.

No one knew what was bothering Adel. And no one asked. She sat through her classes with a sullen, bored, faraway look in her eyes, obviously not interested in the material being taught, and certainly not participating.

Before she entered tenth grade Adel had heard rumors that Mrs. Schwartz was the school's most demanding biology teacher, and it was Adel's bad *mazal* to get stuck with her. She decided from day one that she hated Mrs. Schwartz and would not comply with anything that had to do with her class. Here is where she really let herself seethe with resentment at the world around her, arms folded firmly across her chest, allowing the blackness in her soul to bore daily into the teacher's face.

Mrs. Schwartz was a short, plump older woman with round

spectacles. She considered it a privilege to teach her favorite subject — *nifla'os haBorei*, the wonders of the creation — with ardent enthusiasm. She was especially ebullient about the multicolored tulips she grew in the garden behind her home, which was walking distance from the high school where she had been employed for over twenty-five years.

When Mrs. Schwartz received an official office form accompanying a request that she approve Adel's transfer to a lower-track biology class, she took the liberty of checking her student's past academic performance. She knew Adel hadn't passed any of her biology tests, so she was shocked to see that Adel had been in English and math honors classes since seventh grade. Something was definitely wrong.

The next day she approached Adel with a wide smile and twinkling eyes and asked her to join her in the small adjacent lab room, so they could speak privately for a few minutes while the rest of the class worked on an earthworm dissection. Adel's eyes flashed with anger.

Alone with Mrs. Schwartz, Adel leaned her back against the lab counter, her face grim. She refused to make eye contact with her teacher.

"Adel, I see that you requested to transfer from my class," Mrs. Schwartz began.

Adel stared at a crack in the corner of the floor.

"Do you mind if I ask you why?"

No answer.

"I checked your records, and I noticed that you do very well in English."

Adel's face remained hard and impassive. Inside, mean, angry thoughts churned. *How dare she interfere with my life! I don't want to be here! I want out!*

"Did you know that the material covered in my class involves nothing more than reading?" Mrs. Schwartz continued her one-sided conversation.

Adel refused to respond.

Then Mrs. Schwartz held up and waved a yellow paperback with the outline of a green tree on the cover.

"You see this? It's a basic biology review book. At the end of each chapter is a practice exam. All my tests are similar to the ones in here. All you need to do in order to pass is to read this. It's really not so hard, especially since you're a fantastic reader."

A subtle change in Adel's expression seemed to indicate that she was offended. Indignant that Mrs. Schwartz had the audacity to snoop in her business, she hardly seemed impressed by her teacher's offer to make the material easier to understand.

Mrs. Schwartz did not miss this. Placing the yellow book on the counter, she whispered quietly, "Adel, what's wrong? Why are you failing my class? You are highly intelligent. Is something bothering you that I could help with?"

Adel's brows furrowed, and she kept staring intently at the floor without saying a word.

Mrs. Schwartz offered to lend her a copy of the yellow book, gently suggesting again that it would assist her.

"You'll see. My class will be easy for you!" Mrs. Schwartz beamed a genuine smile of compassionate warmth in the direction of the icy wall that surrounded her student.

Despite the acute embarrassment of being called aside and singled out in front of the class, and her indignation at the fact that Mrs. Schwartz was interfering with her life, a ray of hope managed to penetrate the dreary self-imposed fortress surrounding Adel. Though she had built that subconscious barrier for self-preservation, it did nothing to assuage her misery. She felt agonizingly isolated and alone.

Mrs. Schwartz wouldn't have bothered to say anything to Adel if she wasn't concerned, if she hadn't noticed.

Adel felt an uncomfortable awkwardness as she glanced at the yellow book on the counter beside her, apparent evidence that someone actually cared about her....

In the months that followed there was a barely perceptible shift in Adel's demeanor. It was not an easy transformation, but once it began it gained momentum. Adel felt an unfamiliar urge to try...at least in Mrs. Schwartz's class.

She soon discovered that it was true: Mrs. Schwartz's class work was predictably organized according to the chapters in the handbook she had lent Adel. It *was* easy to follow the progression of the material in order to pass the exams. She allowed herself to open up just enough to enjoy being in Mrs. Schwartz's pleasant, positive presence. It even began to be...fun! This was a safe place in the stormy sea, where she could relax a little and start to smile.

Teacher and student never spoke privately again. Adel never confided what was the source of her agonizing distress. Her painful issues still needed to be addressed, yet Adel now felt more strength to cope in a way that, previously, she hadn't thought possible.

Slowly, she began to surface from her isolation in much the same way that a butterfly breaks forth from the constriction of its cocoon.

●●●

Several years later, when Mrs. Schwartz was retired, her school forwarded a letter that arrived from an address thousands of miles away.

It was from Adel.

Dear Mrs. Schwartz,

I don't know if you will remember me. I was in your tenth-grade biology class.

I wanted you to know how much I appreciate something you did for me then, nearly five years ago. No one can ever really understand how much impact he or she can have on another person through just the smallest gesture, but in a way, you saved my life.

At the time I couldn't stand that you tried to talk to me. I hated you, like I hated everyone, like I hated myself! I didn't want to be in the class of the most demanding biology teacher in our whole high school!

Yet, now, in retrospect, with the benefit of emotional and physi-

cal distance from that dark period, I can say that I deeply appreciate and am overwhelmed with gratitude that you were the only one during that terrible time who took the trouble to try and reach out to me. Your care was genuine, your concern was real…your warmth…in that one moment when you attempted to help me… touched me. Everything that unfolded afterward, my change for the better, my willingness to try, an almost unconscious decision to start applying myself in school…I can honestly say were all because of you. I wanted to do well in your class! I wanted to prove that you were right and to live up to your expectations that I could succeed.

So many good things have happened to me since we parted ways. The world is a much brighter place for me now. I just wanted you to know. Thank you. Thank you. Thank you.

Your student,

Adel Bergman

AN ENDURING LIGHT

Nancy Schwager Hochman

Someone finally hears the cries of a lonely heart.

The first time I met Ruth was on the elevator. A tall, fleshy woman with matted grey hair and glasses that magnified lifeless-looking eyes, Ruth spoke first. "You new here?" she asked.

"Yup," just moved in yesterday," I replied.

She scrutinized me intently. "I'm not feeling very good. I have problems with the board [of directors]. But don't tell anyone I complained to you. I don't want no trouble, okay?"

I might have asked her for more information, but she looked so frightened and spoke with such a sense of finality, I just smiled.

"That's a pretty star of David," I said. "By the way, my name's Nancy."

An Enduring Light / 93

"I'm Ruth," she said, without a hint of a smile on her face.

The name *Ruth* came up soon after that brief encounter. "The people here are all very nice, except there's one woman..." the superintendent said. I couldn't help but notice how, on the elevator or in the lobby, people gave Ruth condescending smiles, frozen nods, or turned backs.

Having grown up in a family that had always rooted for the underdog, and as a *baalas teshuvah*, I made it my business *to say a warm hello* whenever I saw her. But within a few weeks I began to understand why people were dismissive with her.

"Is it going to rain outside?" she would ask anyone in the elevator, or anyone she came across during her strolls down the halls, who would listen.

"If it's a bad storm, can the windows break? Someone told me they could break. Is that true? What should I do now?"

Or: "I didn't get a bill from the lighting company. Am I in trouble?"

"My chest hurts," she told me when I saw her next. "Do I have to go to the hospital? I don't want to go to the hospital."

My greetings became more clipped when she cornered me in the lobby. "I'm having trouble seeing," she said. "Am I going blind?"

By this time it was resoundingly clear that the woman was mentally handicapped. Although I felt sorry for and even concerned about her, at this stage I also felt trapped whenever I saw her and wanted little to do with her. When I heard Ruth's trademark knock on my door — a series of five or six taps, then a pause, then an increasingly louder round of knocks — I pretended not to be home.

If anyone would have told me that within a few months I would reintroduce this woman to the mitzvah of lighting Shabbos candles and extend *hachnassas orchim* to her each Shabbos, I would have been incredulous.

Despite my less-than-hospitable attitude at the time, Ruth persisted. "Can I be wit' you?" she asked several weeks later, while I was sitting in the lobby.

"Sure, take a seat," I said, my tone less than enthusiastic.

As soon as she sat down she began talking.

"Pray for me," she said. "I'm so lonely. You have your husband living with you. I have nobody." She was soon content to just sit. I thumbed through my magazine, waiting to greet a friend who said she might come by. After half an hour of sitting, and exchanging just a few words with her, I told her I'd see her again.

"Please, just be wit' me a little while more," she said, following me to the staircase.

"Sorry, I've got papers to mark and housekeeping to do," I said, virtually running up the stairs.

"What's the matter?" Ruth yelled upward. "Why don't you want to be wit' me? Don't you like me?"

I soon found myself shouting, out of frustration, "Yes, I like you, but I need to go. I'm busy. I'm sorry, but I've got things to do. Good-bye."

Once home, I seated myself at the kitchen table in front of a mound of unmarked papers, frozen. "Pray for me. I'm so lonely," kept sounding in my ears.

Several weeks later, with Shabbos only minutes away and a table yet to be set, I heard the same incessant tapping. Despite the last-minute rush, this time I opened the door.

"Hi, Ruth," I said, breathless from running.

There was no hello. Just words that tumbled from her mouth.

"I'm lonely. I'm scared. Can I be wit' you tonight? Please. Just a little while."

There was a pleading look in her eyes that expressed her anguish: "I'm so lonely. I have nobody."

"It's almost Shabbos, Ruth. Would you like to come in and light candles with me?"

As we lit the Shabbos candles together, her empty-looking eyes glowed with the reflected flame. When I uncovered my own eyes I noticed that she looked far more relaxed; the fear I saw and heard had begun to vanish. Finally, I saw something I had never seen on her face before: a smile, as I hugged her and wished her a warm and beautiful Shabbos.

I made it my business to learn more about whatever Ruth was willing to share. Tears came to her eyes as she recalled her mother preparing Shabbos meals and lighting candles when she was a child. She had lived with her mother up until eleven years ago, when her mother died, and since that time Ruth had indeed been living alone with some assistance from her sister.

I also learned that because of her disability, her stove was permanently disabled. She looked hungrily toward a pot of chicken soup and one of turkey meatballs simmering on the *blech*.

In time I learned other things as well. I learned that Ruth was very able to express compassion, that she had a sense of humor, and that she was unfailingly honest. I also learned that there's seldom a good reason to hide behind a locked door when a neighbor in need is knocking.

That night, a much-belated invitation to come in and light candles bridged the distance between two very different people who share one Jewish heritage. Now, whenever I hear the *tap tap tap* on the door an hour or so before Shabbos, I know it is my friend Ruth, here to help me with last-minute preparations and to share candle-lighting and a warm Shabbos meal.

SEEDS OF COMFORT

By Chaya Klein

Decades later, they learned that it had all been worth so much...

Anna and Lillian met in a university library when they were both studying for midterm exams. Well, actually, Lillian was crumpled on the library's bathroom floor, sobbing brokenly because she hadn't done well on one of her important finals. "My parents will kill me!" she cried.

Concerned for the welfare of this woman whom she vaguely recognized from around campus, Anna stopped what she was doing, sat on the floor next to Lillian and asked if she could help. She tried to lift Lillian's spirits, joking around about plant classification. The two discovered that they had many common interests, and their budding friendship eventually led to their becoming travel partners in the exotic Andes Mountains, exploring the Native American culture of Peru and Bolivia.

On that two-month trek Anna had ample time to share with Lillian her dissatisfaction with the egoism and selfishness of Western society and her desire to learn about authentic Judaism in far-off Jerusalem.

Anna's disclosure astonished Lillian. She wasn't interested in delving into the depths or climbing the heights of the heritage that was the birthright of both of them, but she did amicably agree to accompany Anna to the few Jewish points of interest that they uncovered in Cusco, Arequipa, La Paz, and Lima.

●●●

When Eli and Hannah, a young couple, came to be the Chabad presence on campus where thousands of unaffiliated Jews studied, Lillian didn't even notice their arrival.

It wasn't until three years later, when Anna was coming back from Israel for a visit, that Lillian met the young Chabad couple. A lot had happened in those years since the two women had last seen each other. For one thing, Anna had married Michael, another friend from university who had undergone a spiritual metamorphosis.

Anna and Michael contacted Eli and Hannah, asking if they would mind hosting a kosher dinner for some of their Jewish friends.

Eli and Hannah agreed, and that evening they all enjoyed a memorable meal with lively discussions on a variety of relevant contemporary topics. Despite her hesitancy when it came to anything "too Jewish," Lillian enjoyed meeting Eli and Hannah, who welcomed everyone so warmly. Hannah even served vegetarian miso soup with seaweed especially for her guests, instead of her traditional chicken soup with matzo balls.

Even after Michael and Anna returned to Jerusalem, Lillian would show up occasionally for Chabad-sponsored campus events.

●●●

One Rosh Hashanah years later, Lillian convinced herself to attend High Holiday services, even though she assumed there would be no one there she knew. She went alone and sat beside another single woman, and when the services were over they introduced themselves. It took just a few minutes of playing "Jewish geography" to discover to their amazement that they were actually distant cousins! That was the beginning of the friendship between Lillian Herman and Leslie Rubin.

●●●

Many years passed before Michael and Anna visited America again. They had come for a family celebration and took advantage of the chance to have an emotional reunion with Lillian as well.

Lillian and Anna were sitting together in the shade of a large, green, leafy maple tree, soaking in the natural beauty of the countryside, when Lillian asked, "Do you remember the Chabad couple you introduced me to about twenty years ago?"

"Yes, Eli and Hannah! How are they?"

"They're fine. Let me tell you something that happened," Lillian continued.

"About five years ago I went to Rosh Hashanah services and met a woman named Leslie, whose father was a Holocaust survivor. Leslie grew up with a burden of heaviness from all the horror her father carried with him that had never healed.

"And then, just a few months ago, she called me up to tell me that her father had been diagnosed with a very advanced malignancy that had already spread. He didn't have a chance, and she and her sisters were devastated. The whole family was sucked into a cyclone of despair; they didn't know where to turn or how to cope.

"When Leslie called me she was in a pit of depression. Her father had just been transferred from the hospital to a hospice — the last stop. The Nazis had destroyed so much of his life, and now he was terminally ill — it was just too much suffering.

"I felt compelled to do something — anything to help my friend and her family. They needed a tremendous amount of support — but from where?

"For some reason I thought of Eli. I just pictured his warm, smil-

Seeds of Comfort / 99

ing face, his friendly, outgoing personality, how he welcomed us to his home that time we met so long ago, when you and Michael were visiting from Israel. Remember how happy he was to host us for that meal?"

Anna could picture Eli opening the front door with a huge smile on his face.

"So I encouraged Leslie to contact Eli, but she protested. 'Why? We're not religious! We don't even do anything Jewish! Why should we call a rabbi? How can he help?'

"I insisted that it was a good idea. I don't know why, but that's what I thought she should do, so that's what I told her."

Anna followed Lillian's words carefully, her heart going out to Leslie and her family.

"When Leslie finally got up the courage to call Eli, he agreed to come over right away to meet her father. I don't remember the exact words Leslie told me he said, but I know that he gave them a religious context with which to relate to what was happening. He spoke simple, eloquent words that encouraged, comforted, and helped them cope. He knew what to say and how to say it.

"He was there for them — for her whole family. He helped them right through to the end of their ordeal. He made them feel as if they were his own family, and when her father passed away, Eli drove seven hours to be with them and make all the arrangements for a Jewish funeral. He took care of all the details. He paid the expenses and didn't even ask for compensation. He walked them through every aspect, holding their hands spiritually, in the most sensitive way.

"Leslie told me, 'Eli's love was so palpable, *so real!* He generated so much love, we were all ready to become religious!' That's what she told me, Anna! Isn't that incredible?"

Anna was certainly impressed by Eli's inspiring devotion: visiting the sick, arranging a kosher *taharah*, comforting the bereaved. He had obviously made a *kiddush Hashem* with his genuine *ahavas Yisrael*. She wondered if he was even aware of the impact he had made.

"Just think, Anna! This whole unfolding of the most vital assistance when it was so crucial to their emotional and spiritual survival happened only because of you and Michael!"

Anna stared at Lillian uncomprehendingly and exclaimed, "What? What are you talking about?"

"Well, think about it! The 'seeds of comfort' for my friend Leslie were planted decades ago! I met Eli only because of you and Michael. And I probably wouldn't have gone to Rosh Hashanah services if I hadn't felt good about you two, and then I wouldn't have met Leslie to begin with. And, wow — if we go even further back, I met you only because you stopped to talk to me — a perfect stranger — when I was sobbing on the floor during exam week.

"It's like a whole complex, interconnected system of different details that all come together somehow. It starts with someone just being warm, friendly, and caring, and look what happens!"

SOUTH OF LEBANON

By Gavriel Horan

*All it took was one tiny action…
but the outcome will last for generations….*

Yosef did not recognize the face that stared back at him as he looked in the mirror. He splashed cold water over his face and looked up again at the pair of bloodshot dark eyes surrounded by wrinkles and bags that hadn't been there a year earlier. A few traces of premature grey hairs graced his slightly receding hairline.

What had become of the young man with the thirst for life who used to greet him in the mirror each day? Those same dark eyes had sought passionately for meaning and truth, had led him to distant lands and to places he'd never even dreamed of. Had it all been for naught?

Yosef forced a smile — it had been much too long since he'd

smiled. The smile broke through his gloomy façade, but only for a moment; then his stoic visage returned. It was him all right. He couldn't forget that smile. Back when it all began, he used to smile from ear to ear with every single breath, every *berachah*, every mitzvah. Yosef breathed a deep sigh. He feared he had made a dreadful mistake. Was there any turning back?

◆ ◆ ◆

Joe Johnson was born just south of Jefferson City, Missouri, in a town called Lebanon. It was originally known as Wyota, after the Indians who lived there and were now long gone, leaving behind nothing more than a few river and town names. In the 1850s it was renamed after Lebanon, Tennessee, the hometown of one of the local reverends. Located on the edge of the Ozark Mountains, Lebanon is famous for its "healing" magnetic waters. It was and is a small-time, one-horse town and will probably stay that way forever. Joe's family had been there from just about the beginning.

Family tradition had it that his great-grandfather was the last member of the Johnson clan ever to have been east of the Mississippi River. Joe didn't know that he would be the first to break that tradition. He always wondered what the world looked like beyond the outskirts of his town and across the Mississippi. The farthest east he had ever been was St. Louis — that was when he was a boy.

Joe had always longed to see the world and to find meaning in life. It didn't seem like Lebanon would be the place where he would find the answers he was seeking. Most people there were interested in more important things, like the weather, the local barbershop news, and the Cardinals. There's always been a road that ran through Lebanon — from the time it was just a rough Indian trail till America expanded west from St. Louis. Today that road is called I-44.

For all intents and purposes, I-44 was meant for traveling westward.

But as Joe's fate had it, he would go east. One day he packed his bags and headed toward the rising sun to see what the world looked like on the other side of the road.

He was surprised to see that it just kept on going, farther than the eye could see, so he decided to follow it; and as it turned out, the world was much bigger than he had ever imagined — who needed such a big world? Still, he wanted to see it all and find out what it was all about.

That was the beginning of his journey.

❖❖❖

Joe's travels led him across the great ocean, through many mighty cities and over strange and exotic lands, until eventually he found his way to the Holy Land — just south of Lebanon.

In Jerusalem he discovered, quite accidentally, that there were answers to his questions about what the whole big wide world was for. It took him by surprise and rocked his own world. No one from Lebanon, Missouri, would ever have imagined that he would end up there.

To make a long story short, eventually Joe was directed to a conversion program in New York City, and after extensive study and introspection, he became a Jew: Yosef — Yosef Johnson.

❖❖❖

A few years later Yosef was studying at a large yeshivah in New York, but things weren't quite going as planned. When he had first converted he was blown away by everything he learned; *Yiddishkeit* seemed to answer his every question and fulfill the longing in his heart. He felt special in G-d's eyes for having been chosen to join the Jewish people.

But as time went on things started to change. He didn't find his place in the yeshivah. The students who shared his passion for life and for Torah were miles ahead of him in learning. Since he was still struggling to learn Hebrew, he was placed with the boys who weren't particularly interested in *Yiddishkeit*. He felt like he was in total *galus*, with no one to talk to who understood him or who cared. He felt lower than the lowest element of society, like a wanted criminal forced to dwell among the shadows on the outskirts of civilization — a complete outsider.

Yosef continued to go through the motions, but it was getting harder every day. "Does anyone care that I'm a Jew?" he thought. "I've come from worlds away, but nobody seems to notice me anymore." His depression ate at him day and night. It didn't seem like his mitzvos really mattered to anyone. At times he longed for his old world, where he had a place. Now he felt stuck between two different worlds — somewhere between Lebanon and Jerusalem. He started to wonder about whether he should go back....

◆◆◆

He rode the subway into Brooklyn feeling both trepidation and ambivalence, or something in-between. Yosef had come to the end of the road. This was his final attempt. He looked back and forth through the crowds of nameless people who filled the train during the morning rush-hour crunch, people of all shapes and colors, each one a world unto himself, light-years away from one another despite their physical proximity (which was currently too close for comfort — even for close friends). He imagined that, at the end of the day, each of them had his own family and community to return to, where each one mattered and where everyone looked and thought like them. Now, on the train, each one was a nobody, and it was somewhat comforting to Yosef to be surrounded by them.

The sunlight jolted him out of his silent reverie as the train shot into the open air across the East River, the tenement houses flashing by, reminding him that he had arrived in Brooklyn.

It hadn't taken much to convince him to make the trip. Someone in yeshivah had mentioned that he should go to see Reb Chaim Eliezer, one of the older chassidic Rebbes of the generation, who might be able to help him find his place in the world of Torah and Judaism. Figuring he had nothing to lose, Yosef called the *gabbai*, who told him curtly to come to daven with the Rebbe in his shul in Borough Park. After *Shacharis*, he was told, he might be able to speak to the Rebbe for a few minutes.

Yosef wasn't expecting much. He had already started packing his bags. He didn't think he would be missed.

Yosef got off the train at 13th Avenue and followed the directions the *gabbai* had given him to a street lined with old houses built close together in the Brooklyn fashion. He hardly noticed the tiny shul.

He walked into the old *beis medrash* to find a motley crowd of elderly Jews donning *tallis* and *tefillin*, preparing to daven. It looked like a scene straight out of a Yiddish folk tale. Yosef took a seat in the back of the shul and started to put on his *tefillin*, feeling as though he had been transported back 200 years to Eastern Europe.

Then the Rebbe walked in.

He was a small, unassuming elderly man enwrapped in a long white *tallis*. He walked slowly to his seat at the front of the shul and then turned to face the crowd. He scanned the room quickly, like a shepherd surveying his flock. His gaze fell briefly on Yosef, and for a split second, which seemed like an eternity, their eyes met.

Yosef felt as if the Rebbe were looking into the depths of his soul. For the first time in ever so long he felt understood, and he longed for that feeling never to end, but a moment later the Rebbe broke the link and continued his circuit as if nothing had happened. Yosef was alone again. He felt certain that the Rebbe had learned everything about him in that second but that he too must have deemed Yosef unworthy of his attention. Yosef was left feeling even lonelier than before.

The congregation began to pray and Yosef joined them, though he felt, as always, like he didn't belong. His heart lay in a pit of despair. Yosef spoke to Hashem in his own words, in the language that he understood. "Hashem, what do You want from me? I traveled the world in search of meaning. I left my home and my family and everything I knew — to find You. Now what do I have? I'm all alone in the world; I have no family, no friends, no home. Please help me!"

His voice rose and intermingled with the voices of the others in the shul. Tears formed at the corners of his eyes and trickled down his cheeks. "All I want is to serve You, but it doesn't seem like anybody cares about me. It doesn't seem like my mitzvos matter at all.

What do You want from me? Where should I go? What should I do?" he cried out from the depths of his heart, completely lost in prayer. He forgot his surroundings — the room disappeared, along with the congregation, the shul, the entire city. He was all alone with Hashem. "Please send me a sign," he cried. "Send me a sign that I matter, that I belong to the Jewish people. Send me a sign that You love me....!"

Suddenly, a hand on Yosef's shoulder wrenched him back into the world, back into time and space, back into the musty room. Someone was standing behind him, gently adjusting the strap of his *tefillin shel rosh*, which must have gotten twisted. Yosef turned around and found himself face-to-face with the steel-blue eyes of the Rebbe.

The Rebbe looked him in the eye and smiled the warmest smile Yosef had ever seen. That smile caused an explosion of wrinkles across the Rebbe's face and sent ripples of love into Yosef's heart. In an instant all his feelings of loneliness and despair melted. Hashem had heard his prayer. Someone cared. Yosef was not alone.

◆◆◆

After that first day, Yosef moved into the Rebbe's *shtiebel*, where he slept and learned. The Rebbe took him under his wing and spent many hours learning privately with him, until Yosef became a *talmid chacham* in his own right. The Rebbe encouraged Yosef to complete his degree and helped him get married.

Today Yosef Johnson is a chassidic Jew living in Borough Park. His many children are upstanding members of chassidic communities all over the world.

A WELCOMING WORD

By Chava Dumas

She had a feeling she should make that call, and it's a good thing she didn't hesitate!

It was Elul, the auspicious month that precedes Rosh Hashanah, when people work at healing difficult relationships. Laya was busy ironing her husband's white shirts. She was almost done with the pile when an image of her acquaintance, Gittel Horowitz, breezed through her mind. She realized she hadn't seen Gittel for quite a while; it had been several months since the last women's group meeting.

Gittel was born in Germany in 1936. When she was 4 years old, after a harrowing escape from the misery of the Holocaust, she and her parents were able to board the Westerland, which sailed safely to the shores of America. The next time the Westerland sailed from Europe, it was sunk by the Germans, leaving no survivors.

Gittel knew how to live frugally, to make ends meet, and she was aware of what was important in life and didn't complain. She was blessed with a positive, upbeat outlook that can keep a person going through almost any difficult life-circumstance.

When she was nearly 20 she met Shmuel Feldman. She thought he was a wonderful young man with good *middos*. Eventually, though, they decided not to marry. They parted amicably and went their separate ways.

Several years later, in 1961, she met and married Hershel Tzvi Horowitz.

◆◆◆

In the beginning of their married life everything was great. Normal. Stable. Life functioned smoothly. They started off in a one-bedroom apartment in Queens, and Hershel Tzvi worked as manager of the kosher deli section of a local supermarket. Gittel was an assistant for elderly care in a nearby old-age home. A few years later they moved to a larger rental before they were finally able to buy a home in the suburbs, in 1972. By then they had three young children, Sarah, Adel and Simon. After they settled in, Gittel quit her job in order to stay home and devote herself to their children.

Always looking for opportunities to give, Gittel joined a local chapter of Hadassah and also became very active in a number of *chessed* projects organized through their synagogue. She was always there for others in any way she could manage, even if, in some cases, all she could do was to share a smile to help people feel good.

Laya Freeman, another volunteer at the women's group, was drawn to Gittel's bubbly personality. They enjoyed seeing each other at the various Jewish events in their area. Though they were both busy raising their families they tried to keep in touch with occasional phone calls.

◆◆◆

Gittel knew how to balance a budget, an essential skill she had learned early on from her parents. She knew how much Hershel

Tzvi earned, and she trusted him to pay their bills and monthly mortgage. She couldn't understand why his salary wasn't covering their expenses when she recorded everything so meticulously, but she didn't question how he managed their finances, naively assuming that he was just as responsible as she. Yet money constantly seemed to be disappearing

If he had been an alcoholic she might have smelled that something was wrong, but she couldn't figure out what was amiss. When their oldest daughter Sarah was having a birthday party, all the family was there, but her husband didn't show up. He disappeared for two weeks. He would call every day with explanations for where he was and what he was doing, and he talked to the kids, as though everything was fine and he was just busy with some lucrative business adventure.

Gittel's top priority was to keep her marriage intact. She thought that was best for the children. She tried to avoid confrontation with her husband. She decided to go back to work part-time, while her mother helped out with watching the kids. Her parents also pitched in with the monthly mortgage payments. They didn't want to see their child or grandchildren suffering.

◆◆◆

Over the years she noticed lots of clues, but she still had no concrete evidence — no real proof of what was actually going on. Maybe she was simply in denial and couldn't accept the fact that her husband was sick, thinking he had a "little problem" that could just go away by itself.

Her parents' financial support didn't save the Horowitzes from losing their home in 1984. That shook Gittel to her core.

First the county Marshals appeared at their door — the ones in charge of carrying out eviction notices. She and her children watched, heartbroken, as the Marshals carried off their furniture and appliances. "Losing our home was horrendous!" she exclaims. Confused about her options, devastated as a result of what had hit her, she had no idea where to turn.

Debt collectors were calling all the time. Her husband was constantly borrowing money from people he knew, to cover the costs of keeping his habit secret, while Gittel cheerily tried to adjust and keep the family together when they were forced to move into a small, cramped apartment in a low-rental project. She was as sweet as could be, as optimistic as the twittering birds singing at dawn — but it wasn't changing the situation. She could no longer ignore the truth: her husband was a chronic, compulsive liar and gambler.

The facts that she had to face were dismal: Their life savings were gone and they were drowning in bottomless debts; the interest they owed was astronomical. Behind her back, Hershel Tzvi had lost everything.

The years of grievous deception lay heavy on Gittel, and her world turned dark. Her husband had built a colossal web of fabrications to "protect" her from the truth.

They had been married for twenty-two years and their children were older teenagers when they finally joined Gamblers Anonymous. "I was praying all the time for G-d to save me. Getting into GA helped for a while. For a number of years things actually got better. I was in charge of all the money. We had about four good years after that initial blow-out crisis of losing our home. We even went together to speak in high schools and warn kids about gambling addictions."

◆◆◆

But then he got back into it. Quietly at first, so she wouldn't be suspicious, but now Gittel knew what odd behavior looked like and what the warning signs were. She knew that he was gambling again.

"I was trying *so hard* to keep everything good for the sake of the children. I didn't want to confront him. It was only when I joined a support group for women whose husbands were in GA that I learned to identify how my own actions could be 'enabling' him to continue with his addiction. I met other women in the same situation, whose husbands gambled on the stock market, bought lottery tickets compulsively, or bet on horses at the racetrack — all manifestations of the same illness. Yet I was so scared to put my foot down, scared to make him accountable for the money he was losing.

"I would threaten to leave him, but my threats were just empty words — I never did it. The few times that I really confronted him — 'What are you doing with our money?!' — he would go belligerent, screaming loudly, and I hated that and hated that the kids had to see a scene. It was so ugly, so painful. It wasn't physical violence, where you can see external wounds, but verbal abuse rips you apart internally."

Gittel knew she shouldn't try to rescue him by bailing him out and giving him money to pay back the people they knew. She was just so embarrassed! She tried to encourage him to get into therapy — GA wasn't enough. She knew gambling was only a symptom of a deeper problem. Being browbeaten by his own parents, emotionally abused as a child — he needed to heal. She understood that he needed help, and she loved and cared about him. She wanted to stand by his side and help him confront his problems, but it was too much for her.

The vicious cycle continued. After they lost their house, they moved three more times.

Finally, in 1992, when they were living in a dinky place on the South Shore, another eviction notice showed up in the mailbox. Gittel was alone when she read it.

Staring at the black letters on that white slip of paper, the years suddenly weighed too heavily on her. She couldn't stand. She turned around, walked straight into the coat closet next to the front door, collapsed on the floor and cried her heart out. There was no way she could handle this anymore. She would rather have a nervous breakdown than face this life.

◆◆◆

"I wonder what's happening with Gittel lately?" Laya was thinking as she hung the last ironed shirt on a hanger. She knew that Gittel didn't have an easy life, though she had only surmised this from occasional quiet comments her friend made. They didn't usually speak on the phone, but she suddenly felt an overwhelming wish to say hello — *now*. Too much time had passed since she'd last heard from Gittel. Okay, it would be kind of an out-of-the-blue call, but *why not?*

The phone rang and rang for a long time. No one was answering. Laya was just about to hang up when she heard someone pick up.

"*Hello, Gittel!* It's Laya Freeman. I just called to say hello. *How are you?*"

Gittel was stunned. How could Laya know to call *now*?

She had heard the phone's incessant ringing while she was submerged in the dark closet where she had been lying for hours crumpled like a dirty dishtowel. Beyond exhausted from her emotional outpouring, it was hard to believe there was such a cheerful voice greeting her. Someone cared enough to call her?

"Oh, Laya!" Gittel started to sob.

"I…I…I can't believe you're calling…to say hello! I'm…I'm…not okay. I'm in trouble," she managed to blurt out. Gittel, always the caregiver, found it very difficult to admit that she needed help from others, but she had nowhere to go. "It's so wonderful to hear your voice! Thank you — thank you for calling."

Laya's spontaneous response changed Gittel's life forever.

"Gittel, what's wrong? Pack your stuff and come right over and stay with us!"

"Laya!" Gittel cried again. She knew her friend was serious. "I do need to come right now! We've been evicted again! I have nowhere to go."

"So come! Come now! I'm waiting for you!"

While Gittel hastily packed a few belongings, Laya sprang into action. Her five children were married, so she had plenty of space for Gittel to stay with them indefinitely. In fact, they would enjoy having her company. Laya enjoyed the opportunity to prepare the guest room with new sheets and a bright-colored pillowcase.

Hershel Tzvi arrived home that night and watched as Gittel walked out of his life. "How can you leave me after thirty-two years? Don't go!" he begged.

The foundation of a Jewish home is the solid structure of truth and honesty. They had been married for over thirty-two years — 32 — the numerical value of the Hebrew word *lev*, heart, and Gittel had invested her heart and soul into her marriage, her children, and a husband who had never stopped deceiving her. She had painstakingly tried to salvage their marriage, but it had irrevocably fallen apart.

Gittel dutifully called her grown son in another state and arranged for her husband to go live with him, while Gittel began a new chapter in her life.

By the time the doorbell rang at the Freemans' home, Laya had a hot, healthy minestrone soup ready and a pot of herbal tea simmering. She opened the door and welcomed Gittel into her heart and home.

With the Freemans' unconditional love and acceptance Gittel began to undergo a transformation. Never made to feel like an intruder, Gittel was embraced as though she were a long-lost member of the Jewish family, and it had a wonderful healing effect on her battered soul. She was able to work and save money while she stayed rent-free with the Freemans for over a year. During this time the sticky details of her divorce were negotiated and finalized.

When Gittel first moved in with the Freemans, the *Yamim Nora'im* were nearing. She joined a women's choir, and as they sang the Yom Tov prayers together the Hebrew words of the liturgy uplifted her. Hashem had helped her through a dark, incredibly painful period of her life, and now, with faith, renewed hope, and the Freemans' support, she could make a new beginning.

◆◆◆

Eight years later, through a number of unusual circumstances, Gittel heard that Shmuel Feldman was also divorced. In a bizarre way their lives had run along parallel lines — almost as though an invisible bond had run between them. They had raised families with children the same ages, with almost identical names, who had remarkably similar personalities. Unbeknown to either of them, they had even used the same pediatrician!

Though more than four decades had passed, they agreed to meet one another again.

Shmuel had been married for thirty-four years to a vindictive woman and had suffered miserably before realizing that the most rational albeit difficult solution was to part.

They didn't want to rush. They had both been through a lot. In time they decided to take a chance and start a new life together. They married in September, 2001.

●●●

During that tragic afternoon when another eviction notice arrived, when Gittel lay on the floor covered with tears, it had seemed like the end of the road. How could she have known how much her life was about to change as a result of one timely phone call?

Within the love of their sacred home, the Freemans provided Gittel with a safe harbor in a turbulent sea. Seeing the strength and solidity of their marriage and the way they worked as a team inspired Gittel and gave her the courage to remarry. To this day she carries with her that year of witnessing the Freemans' goodness and kindness. "Only G-d knows why we go through horrible experiences," Gittel says. "I firmly believe that there are reasons G-d puts us in places. I've learned to be strong. To begin again. I learned from my life-experience that G-d brought me down this path, and whatever He has planned, I can trust Him."

JUST SAY YES

By Faigie Horowitz

A small detour from what she had planned enriched her life and the lives of many others.

am not going to be nice, I decided. *I don't always have to go out of my way*, I kept telling myself. *There are other frum people in the room. They can go over to that young woman. Let them welcome her.*

Tiffany was introduced by one of her superiors from a secular Jewish organization. We were at one of those sporadic meetings that included several Jewish social service groups. "This is Tiffany, who just returned from a year of study in seminary in Israel."

I had seen her at some meetings on 59th Street the month before, and the introduction was the same. It seemed to be a tagline. "Look at us! We also have an observant Jew working here." But there seemed to be more to Tiffany's story than her year in Israel. There were signs that her Jewish journey was not yet complete.

A heated argument took place in my brain, and logic won over my sense of responsibility. There were other community professionals in the room who could reach out to her, and I had a lot on my plate. I just didn't have the time. There were my full-time job responsibilities, from which this meeting was taking time away. Grant-application deadlines loomed. My son was starting school and needed his supplies bought and his books covered. Besides, there was Yom Tov to be made in my house and in my father's house. And there were lots of guests to prepare for. This was the busiest time of the year for me, and I couldn't think of adding to my endless Tishrei lists.

Then the call came. It was during those very short days between Yom Kippur and Succos, when there just aren't enough hours in a day. At first I didn't even recognize her name and confused her with her boss, who was also a new hire. I assumed she was calling to schedule some meetings. Only Tiffany had a family issue; this was not a work-related matter at all. Someone from her workplace had suggested that she talk to me about "protektzia" for getting an elderly family member admitted to a particular residence. After a half-hour recitation of all the particulars that might contribute to a fast-forwarded acceptance, my sense of responsibility finally won out.

I asked Tiffany where she was spending Succos. For the first days she was going to a former roommate's cousins in New Jersey, she said. For the last days she was invited to Crown Heights. And she quickly accepted my invitation for Shabbos Chol HaMoed, explaining that there would be no celebration in her home, which was not even kosher.

I really wasn't in the mood. Shabbos Chol HaMoed was the only downtime for our family all Yom Tov long; it was the only time we would be in our own *succah* that year. I had planned on serving only my immediate family. I had to be in shul Shabbos morning. I wasn't interested in hosting a single young woman whom I didn't know at all and with whom I would need to have a professional relationship in the future. I didn't want to cross professional boundaries, as she was an administrative assistant with a fancy title in a place where I could not always trust the people. So I made sure to invite neighbors who had a *kiruv* home over for dessert that Friday night. They were the warm, friendly type and would certainly engage her with humor and scintillating stories.

To my surprise, the relationship that developed felt very comfortable before a few hours were up. In Tiffany I finally had someone who knew many of the players in my work life. In the short time that had passed since she had become observant, she had learned what it was like to function in an environment where you are the most observant *frum* female and everyone is watching you. The boundaries disappeared as we spent all Shabbos afternoon on the couch sharing war stories.

Tiffany came back to our Boro Park home often and spent many *chagim* with us. She was still living at home in a non-Jewish section of Manhattan. She did not eat hot food at home during the week because family members were wont to uncover the crock pot and take a taste of her delicious-smelling food. After Shabbos she would gratefully accept the leftovers I happily bestowed on her before she headed for the train. Her former *madrichah* began to join her in our home, and we would all work side by side preparing and serving meals.

I badgered and nagged one of the frum JCC directors to invite Tiffany for Shabbos. Rabbi P. was into *kiruv*. But he had a large and growing young family and not much time to spend with them. I understood that he too had many pressures, both personal and professional. Eventually, Tiffany was invited to the annual Shabbaton Rabbi P. held for Machon Academy for Girls in Queens.

And that one Shabbos in the Catskills became the link to the next chapter in Tiffany's life. She was mesmerized by the dynamic personality and inspiring words of the late Rebbetzin Judy Young, *a"h*, whose husband ran the school. Tiffany jumped at the invitation to the Young home in Lawrence and immediately became a *bas bayis* there as well.

And what a match it was! Judy took Tiffany shopping for her first Shabbos coat, introduced her to the young man who would become her *chassan*, and made her *l'chaim* in her home, all within nine months of first meeting her. We divided the wedding preparations between us. Judy dealt with inevitable crises that came up, gave the *kallah* classes, and made Shabbos *sheva berachos*. She mothered the young woman and set her on her way to establish her home on a firm Jewish foundation.

Tiffany currently runs programs for special-needs Jewish children in upstate New York and has three lovely children of her own. Rebbetzin Judy Young has passed from this world, leaving behind a legacy of inspired Torah learning and living for hundreds of women. And I am left with the lesson that it is worthwhile to listen to my inner voice when it says, *Engage. Reach out. Reach out even when you don't want to.*

A FIFTY-DOLLAR BLESSING

By Arel Mishory

A practical gesture can be life-giving.

Some years ago, I was exhibiting my artwork in national wholesale gift shows. On one occasion, unfortunately, all my inventory was shipped to a warehouse several states away from the venue of the exhibit. At the time, no one had a clue as to where the material had been shipped. The promoter of the show observed me leaving the event in tears and persuaded me to stay. She thought people would be so sympathetic that they would order from me anyway.

So for five days I sat in an empty booth that had cost me over $5,000 to rent and tried to sell work that existed only in photos. Person after person would stop by, read my story, or listen to me tell it yet again, and say "tsk tsk tsk — that is a nightmare," and then walk on. At some point my neighbor in the next booth couldn't take it anymore and shouted out, "Stop with the sympathy already!"

Finally, another exhibitor came by and said, "I can't do much, but here's something to help you out." It was a $50 bill.

This act of kindness was such a huge lesson for me. It made me realize how beaten down I was after five days of hearing "tsk tsk tsk." Not one person had said to me, "Here's a cup of coffee," or, "Is there anything I can do?" or, "I'd like to order your work for my gallery — I'm sure I'll love it," until this man came and gave me the $50. I saved that $50 bill and used it to start my son's bar mitzvah *tefillin* fund.

This exhibitor's act inspired me to follow up my own words of sympathy with action. I now try to make that phone call, make a meal or part of a meal, give a ride…whatever I am capable of doing at the moment. At the very least, I put that person who needed my help in my prayers and thoughts.

I once learned that a *vav* is an extended *yud*. The *yud* represents the thought, and the extension represents the action necessary to carry out the thought. I hadn't really understood the lesson that a thought is so often enhanced by a follow-up action until that painful experience I had in an empty booth, and it made me pay attention to how I greet someone. Do I truly take into consideration what that person might be feeling? Have I judged that person's state of mind adequately? Am I really responding to him or her as a human being, or am I responding only to my own feelings?

What was at the time a traumatic week offered the blessing of an important learning experience.

A BEGGAR'S PAST... AND FUTURE

As told to Sorole Friedman

Behind every pair of sad, vacant eyes lies a powerful soul.

It was one of those hot, humid mid-August days. The sun beat down without mercy. I was standing at a bus stop fanning myself with a folder when I noticed a beggar rummaging through a nearby city garbage bin. It was a grotesque sight, and my heart went out to him. Maybe it was the swarm of flies that surrounded him, or the dirty sweat pouring down his face; but whatever it was that most disturbed me, I couldn't just watch a fellow human being search for food in a garbage can. I walked over to him and tried to hold my breath as I nonchalantly struck up a conversation.

"Hi. How are you?"

He looked at me wildly.

"I'm so pathetic," he shot back.

I had absolutely no idea what that meant, but what I did know was that this guy seemed like no ordinary beggar. I was determined to get to the bottom of this.

"Can I invite you to lunch?" I asked him. "There's a pizza shop right around here."

His eyes narrowed and he started shouting at me. "Who do you think you are? Do you think you're better than me just because you're wearing a suit?"

I was taken aback, but I continued trying to persuade him to join me for lunch. Finally, we ended up in a small pizza shop a block away.

After he had consumed two slices, an order of French fries and a soda, we started talking. When he told me his name I was shocked. It was a very prominent Jewish name. I questioned him, and he began to tell me his story.

"I was once an extremely successful entrepreneur in the oil business. I was supporting my wife and kids comfortably. But my business took a turn for the worse and my financial status took a sharp dive. Eventually, I was left with almost nothing. A terrible dispute broke out between my family and me. In a rage I stormed out of the house.

"It's hard to explain what happened next. I was in a heavy depression, and I sunk lower and lower. I felt like a complete failure. There was no way I could go back home. And now…well, this is what has become of me."

I felt terrible for him. I took him to my office, showed him where he could shower and gave him a clean tracksuit that I found there. When he was dressed and refreshed, we sat down to talk again. "I have a beautiful wife," he told me, "and beautiful children, and a big house in Flatbush."

At this point I was starting to get a little cynical. Maybe this guy was totally loony and was making all this up. Living out on the streets like a beggar for six months can drive a person crazy.

"Why don't I call your wife and tell her that you're here and that you want to come home?" I asked him.

Instantly, the wild look returned to his eyes, which opened wide with fear.

"No, no, no," he said, trembling fiercely. "I can't face them. They'll never want me." He broke down and sat sobbing in his chair. I patted his arm and tried to comfort him.

"Money isn't everything," I said. "I'm sure they're waiting for you to come back to them. Your children need their father!" I spoke to him for hours, wearing myself out trying to persuade him, until at long last I convinced him to allow me to call his wife.

The entire time as I spoke with his wife he sat inert, a stolid expression on his face.

When I explained to the woman on the phone that I had her husband with me, she burst into tears and became hysterical.

"I can't believe it!" she told me with intense emotion. "I've been searching for him for over six months. The police have sent out countless search teams, and I've been doing everything in my power to locate him. Of course we want him to come home as soon as possible!"

He sat silent beside me as we drove, but I could almost hear his heart beating. When we arrived at his home his entire family was standing outside waiting for him. A huge smile spread over his face and, as if he were a child returning home after a long absence, he flung open the car door and ran to meet them in an emotional reunion.

I sat in my car watching the scene, tears rolling down my cheeks — tears of sadness for what this man must have gone through during these past months, and tears of happiness over the fact that I'd had a part in reuniting this beautiful family. I watched him hug and kiss each of his children as if he were seeing them for the first time.

"You have no idea what you've done for us," his wife told me later as I sat in their kitchen. "We are forever indebted to you."

"It was my pleasure," I told the family. "But before I leave, please, promise me one thing: Promise me that from now on you'll keep Shabbat every week."

Without hesitation, they agreed.

We exchanged phone numbers, and as I prepared to leave, my new friend gave me a huge bear hug. "There are very few special people like you in the world," he told me. "Not too many people would actually stop and say hello to a disgusting beggar searching for food in a garbage can. You saved my life. Thank you."

"Call me if you ever need anything," I told him. "I'll help you with everything. It's really my pleasure."

After that, we spoke frequently. I helped him get over his ordeal; I lent him money and helped him pick up his life where he had left off. I gave him encouragement when he needed it and helped him fulfill his promise to me.

Eventually we lost touch. He had his family and business to tend to and I had mine. Life went on uneventfully, and the memory of this incident faded.

● ● ●

A couple of years later I was in my office when my secretary informed me that I had a visitor. A tall, well-dressed businessman walked in. "Hello," he said with a smile. "Do you recognize me?"

I racked my brain as I stared at him. "No," I answered. "Not really."

"Are you sure?" he pressed. "Look at me closely." I squinted at him for a few seconds. I knew the face from somewhere. He smiled at me, and suddenly it all came back. I stood up.

"Aren't you...?" He nodded, and we fell into each other's arms, laughing.

"I have something for you," he told me. Out of his leather briefcase he extracted a box and handed it to me. "Open it," he urged.

In the box was a lovely silver wine goblet. I stammered. "Wow! You shouldn't have. Thank you so much. It's beautiful."

"No," he said, "thank *you*. You picked me up from the dumps and put me back on my feet. I'm a lot more religious now, and I keep Shabbat every week. I am the happiest man ever."

Tears of joy blurred my vision as we sat on the couch to catch up on each other's lives.

TEARS OF CARING

By Michelle Tendler

Don't think that no one cares.

My mother, Rebbetzin Dr. Jean Jofen, *a"h*, was a *shadchanit*, a psychologist, a college professor, and a Shakespeare scholar, among other things. With a short blond *sheitel*, sparkling blue eyes and an attitude to match, she was a woman who constantly amazed those around her with her energy, love of life, and desire to give to others. As a *shadchanit* my mother didn't just make *shidduchim*. She took singles under her wing, guided them through the dating process, and opened her home to them every Friday night.

When we were sitting *shivah* for my mother, a former "single" of my mother's told us her story: "I remember attending a singles' event that your mother hosted — both to raise money for Yeshivas Beis Yosef and to try to match people up. I will never forget how she got up to speak, looked around at the room full of singles, broke down and began to cry. That was how she greeted us.

"She was a professional orator, an accomplished scholar, and a professor, but that didn't stop her from crying. When she composed herself she explained that she had been crying for the pain of every single who had not yet found his/her mate. It made a tremendous impression on all of us and showed us that someone really cares.

"Throughout the next three trying years, until I met my husband, I held on to your mother's tears. Whenever things got really hard and I began to feel that nobody cares, I would picture your mother's warm blue eyes filling up with tears, and I would remember that somebody really did care."

"YOU SAVED HIS LIFE!"

As told to Chani Wagschall

Often it doesn't take more than open eyes combined with a sensitive heart.

I entered my local shul one day and noticed someone sitting with his head down, barely davening. His face was drawn, which I found especially surprising, since I knew that his first child's *aufruf* had taken place that past Shabbos. Hesitantly, I extended my hand to him with a *"Mazal tov"* and a *"Shalom aleichem."* His face lit up and I was able to engage him in conversation. I inquired about his *mechutanim*, which *kollel* his son would be learning in, and so forth, and wished him all the best. When I walked away he looked a bit better, but…

As soon as I got home I phoned his *rosh kollel* and made him aware of how worried the soon-to-be *shver* appeared. He reassured me that there was nothing to be concerned about. This *avreich* was a genuine *ben Torah*, he said, with a beautiful family, and he was sure that the man was simply suffering from "the pre-wedding jitters." Yet I repeated my concern that something was amiss and suggested he look into the matter.

A few weeks later I happened to meet the *rosh kollel*, and he told me reverently, "You saved his life! That man was on the brink of a breakdown, overwhelmed by unbearable financial responsibilities. Because of his concern for *shidduchim* for his other children he was too embarrassed to seek help, and terribly distraught. As soon as I spoke to him he opened up and shared his problems — for which we found solutions. Your *shalom* gave us the opportunity to help him."

ONE SMALL ACT

Rabbi Shlomo Borenstein

A small act of chessed paid off in a big, big way…

When my college roommate asked me if I would like to join him as an advisor at a Shabbaton for high school kids, I was eager to accept. I myself had become *frum* through this organization a number of years before, and I felt it would be a great opportunity to give back a little of what I had gained. Most of these kids were already *frum*, but I hoped that my presence there would serve as a catalyst for making a difference in someone's life; you just never know which of your actions will inspire someone to really want to turn his or her life around. I just wanted to lead by example, to show them that Judaism can be cool and fun and fulfilling all at the same time.

Friday night and Shabbos morning went well. I made quite a few friends. I have an outgoing personality; meeting new people has never fazed me, and I love playing games of all kinds, so we really hit it off. They were all welcoming and friendly, and they accepted me as one of the gang.

The program was packed, but there was a break in the schedule on Shabbos afternoon. Some used the time to sleep, others explored the neighborhood. Most planned to hang out at one of the homes, playing Ping-Pong, schmoozing, and noshing. I felt flattered to be included. When we walked into the house I made sure to give our hosts a warm, appreciative greeting. They responded in kind, and the subtle magic our few words created made me feel a pleasant connection to this fine family.

We all had a great afternoon, and the time passed quickly. Before we knew it we were due back at the shul for *Minchah*. We thanked our hosts and everyone began heading out the door, when I took a good look around and noticed the state of the house. Simply speaking, it was a wreck! I detected just a touch of frustration in the eyes of our host, and my conscience wouldn't let me leave….

I started helping the parents put their home back into place. We chatted as we worked together. They seemed very sweet. They were accustomed to this annual invasion and opened their home for it happily. The mess didn't seem to faze them at all. Their laid-back approach impressed me a lot!

When we were done I wished them a good Shabbos and hurried back for *Minchah*. The rest of the Shabbaton flew by, and I left with good memories, hoping the kids had enjoyed it as much as I had.

●●●

Fast-forward two years. I had taken a year off after college to learn in a yeshivah in Israel, and that year quickly led to a second. I found myself sitting in a *beis medrash* learning day and night. I loved learning and took to it like a fish to water. I knew where my heart was, and there was no turning back. The world of learning was where I wanted to spend the rest of my life. My current problem was: with whom? Even though I was still fairly young, I felt the time had come to search for my *bashert*.

With great trepidation I approached my *mashgiach* and informed him of my desire to enter the world of *shidduchim*. He allayed my fears, encouraged me, and gave me the number of a former student of his who had become quite well-known as a *shadchan*. "Don't worry," he assured me, "everything will be all right."

I was greeted warmly at the *shadchan's* home, and a short conversation ensued. He asked questions, listened to answers, and put some good, old-fashioned intuition to use, and he quickly reached an understanding of who I was and what I wanted in life. He then whipped out two sheets of paper with lists of names on them — on one were names of single girls, on the other of single boys. With an air of confidence he perused the pages.

Am I really entrusting this young rabbi with helping me find my future wife? I wondered to myself. I felt as if I were watching him going through a shopping list. The only difference was that I knew the cashiers at the check-out counter longer than I had known him!

But he seemed pretty sure of himself. Setting aside his lists, he looked up with a smile. "There are quite a few good choices here, but one definitely stands out from the rest! I've got a good feeling about it," he informed me.

I was glad *he* had a good feeling about it! Personally, I wasn't sure if the feeling I had in my stomach was more nervousness or nausea. When he told me the girl's name, however, I recognized it immediately. I had met her in my "before yeshivah" life, and I had known she was in Israel.

The *shadchan* told me that she too had grown a lot over the past two years. She too dreamed of a future similar to the one I envisioned. But I'd heard enough *shmuessen* about *shidduchim* over the years to know that I had to check this out myself. I asked for a couple of days. We'd be in touch.

I made my calls and heard wonderful things about this potential *eishes chayil*. Incredibly, it seemed the *shadchan* had really hit the mark. When I called back I gave my enthusiastic consent.

I was in for some disappointing news, however. He had spoken to the young woman about the idea of going out, and she had responded that she wasn't interested. I admit that I was a little hurt that she had said no to me; after all, it wasn't as if we were total strangers. But the *shadchan* was quick to reassure me. It had nothing to do with me personally; in fact, he hadn't even mentioned my name.

Apparently, before her parents had given their consent for her to return for a second year in Israel they had made her promise that she wouldn't go out on any *shidduchim* while she was there. Her parents wanted to meet anyone she was going to date before she went out with him. They were very concerned about their only daughter and weren't taking any chances of allowing her to be swept off her feet by some city-slicker yeshivah *bachur*. I definitely understood.

I might do the same thing one day for my daughter.

The *shadchan* then asked me if there was any chance I might be flying to the States in the near future. I informed him that it would be a good few months before I returned to the good old US of A. Anyway, as good as this *shidduch* sounded (and it sounded very good), I knew that the *shadchan* had that list of his, and I didn't see any purpose in flying to the States just to meet one girl's parents. He was a bit disappointed but decided he wasn't giving up. He asked me to give him a little time.

True to his word, he approached her again. She reiterated her promise to her parents, but just out of curiosity asked what the boy's name was. When the *shadchan* told her, a small smile appeared on her face. She said she would speak to her parents but couldn't promise anything.

● ● ●

Back in those days you didn't just pick up a phone and call home. It was very expensive, and usually you would arrange a time to call to make sure that someone was there. When the day arrived for her to call home, both her parents were eagerly waiting to hear from their daughter.

The conversation started off nicely, but when she got to the point about the suggested *shidduch*, there was silence on the other side. A promise is a promise, her father reminded her, and there were plenty of nice boys back home for her to go out with. Her mother quickly chimed in that it was very important to them to first meet any prospective young man. After all, this was their future son-in-law they were talking about.

That's when she shared her secret. "But you *have* met him!" she replied. "Do you remember that Shabbaton two years ago…and how everyone came over to hang out…and one advisor stayed and helped us clean up the house afterward? Do you remember how impressed you were with him? You kept telling me how nice it would be if I found someone like him one day.

"Well," she said, "I did. I found *him!*"

Her parents happily gave their *berachah* for our date.

Twenty-three years and eight children later, I can truly say that the rest is history. Picking up a few pieces of popcorn and tidying some chairs is still the best investment I've ever made.

3
BE A MENTSCH

A MIGHTY POWERFUL WEAPON

Yaffa Ganz © 2009

Sometimes a person does something without even thinking about it — it can be just a tiny thing…and then, all at once, everything is different…

Hila drove slowly, weaving her way through the puddles and the slush of the Midwestern town where she lived. The grey sky matched both her mood and her battered, tired-looking grey sedan.

Hila was tired too. A petite, pleasant-looking woman of 45, she felt like she was 80. She was tired of everyone telling her it was time to get on with her life, time to change her job, time to go out and meet new people. She was tired of a well-paying but boring, demanding job. She was tired of hearing about other people's husbands and children. And most of all, she was tired of being told that the time had come to remarry. Even if she had ever thought of remarrying, no one had any suitable suggestions. All they offered was well-meaning but worthless advice. Nothing made her feel more tired or grey than unsought, useless advice. And today she was especially tired of just about everything. But that was to be expected. Today was the third *yahrtzeit*, and nothing had changed.

This is no way to live, she thought. If I don't want to become a national statistic for depression, I have to *do* something!

But what? Her husband Yochai had died of a sudden, massive, thoroughly unexpected stroke, behind the wheel of that grey sedan while on his way to work, leaving his wife in a state of prolonged shock. There were no children, but they had been a family nonetheless. Their home had always been filled with light and love; with friends, relatives, guests. Now everything was quiet, lonely, sodden grey — just like the sky, the slush, the old sedan.

Hila had a responsible job as a comptroller at a large manufacturing company. Screws, nuts, and bolts were their specialty. The salary was good but the work was unbearably monotonous. Hila hadn't minded it before the accident; her real life began at home. But now it was all she could do to drag herself to work. Only the thought that she was responsible for parts that would be used in a vast array of vital machinery — and if they were poorly constructed they might endanger someone's life — kept her from falling asleep. But at this stage in life, what else could she do? She'd been at this job for nineteen years and hadn't the faintest idea what else might be out there. Besides, who would hire a 45-year-old woman, no matter how responsible she was?

Hila sighed. She looked at herself in the rear view mirror and didn't like what she saw. The light was gone from her eyes and she looked old. What I need, she thought bitterly, is one of those small, everyday miracles, the kind that happen in stories. Something simple that makes everything turn out well. The kind of thing, she thought sadly, that rarely happens to real people in real life. All I need is one.

Suddenly, on an impulse, she made a face at the unhappy

image staring back at her from the mirror, stuck out her tongue and promptly drove right into the car in front of her.

Oh, great! Just what I needed to end a perfect day, she thought with a groan. She braked and pulled over to the curb, not knowing if she was going to scream or burst into tears.

A tallish, respectable-looking man in a business suit came out of the car. He looked at Hila, at his smashed back fender and at her crumpled front one. He frowned. Hila braced herself. But instead of shouting, he began to apologize.

"Are you all right, ma'am? I'm so sorry. It was all my fault, of course. You see, I was daydreaming, sort of meandering along without really concentrating on the road. I was thinking that I could use a little Divine assistance for a problem I'm dealing with, and then I saw you stick your tongue out at me in my rear view mirror. I was so surprised that I braked without thinking. But that's no excuse for stopping so quickly. I'll cover the cost of any damage, of course. Are you okay?"

Hila was taken aback. It wasn't often that one came across such gentility on the road. "Stick my tongue out at you? Oh, no!" she said with fervor. "I wasn't sticking it out at you — I was sticking it out at myself! I mean, I don't usually stick my tongue out at anyone! It's just that I was so busy feeling sorry for myself that I didn't even notice you. I'm so sorry. It was all my fault. A driver is supposed to pay attention to the road, and the car in back is always at fault."

"Not at all," said the man firmly. "One can't just slam on the brakes in the middle of traffic for no good reason. Here's my card. Can I have your name and information? We can stop off a repair station right now and get an estimate if you'd like."

"No way," insisted Hila. "This was my fault. I pay for any damage." She looked at the card. *Fishel Mintzer, CPA.* It had an address she didn't recognize.

Mr. Mintzer hesitated for a moment, but he was adamant. "Look," he said a bit uncomfortably, "am I correct in assuming you're an Orthodox woman?"

Hila smiled. What else could she be with all of those stickers about Shabbos and G-d and *taryag mitzvos* on her bumpers? Her husband Yochai used to collect them. And of course her tired-looking wig was a dead giveaway. She nodded.

"Well then," said Mr. Mintzer, "let's not argue. What's the name of your *rav*?"

"My *rav*? Rabbi Slutz. Mordechai Slutz. Why?"

"We'll go to him and ask who pays the damages," said Mr. Mintzer.

"No way," said Hila. "There's nothing to ask. You're a very generous man, but if you go around paying other people's bills you'll bankrupt your family!"

"I'm afraid not," Mr. Mintzer said sadly. "My wife was much more generous than I am."

Hila picked up on the past tense immediately. "She *was*?"

"Yes. She was a special soul. She gave *tzedakah* with an open hand and an open heart. Her purse was always ready and waiting for someone in need. If anyone could bankrupt a family by giving money away, it was her, not me. Today is her *yahrtzeit*. I just came from shul; I said *Kaddish*. She died three years ago today. It still doesn't seem possible."

Hila gulped and raised her eyebrows. "How strange. Today is my husband's third *yahrtzeit* too. We didn't have any children, so his brothers say *Kaddish* for him. It's a hard day for me."

Now it was Mr. Mintzer's turn to look surprised. "How unusual. I mean, we didn't have any children either."

They were both silent for a moment.

"Um…would you like to go to your *rav* now about the car?" asked Mr. Mintzer.

"It's really not necessary," said Hila. "It's an old car. And it has sad memories for me. I was just thinking it's time for a new one. I need something more cheerful-looking, something that's not so…grey."

"Well then, I'll check it out with *my rav*, Rabbi Moshe Greenman. Can I have your contact information?"

Now it was Hila's turn to hesitate. Then she stuck her hand into her purse and pulled out a business card. *Hila Ross, Comptroller.*

National Engineering Corporation. Manufacturers of Screws, Nuts & Bolts.

"Just don't stick your tongue out at any other unsuspecting drivers," Mr. Mintzer said with a smile.

"I wouldn't think of it," Hila answered emphatically. "Not even at suspecting ones!" She smiled back as he put the card in his wallet. They wished each other well and drove off in different directions.

That week Hila bought a car. A new-used car. It wasn't sodden grey, but it wasn't particularly bright, either; still, it was an improvement on her old one. It was a respectable, neutral white. Sort of like the sky. And she went looking for a different job. To her surprise, she actually found one, and soon she began working as the director of a welfare agency for underprivileged children. It paid much less than nuts and bolts but it was definitely more interesting.

Time crept on. The holidays were especially hard. But Hila reminded herself constantly that even if she didn't have everything, she still had much to be thankful for — a house, a job, family, and friends. She tried to remember that she was infinitely better off than the people she saw every day at the agency. Sometimes she wondered how Mr. Mintzer was faring. Poor man. He had seemed so unhappy.

Meanwhile, although busier than ever with his accounting firm, Mr. Mintzer found time to make an appointment with his rabbi. He described the unpleasant accident with the pleasant widow. He wondered if perhaps it was a message — or, who knows...a gift? — from G-d. It wasn't the usual way to meet a *shidduch*, but then again, who can know the ways of G-d? His ways are endless, and stranger things have happened.

Rabbi Greenman thought it was definitely worth pursuing, and he wasted no time. He called Rabbi Slutz. The two rabbis met several times to discuss the situation more thoroughly but weren't quite sure how to proceed. According to her friends, Mrs. Ross did not seem to be quite ready for *shidduchim* yet. If Mr. Mintzer called she might just refuse him.

One day Hila received a check in the mail for $1,500, together with a short note from Mr. Mintzer.

"Dear Mrs. Ross," he wrote, "The matter of your car has been on my mind ever since the day of the accident. My mechanic said this amount should cover the damage. Please accept it with my apologies. All the best, F. Mintzer."

Hila called Rabbi Slutz. "Take the money," he said.

"It's wrong to take it!" she answered fervently. "There's no reason he should pay for damage caused by my idiosyncrasies!"

"But your *idiosyncrasies* are causing him concern. Take the money. You'll be doing him a *chessed*," said Rabbi Slutz.

A *chessed*? That put things in a different light. "I suppose I owe him a *chessed* or two after causing him to bang up his car. And he was so nice about it, too!"

So she deposited the check in her account and immediately wrote out a check for the same amount to the welfare agency she worked for. A week later Mr. Mintzer received a receipt for $1,500 in the mail, thanking him for his generous donation. It took him a few moments before he realized how and why it had been sent to him. He called Rabbi Greenman, who called Rabbi Slutz.

"What a waste," sighed Rabbi Slutz.

"A waste? The money went to *tzedakah*. It wasn't wasted. Do you mean the damaged cars?"

"No, I don't mean the cars. I mean the lives of the people who drive them," answered Rabbi Slutz. "Sometimes smart people don't think straight! We really must do something about this. I have an idea," he continued. "It's so simple and straightforward that it's slightly unconventional, but it just might work.

"What we need here is a little communication. You will agree with me, of course, that the tongue is a powerful weapon. In this particular instance, it even caused an accident! Fortunately, all it damaged was two cars. Now let's see if we can wield its power to heal two damaged lives." And Rabbi Slutz proceeded to explain.

"It's like this," he said. "Hila told me that her welfare agency is always in need of a few volunteers. And Mr. Mintzer told you that he could use something to add a bit of *simchah* to his life. Now if we can get him to offer his services to the children at the agency a few times a week…"

"Brilliant idea!" Rabbi Greenman exclaimed. "You needn't say another word. Let's get started!"

Several months, many phone calls and quite a few meetings later, the deed was done. It happened on a bright, sunny spring morning. Rabbis Slutz and Greenman were standing at the entrance to Rabbi Slutz's shul surrounded by a group of happy-looking people. They were all waving toward the parking lot where a tall, smiling man and a lively, petite woman with a smartly coiffed wig were entering a brand-new bright-blue sedan. A big sticker on the bottom of the back window proclaimed:

"The tongue is a mighty weapon indeed."

Rabbis Slutz and Greenman shook hands enthusiastically. Their job was done. The blue sedan passed the two rabbis on its way out of the parking lot. For a mini-moment Rabbi Slutz was tempted to stick out his tongue jokingly as a send-off to the new couple.

But he refrained. The tongue is a mighty powerful weapon indeed. One can never be too careful when using it.

OPEN THE DOOR AND LET ME IN!

By Faigie Horowitz

Just being noticed gave her another chance at life.

It was the day before school opened when she presented herself for the interview with the principals at Bnos Mushlamos High School. Zahava was not yet enrolled in a school and was desperate to get in. Last year's school, Shoshana Academy, did not accept her registration for the new year. It just hadn't worked out, they said. Shoshana Academy wasn't a good fit for her.

They were right. But where was Zahava to go? She was an observant eleventh-grader who had been raised in a *frum* family. Her academics were okay but not outstanding. Zahava had been in four schools in three years. She didn't belong in the schools for at-risk kids. Your standard Bais Yaakov certainly wouldn't look at her. Zahava, together with the staff of Rachel's Place, had applied to at least four schools for the coming year.

Rachel's Place is a Brooklyn residence for girls who cannot live at home. It was founded by several tireless women who fought apathy and government bureaucracy to provide a home for girls who need one. Staffed by professionals, it functions as a restorative haven where young women can get past family issues and move ahead with their lives.

Two board members of Rachel's Place had a conversation the day before Zahava's interview. Rivka was a hands-on board member; Dinah was involved primarily in advocacy and politics. She was rarely involved in day-to-day operations. After concluding their business concerning a prospective resident, Dinah asked about Zahava. She knew a little about Zahava and had been contacted when it became clear that Zahava should no longer be at home.

"We have a problem with Zahava," Rivka said with a sigh. "She is doing really well, but we don't have a school for her. In two days the school year begins and we've exhausted all the options."

"What about Bnos Mushlamos?" countered Dinah. "They're open to accepting transfer students. I just spoke to the director last week."

"We never considered it. Let's give it a try."

Dinah, who was quick to use her connections, immediately placed a call to Bnos Mushlamos' director. A staffer from Rachel's Place followed it up and scheduled an appointment for an interview the next day. The director of Rachel's Place was on vacation, so a counselor named Ilanit was slated to drive Zahava over for the interview and meet the principals with her. Normally this was not Ilanit's role, but it was the eleventh hour for school registration and they had to make do.

Zahava's appearance didn't help. Her garb was technically *tzenius* but certainly demonstrated attitude. The skirt was long enough but denim and decorated with rips and fringes. The T-shirt had the required sleeve length but it was the latest ghetto look. Here was a girl who wasn't looking to hide anything. *Take me as I am*, she seemed to be saying.

The two high-school principals took her at her word and her

appearance. In other words, they were underwhelmed. They were not eager to admit a student who resided in a shelter for girls without a home. They knew Rachel's Place did good work with its girls and helped them transition to independent healthy living. But this particular resident wasn't for them, they told the counselor Ilanit. It just wouldn't work out for either Zahava or the school.

During that part of the discussion the anxious Zahava was waiting outside in the hall. Suddenly, a booming voice greeted her effusively. "Zahava, how *are* you?" She was pleased to see a familiar face in the austere hallways of the unfamiliar Bnos Mushlamos.

It was the elderly, bearded man who had struck up a conversation with her one night while she was in a kosher pizza shop with her siblings. She explained to him politely that she was here applying for acceptance to the school. "They don't seem to want me" somehow slipped out in the conversation, although Zahava had not yet been given the bad news. Ilanit was still inside, trying to persuade the people in charge.

The octogenarian with the long white beard schmoozed with Zahava for a few minutes and then took his leave. He strode purposefully into the meeting going on in the Hebrew principal's office. He was none other than Rabbi H., dean of the school.

As soon as he walked in, the atmosphere thawed considerably. Rabbi H. had known Ilanit's family since before she was born. He and Ilanit's father had been friends for years before the latter's passing. He was pleased to hear that Ilanit had gotten her credentials and was now a *madrichah* and social worker at Rachel's Place.

After catching up with Ilanit, Rabbi H. got down to business. He told all those present how he had reached out to Zahava that night in the pizza shop. She was dressed in similar, off-putting fashion but gave off warm, sincere vibes while interacting with her siblings. Her engaging personality prompted him to start schmoozing with them.

Despite the growing convivial ambiance in the office, the principals firmly stated their position about Zahava's acceptance — or lack thereof. It was just not a match. Rabbi H.'s position was simple and direct: What would it take to make this work out?

It took a just a few more minutes. The school officials finally stepped out into the corridor and invited Zahava back into the office.

The English principal delivered the good news. "Congratulations, Zahava. You are accepted to Bnos Mushlamos High School. We want to see you in school tomorrow. We thought at first that we would not accept you, but we know now that you are a striving person and a good person. You do belong here."

"Why do I feel like I just encountered Eliyahu Hanavi?" Zahava mused to Ilanit on the way home. "I met him once and then again. That first time, in the pizza shop, I thought he was a clean homeless person buying himself a meal! And he is none other than Rabbi H., founder of the school, with the power and trust in me to convince everyone to give me a chance! Hashem sent him my way just a few nights ago, and then again today in the hallway, to guarantee me the opportunity to go to a good school and grow into the person I want to be.

"Hashem wants me to succeed," she concluded.

Ilanit added the other, less obvious manifestations of *hashgachah pratis*. "Dinah," she pointed out, "doesn't usually play an active role in the girls' lives; her input is rarely directly connected to the residents. Without her, we wouldn't even have considered applying to Bnos Mushlamos. What would have happened if the director of Rachel's Place would have escorted you to the interview? She doesn't know Rabbi H. and has no extra credibility with him. How miraculous is it that I came along to the interview, something I never do?"

When they got home to Rachel's Place, Zahava got busy buying her uniform skirt and gathering school supplies for the next day.

She now knows what Hashem is busy doing during this time of year. He is opening multiple doors for those who knock on them.

JUST A CLAP ON THE BACK

By Brachah Stern

Have you noticed someone today?

I was sitting in the car waiting for my husband to come out of the bakery with some early-morning baked goods. The radio announcer's voice droned on, but I was barely registering what he was saying, as all my attention was focused on an elderly man who was passing by. He was bent over and disheveled beyond belief; his ancient, patched clothing was long out of style. He was so skinny, his clothing hung on him like a scarecrow's. His face was grey and his hair was badly in need of a wash. He looked like he might collapse on the spot.

I felt a little guilty but couldn't think of what to do for him. Here I was, comfortably ensconced in my plush car, waiting for my husband to return with delectable goodies, and right in front of me was this man who looked like he hadn't had a decent meal in weeks.

As I watched all this, a young man happened to walk past. He strode right over to the elderly man, gave him a warm *hello* and clapped him on the back as if they were the closest of friends.

The young man then walked on without a backward glance. He never even noticed what he had accomplished with his actions.

The elderly man was reborn. His clothes were still the same, but his attitude was totally altered. He stood up to his full height, proudly taking on the world; he was no longer a misfit — he was a man who had friends, a person to be noticed. I watched agape as he walked away, a changed man, all because a young fellow had clapped him on the back and treated him the way we ought to treat each and every member of *Klal Yisrael*!

MRS. HAPPY'S NICKEL

By Leah Herskowitz

With a heart full of love, a positive outlook on life, and a smile for everyone, even a nickel is enough!

Everyone knew 143 Taylor Street in Williamsburg, New York as a home that always had an open door for guests and that was a beacon of light to thousands. Everyone was always welcome at the Herskowitz's home, whether for a short or a long stay. The Shabbos table was always full; the poor, the downtrodden and the outcasts were welcome equally. Children from broken homes were taken in and raised, and Mrs. Herskowitz would take care of their bar mitzvahs and weddings.

Mrs. Herskowitz ruled her kitchen, where she would cook, organize tzedakah appeals, and perform countless mitzvos, all the while lending her ear to all who chose to unburden themselves at any time of the day or night.

Mrs. Herskowitz would visit the hospitals, checking up on her "patients," making sure they were eating and feeling better. She had her list of "friends" whom she would call daily to offer words of encouragement and to give them something to live for. She raised huge sums of money, year after year, enlisting her entire family's assistance to help feed the many needy people she had adopted anonymously.

Mrs. Herskowitz, a daughter of Reb Binyomin Wilhelm, founder of Yeshiva Torah Vodaas, was distraught over the fact that there was no Jewish education available to the neighborhood children, so she single-handedly launched an afternoon Talmud Torah, where hundreds of secular children were imbued with a love for Hashem and a sense of Jewish identity. She personally taught many brides the laws of family purity, initiating them to a life of holiness and happiness. She authored numerous children's books, filled with stories designed to instill proper Jewish values and fine character traits. Her stories were published frequently by the children's magazine Olomeinu and read by thousands of children and adults around the world.

After Mrs. Herskowitz's passing, her family found this unpublished manuscript, which had been written many years earlier in her distinctive handwriting. The story shows how even when we have so little, we can still give so much — especially dignity and a feeling of importance May this story bring merit to the souls of Leah bas Binyomin, a"h, and her husband, Yonah Zev ben Tzvi, z"l.

"There is a family I know well," Mrs. Mintz, *a"h*, used to tell her Talmud Torah class, "with lots of children, but they live in a small house. They have no drapes on the windows and no rugs on the floor. Do you know what the mother's name is?"

Here Mrs. Mintz would pause a moment.

"The mother's name is Mrs. Happy."

Now I am going to tell you a story about Mrs. Happy that even Mrs. Mintz didn't know, because I knew Mrs. Happy even better than she did.

◆◆◆

Naturally, with lots of kids in the family and a couple of extra ones staying with them now and then, the money in Mrs. Happy's purse usually left quicker than it came in. But food was bought and paid for, and tuition for yeshivah and Bais Yaakov was paid — maybe a little late sometimes, but it was always paid up with pride. Clothing was not a major expense, because of the special packages they received from time to time.

Every morning each child was given a snack to take to school for recess, such as a tangerine, a bag of potato chips (bought by the case), or some other type of nosh. Who could ask for anything more? And every Sunday morning — or almost every Sunday morning — Mrs. Happy distributed allowances to eager, outstretched hands. There were 20 cents each for Moshe and Shanie, 15 cents for Shloime and Tzvi, 10 cents for Shragie, Avrohom Abba, and Chaneleh, and 5 cents each for Shimon and Yehudis. Some of the kids pocketed their money and spent it all the same day. It was good to feel rich for a day (though none of Mrs. Happy's children ever felt poor on days when there was no allowance).

At the beginning of the week when this little story took place, on that Sunday morning when the kids were crowded around the breakfast table, Mrs. Happy turned away from the sink and dried her hands. "Who didn't have an egg?" she asked. "There are two left. Shlomie, take out another bottle of milk. Shanie, did you *bentch* yet? Finish your cereal. Let's see, where did I put my wallet?... Okay, let's see...uh-oh. I'm sorry, kids. I guess I forgot that I had watermelon delivered on Erev Shabbos ["and the pickles," Zvi chimed in], and I don't have quite enough to give everyone allowance. So I'll owe it to you all."

"Hey, look at the time!" called Moshe. "I'm late!"

"Wait!" said Mrs. Happy, and she ran along with him, stuffing his recess snack into his briefcase just as they reached the door.

Now, let me tell you a little secret: The "not quite enough money" that Mrs. Happy found in her wallet that Sunday morning was *one lonely nickel*.

After the kids left and the baby went in for his nap, Mrs. Happy sat down to the warmed-over cereal and a cup of coffee. "Yes, this week will be a challenging experience," she thought. "Hmm, now how did I manage last time when something like this happened, about four months ago? This time I'm lucky — all the children are well, *b"H*, so I won't have to run up a bill in the drug store. And fortunately, our page in Mr. Itzkowitz's book was all crossed off last week — paid up to the last penny when Poppa gave him the check he had gotten. So, I'll need some bread or milk during the week... *nu*, we'll start a new page and pay it off again soon, with G-d's help. And we have so much food in the house! If only all Jewish children all over the world had food to eat like my sweet children have.

"Now, let's see. I'll make a good potato soup tonight, and with a bit of meat and cholent left over from Shabbos, it will be plenty for supper. Tomorrow night we'll have tuna casserole and potatoes. And here are two packs of franks — great! Tuesday, paprikash potatoes with franks. The kids love it, and it sure stretches far. I'm not going to say a word to Poppa about the money. I saw him open his wallet this morning as though he wanted to give me some cash, then he just put it back into his pocket.

"And if Poppa still doesn't get paid on Thursday...thank G-d my kids love the pizza I make — it's good for them, and it's cheap. Yes, food is no problem. But this lonely little nickel will have to cover everything else this week."

That afternoon Shanie's friend called to ask if she wanted to go ice skating in Prospect Park. And — good! — Shanie remembered about the morning's "no allowance" and answered, "Sorry, Faigy, I just don't feel like freezing out there standing in line waiting to rent skates. How about if you come over to my house to bake cookies with me? You know we can eat as much as we want when we bake... Great! Make it 3 o'clock. See you!"

Mrs. Happy was proud of her.

"Ma, can I have 25 cents for a compass?" Avrohom Abba asked the next morning.

"Let's see if there's one in the box first." They took a look, and, sure enough, down under the colored markers, scratch pads, glue, crayons and other supplies were not one but two old compasses that were still good.

Tuesday night after supper Shraga asked, "Ma, can I look through the coins in your purse tonight? Maybe I'll find another silver quarter like I once did."

"Sorry, I've just used up all the small change in my purse at the moment. How about checking these stamps that Tante Perel brought from her office? Here, look at this new China stamp. Isn't it gorgeous? Okay, you can look at the stamps for 15 minutes, and then *Krias Shema*."

Wednesday morning Yehudis was packing her briefcase. "Oh, I almost forgot — I need $3.50 for the Williamsburg Shabbos our grade is having."

"Three-fifty? Um, okay. I'll give you a check. Just a minute. Here it is. Please show the girl in charge that it's postdated for next week. I'm sure it will be all right. How many girls are we having here for Shabbos? Six? I'd better prepare my earplugs if I want to get some sleep Friday night!"

As the kids tumbled into the house after school, Mrs. Happy asked, "Shloime, what happened to your coat buttons today?" That reminded her that she had wanted to go to the notions store for some buttons for Moishe's jacket. She opened her purse and found the button sample lying there right next to the nickel. "Well, at least the nickel has some company," she thought. The buttons could wait; she decided to sew some knee patches on pants instead.

It was wonderful — so much free time to catch up, since she wasn't doing any shopping that week. She hummed a tune as she sat in the gate mending, keeping an eye on the baby as he played happily in the carriage. Tomorrow, yes, tomorrow her husband would be paid the big, overdue check his boss owed him. But, you see, they had managed without spending a penny. *Baruch Hashem*, they had everything they needed.

On Thursday morning Itzkowitz's boy Jose delivered her grocery order. What would Mrs. Happy do about tipping him? But first, quick as a wink, there was a cup of hot cocoa on the table for him. As Jose held it to warm up his freezing hands, Mrs. Happy bent over him and whispered, "Would you mind waiting till next week for your tip? I'm just short on change."

Jose jumped up from the chair, took off his cap, and bowed to Mrs. Happy. "Lady, I don't need any money tip. I love to deliver orders to this nice house. *Muchas Gracias.*" And Jose pulled on his gloves and cap and flew out of the house before Mrs. Happy could answer.

After the kids left for school Mrs. Happy decided to bake scotch-bread cookies (they had no eggs), which the kids loved and which also served the purpose of warming up the house without raising the thermostat. Suddenly, the doorbell rang. "I do hope it's not anybody trying to sell me something," she thought. "Please, not until tonight."

At the door stood a shabbily dressed man holding a thin coat tightly around himself for protection from the biting cold. He held out a plastic-covered letter for Mrs. Happy to read, and she recognized immediately that this was one of the poor Jews from Eretz Yisrael who had come to America trying to raise money for someone who was sick, or for some other important purpose.

"Come in, come in, Reb *Yid*, and I'll try to help you."

And in a minute the unfortunate man was seated at the kitchen table sipping a cup of steaming coffee with some of the fresh cookies that were already out of the oven. As the man was stammering his hard-luck story, Mrs. Happy nodded in sympathy, but her mind was searching feverishly; where, oh, where could she find a bit of money for the poor man! "Excuse me a moment," she said. Mrs. Happy had an idea. Let's see if there was anything she could borrow from her kids' banks. This surely was an emergency that called for drastic action.

There was some change rattling in Moshe's "Kanana Banana Flakes" can. Mrs. Happy pried the cover open and dumped the contents onto the kitchen table. Fifteen cents! "Well, it's a beginning." Mrs. Happy ripped a sheet from a pad of notepaper and wrote on it, *IOU 15 cents*, put it in the can, and snapped the cover back on.

In Shanie's little Diamond Walnuts can there were just 5 cents. Better than nothing. Well, another IOU.

In Chaneleh's glass piggy bank she could see quite a bit of change, but she couldn't borrow anything from that without breaking it. "No wonder it's a piggy," Mrs. Happy thought to herself.

Shragie's little plastic purse yielded a fortune of 50 cents. "He must be saving up for something," Mrs. Happy said as she wrote an IOU. "But he'll get his money back tonight, when Poppa gets paid."

"Nope, this jar's empty, and this one, too. No more money here."

"Wait, I remember seeing a quarter on the shelf somewhere in the hall where someone must have emptied a coat pocket last Erev Shabbos." Mrs. Happy went and got it, making a mental note to find out whose it was.

The coins on the table added up to 95 cents. "*Nu*, of course! This is what my nickel has been waiting for!"

And there it was — one whole dollar, which was presented to the visitor with profuse apologies and, at the door, sincere good wishes for his good health and success in his mission and a good trip back to the Holy Land.

Soon she was back in the kitchen, busy once again baking cookies.

So, as Mrs. Mintz used to say, there were no rugs on the floor and no drapes on the windows; and Mrs. Mintz didn't even know that there were times when there was no money in her purse...but the mother's name was Mrs. Happy.

YOSSI'S BAR MITZVAH

By Faigie Horowitz

It always pays to make others feel as if they belong.

A sober atmosphere characterized the *simchah*. My brother was making his first bar mitzvah; his eldest was the star. Yet the overall ambiance of the event was tinged with an extra dose of solemnity: My mother, the Novominsker Rebbetzin, *a"h*, the bar mitzvah boy's grandmother, was seriously ill with lung cancer. The prognosis was grim, and everyone who knew her kept her name constantly in their *tefillos*. To add to her merit, numerous *Tehillim* groups had been formed and various initiatives were undertaken by her broad circle of family, friends, and those who had benefited from her kindness and wise counsel.

The family converged from near and far for the *seudah* at Schick's in Borough Park on that cold Sunday night. Rebbetzin Perlow was noticeably pale; she lacked her usual energy and vibrancy. Nonetheless, from her seat she greeted all the guests, both foreign and domestic, with a gracious smile and accepted all the good wishes.

Among the invitees were cousins Dovid and Rosalind, who drove in from Boston. Despite the fact that their invitation had been misdirected so they had not heard about the *simchah* until the previous evening, they headed down to New York with their five young children in tow. Their commitment to family was paramount, and they wished to see Aunt Yehudis and wish her both *refuah sheleimah* and *mazal tov*.

Zahava, Rosalind's sister, was living in Manhattan at the time, seeking her *bashert*. When Rosalind asked her at the very last minute to come along to the *seudah* sans invitation, she hesitated. She felt uncomfortable attending a prominent family's intimate *simchah* when she had not been formally invited.

What to do? Zahava decided to place a call to Switzerland, where her wise mother lived. Zahava's mother strongly urged her to attend the *simchah*. Zahava listened and gingerly "crashed the party."

Upon her arrival at the *seudah*, thoughtful Cousin Rochel saved her the embarrassment of trying to find an unassigned seat. Unprompted, Rochel gave up her own seat at the head table, so Zahava sat with her sister Rosalind on one side and Rebbetzin Perlow on the other.

My mother sensed immediately the strong discomfort of this last-minute, uninvited guest who squirmed in her ridiculously prominent seat. Her tone changed and her voice became strong as, in her declarative style, she firmly pronounced these unforgettable words:

"This is your family. This is where you belong. Go and wash."

The food platter no longer seemed so forbidding as Zahava was quickly infused with a sense of belonging, and she found the company and atmosphere to be genuinely warm, welcoming, and enjoyable.

The next day Cousin Rochel, who had so sensitively given Zahava her seat at the bar mitzvah, phoned her to suggest a *shidduch*. Rochel was newly widowed but did not let that stand in the way of her attempts to help others. She was an accomplished *shadchanit* and had once worked for the Orthodox Union in that capacity. She did not give up when the names she offered were unsuitable. She called a friend, way down on her *shidduch*-networking list, who suggested Moshe B., a refined professional from Manhattan who was also well-known to the Perlow family.

Several weeks later Zahava and Moshe met. Zahava was ambivalent about this *shidduch's* chances. She wanted more information about Moshe and decided to call the Rebbetzin directly. Rebbetzin Perlow was a wise woman whose counsel was sought professionally and personally. Her information was known to be trustworthy, her opinions on the mark, her words pithy — and she knew Moshe B. well.

At this point it was hard for my mother to speak on the phone, but she insisted on taking this call. She endorsed Moshe's credentials strongly, her choice, reassuring words forming a delightful description.

The next morning she called Moshe in his office. She spoke in her signature style: powerfully and concisely, in words that are unforgettable:

"This is the one. Make it happen."

Moshe was left with the phone dangling in hand, dumbfounded. The message could not have been clearer. She endorsed the *shidduch* unequivocally.

Shortly afterward Zahava and Moshe were engaged. The Rebbetzin was gravely ill at the time of the wedding, which was held in Switzerland. Yet the warmth of her outreach at the bar mitzvah never faded. Zahava would frequently recount the story to the Rebbetzin during her final months, giving her *chizuk* by telling her that her hospitality and wisdom had been so fruitful. Although my mother, a"h, passed away soon afterward, Zahava regularly reminds family members and friends of the power of friendliness and of the Rebbetzin's compelling hospitality and how it resulted in the start of a Jewish family.

THE GYPSY WOMAN

By Brachah Stern

Sometimes we catch a glimpse of just how significant our small actions can be.

I am at a supermarket in Switzerland, and a Gypsy woman is there, selling some silly magazine.

How miserable she looks! No one is buying; everyone just passes her by with their full carts, not even glancing her way.

Ten years ago, I was pickpocketed by a Gypsy woman. As I look at the poor Gypsy woman at the supermarket, I can't help but remember that long-ago but still painful incident.

Her magazine holds no interest for me, but I will give her a couple of Swiss francs.

I approach her and she looks hopeful. I greet her nicely.

A smile begins to form on her doleful face.

I take out some money, but before giving it to her I tell her, "Do you know why I am giving you this money? It is because I am Jewish, and our religion teaches us to give charity." If I am giving her a donation, I can give a lesson while I'm at it.

She looks at me, dumbfounded. I imagine that she sees me as someone who has just landed from outer space. Perhaps, I think, she did not understand me, as I do not speak her Gypsy language well. Whatever the case, I look into her uncomprehending eyes, give her the money and walk off.

●●●

As I go back to replace the shopping cart in its stand, she calls me over with her finger.

All right, I am willing to go and hear what she has to say, keeping at a safe distance.

She looks deeply into my eyes.

"You religious…you believe in G-d…you…" and she makes a motion as if trying to ask about *tzitzis*. "That is you?"

"Yes," I answer. "Yes, absolutely."

In a loud, clear, and very incorrect German she says, "For you — for your people — the world was created. Everything for you!"

Now it is my turn to be dumbfounded.

AN INFUSION OF SHABBOS

Rabbi Yitzchok Kornblau

Sometimes even a song can move worlds...

Reuven isn't your typical guy. Most people sort of let life carry them along as passive passengers, but Reuven *lives* life, savoring every twist and turn, every peak and rut.

This may be somewhat charming to read about on paper, but in person...I'd call Reuven a jet engine. Vitality could very well be his middle name.

This story happened in a setting that far from suited Reuven's persona: a hospital shul. Reuven's wife had just delivered their first child, and he had spent most of Erev Shabbos in the hospital with her. With Shabbos approaching, instead of trekking back to his neighborhood shul Reuven decided to daven *Kabbalas Shabbos* and *Maariv* at the hospital, then wish his wife a good Shabbos before going home. To say he was drained is an understatement, and davening in a hospital shul definitely wasn't an experience he looked forward to, but this was what life was sending him, and he planned to make the best of it.

Which is exactly what he did.

As he looked around the shul a depressing scene unraveled before Reuven's eyes. The sick and infirm made their way slowly to the pews. The gloomy mood in the room was palpable and getting worse by the minute. Reuven could only imagine the sorrowful davening he was about to share with his shulmates, and he was determined not to let it happen...

Rising from his seat, he looked around to see if anyone would mind if he stepped up to the *bimah* for *Kabbalas Shabbos*. Quickly realizing that this was the last thing on any of these people's minds, he took his place in front of the *bimah*, sent off a brief personal prayer that this would work, and belted out *Lechu Neranenah* as he never had before. But this wasn't a show of *chazzanus* — that was not what was called for here; he sang *niggunim*, lively, uplifting *niggunim*, which he savored as much as he savored each day. All he wanted was to make the best of this moment — not only for himself but for all those present as well.

At first he wasn't sure if his plan was working, but soon the hum behind him slowly picked up, and before he knew it the shul was filled with song as they made their way through *Kabbalas Shabbos*. At one point he was almost overcome with the urge to look back and see what was really happening around him, but something inside him feared he had gone too far, and he didn't feel like facing the consequences just yet.

Finally, though, he mustered the courage and took a peek.... Faces that just moments earlier had been full of despair were now filled with infectious smiles. Young men were lost in song, old men in wheelchairs waved their frail hands in the air; a new life filled the room — something he never dreamed could happen.

Before long *Maariv* was over and Reuven was ready to run upstairs to say "Good Shabbos" to his wife before heading home.

He turned to go, and he couldn't believe his eyes. The whole aisle before him was filled with the infirm, young and old, who had come to wish him a good Shabbos and thank him for the wonderful gift he had brought them. And if that wasn't enough to show how a simple decision can so powerfully change the quality of other people's lives, one young boy in a wheelchair, sick with the unthinkable, removed any remaining doubt.

"*Toda lecha, Adoni.* You made my Shabbat. I...I never dreamed I would have a Shabbat like that again...."

A MOST UNUSUAL SHABBOS GUEST

As told to Miriam Lea Rosenberg

We cannot begin to estimate the precious merit of making a kiddush Hashem, but sometimes we can get a taste of its reward in our lifetime.

We were finally there — our much-anticipated vacation in the Alps was actually happening!

We were in a small hotel — as elegant as Jewish hotels in the Alps get, but it was a delight to be there. Everything was clean, the food was fresh and good, and the crowd was quite small, so everyone there had the chance to get to know everyone else.

It was midwinter, and in the cities down below the weather was bleak. In the mountains, though, the sun shone and everyone enjoyed the crisp air, the sunshine, and the fresh snow.

The skiing was grand, and those who were not skiers could go sledding or just walking in the beautiful countryside, admiring G-d's magnificent creation. The trees were laden with snow; one could take a stroll on a frozen lake, have a horse-drawn sleigh ride, or enjoy so many other possibilities. No matter how tense and overworked we were when we arrived, it was hard not to relax and surrender very quickly to the welcoming atmosphere. We all felt lucky to be there. The only downside to this place was that it posed the very real danger of becoming habit-forming; one really wanted to return again and again.

The hotel was a melting pot of Jews from all over the world. The guests were of Chassidish, Litvish, and Mizrachi backgrounds; they were French, English, Swiss, and American. Those guests who were not old friends would soon become so.

●●●

On Friday nights the hotel was transformed. The feeling of the *kedushah* of Shabbos was strong, and all the guests were dressed accordingly. It was a sudden break from the week's high-energy activities; it was a celebration of Shabbos. You could feel it in the *Shalom Aleichem*, sung in all different *niggunim* at the various tables; you could feel it in the flowers with which some had spoiled their spouses; you could feel the *kedushah* in the air in every aspect of this peaceful milieu.

I was relaxed; the kids were behaving. I was about to make *Kiddush* when all of a sudden I felt the atmosphere change, as if a wave had washed over the place. As I had not noticed what it was that had precipitated the change, I looked around curiously to see what was happening.

Mr. P., the hotel's proprietor, was standing by the door. Ordinarily an exceptionally calm man, now his face was flushed and he seemed most uncomfortable. Behind him was a tall, ruddy-faced man, well dressed with grey pants and a blue jacket with a small hanky peeking out of his blazer pocket. But…he was not wearing a *kippah*, and it was clear that this was not an oversight. Throughout the room there were raised eyebrows and quiet coughing; even Mr. P., who always knows what to do, seemed nonplussed.

Seeing that the other guests were feeling awkward about the situation, I rose from my seat, and with firm steps and a friendly smile approached Mr. P. and asked him who the newcomer was.

The hotel owner explained that the man wanted to eat a meal at this kosher hotel, though he was fully aware that it was a Jewish establishment. It was clear that this guest had no idea what a stir he was causing, so before he could notice anything that might, *chas v'shalom*, make him feel unwelcome, I invited him to join our table, and he accepted gladly.

Our family discussed with our new non-Jewish acquaintance what Shabbos is all about, and he listened attentively. The other people in the room, seeing that the situation was being taken care of, continued their own Shabbos meals in the pleasant atmosphere of this lovely venue.

What was this guest doing there? There were plenty of other hotels in the area. Had he simply blundered and walked into this one on a Shabbos night without realizing that it was a truly Jewish hotel?

It became clear afterward, though, that this man — we'll call him Mr. Springer — was convinced that the Jewish people are superior. His father-in-law was Jewish, and Mr. Springer had an eligible son and was on the lookout for a nice Jewish girl for him; he wanted only the real thing — a girl who was true to her faith. We all knew, of course, that Mr. Springer had not come to the right place. But how to make that clear to this man who was one of the world's precious *ohavei Yisrael*?

Very gently, with a blend of humor, respect, even admiration, and great care, we conveyed to him the message that his son must find a proper spouse of his own kind. The prodigy-son would surely feel more comfortable that way.

This was a great letdown for Mr. Springer, who had thought it through carefully and was convinced that any girl would seize the opportunity to win this brilliant, promising young man. After all, he was a real a catch; he was good-looking and a fantastic skier; he held a high position at one of the largest banks and was earning top dollar.

Mr. Springer remained in good spirits, though. He had thoroughly enjoyed the evening, and before he left he asked if he could keep in touch with our family.

And keep in touch he did — for many years, even long after his son had found an appropriate girl to marry.

As Mr. Springer was a financial advisor, we invited him to give a lecture on financial planning to the girls in a school we support. He was happy to do so, and he spoke beautifully. While he was there he had a chance to see the school and to get to know just what a school like this is all about. He was more than impressed, and he realized what a great need it filled and what a crucial role it played in building the future; these girls would one day contribute, financially and in many other ways, to the homes they would establish.

Sensing his level of connection to the place, we deemed it appropriate to offer him the opportunity to contribute to the cause, and Mr. Springer came through with a generous donation. In fact, he became something of a regular donor to this Jewish school that had been so deeply in debt, and to this day he has remained a good friend of the school and of our family.

AN EXPRESSION OF THANKS

By Eliezer Leaman

How do you create a channel into the heart of someone who has given you the coldest reception imaginable?

I am involved in an organization for children, and we are always in the market for games, toys, and other items that appeal to children. We purchase large quantities several times throughout the year, as there is always another project, contest, or raffle. We are constantly thinking of new, innovative prizes for the kids. We want them to look forward to being with us and to get excited over what we have to offer — both the Torah they learn and the prizes they receive.

At one point we were in the market for a huge order of a certain innovative board game from the largest manufacturer of board games in Israel. We found that the owner of that company was no friend of religious people. We came to his office to place a substantial order, and not only did the man show no appreciation for the fact that we had chosen to take our business to him, he showed no warmth at all, and it made for a most uncomfortable venue in which to do business. His cold manner was informing us in no uncertain terms that he wanted no part of our way of life.

Regardless of his attitude, however, his factory was top-of-the-line, his production crew produced high-quality products, and we were very satisfied with his service. I wanted to reach out to him and also to thank him in a way that would show our genuine appreciation and that might perhaps slide the door to his heart open a fraction of an inch. I racked my brain for an idea, something that would strike a chord, that would get through to this man who was light years away from us.

And then, like a bolt of lightning, it hit me.

I had noticed on one of my visits to his office that there was no *mezuzah* on the door. I wasn't sure about the rest of the company, but one has to begin somewhere, and his office was as good a place as any. I knew, however, that a simple *mezuzah* in a standard wooden or silver case wasn't going to do it here. His secretary had told me that he loved the game Rummikub, so I knew I could come up with something close to his heart. The *mezuzah* case that would hang on his doorpost was going to be constructed from pieces right out of the Rummikub game. It would be a great, one-of-a-kind conversation piece, and he would absolutely love it!

I special-ordered the *mezuzah* case and sent it off with a prayer on my lips and hope in my heart.

He sent me an e-mail thanking me for my kind gift.

Several months later I received a phone call from him. After some preliminary small talk he coughed a little and then came to the point. His company was moving into newer and larger offices, he told me, and would I be so kind as to supply enough *mezuzahs* for all the offices in the building, because *he needed them*! Since I had provided him with his first *mezuzah*, would I continue to do so....

THE PERFECT GIRL FOR MY SON

As told to Malky Lowinger

> *"Perfect" and "imperfect" are very relative terms.*

Like it or not, when it comes to *shidduchim* in our community, it's a boy's world. It's not really something to be proud of, but the bottom line is that there seem to be many more eligible young ladies than *bachurim* "on the market" at any given time. This means that a good, *"geshmak"* learning boy has plenty of girls to choose from; the deck is stacked in his favor.

When it comes to our girls, our best defense is to daven a lot, to do our *hishtadlus,* and to hope for the best.

So when my oldest son Ari turned 20 and someone approached us about a *shidduch* for him, I laughed. He wasn't ready, I wasn't listening, and the time just wasn't right. Thank you very much, I said. Call me back in about a year.

But the *shadchan*, Duvie, who had seen Ari in yeshivah and liked what he saw, was persistent. He actually waited out the year and called again. At that point Ari was still learning well in Eretz Yisrael, was perfectly happy with things as they were, and was still relatively young for *shidduchim*, at least in our circles. I decided to pass on the *shidduch* again.

By now Duvie already had a "resume" written out for the young lady in question — that is, he had a page filled with all the relevant information about the suggested girl. Our would-be *shadchan* decided to fax it to me ("just in case," he said. . .). More out of curiosity than anything else, I scanned it quickly, looking for some interesting detail that might catch my attention or tickle my fancy. Was she especially lively? Did she have an amazing talent? Was she outstanding in her *middos*? Would she be the ultimate *balebusteh*? Did she come from a prestigious family?

As I glanced through the references, something caught my eye. It was the name of an esteemed rebbetzin whom I knew personally. I trusted her opinion, and felt instinctively that she would be honest with me. I decided to call the rebbetzin and run the idea by her.

Our conversation was warm and friendly, but it didn't go quite as I had expected. The rebbetzin did indeed know the girl in question, as well as her family. Yes, they were wonderful people. Yes, they got along well with all their *mechutanim*. Yes, she had outstanding *middos*. Yes, she was *ehrlich* and *eidel* and mature. And, yes, she would make an exceptional wife and mother.

So far, so good. But then she said something that threw me off for a moment. "Only one thing, Batsheva. I suggest strongly that you go and see the girl yourself before the boy meets her. I happen to know that she'll be at a *simchah* tonight. Go and check her out. Don't give a yes until you do so."

Could the rebbetzin think I was so shallow that I needed to see if a girl was pretty enough for my son? Did she really think I was one of those mothers who ran to weddings to spy on the girls? It's no secret that there are women in our community who won't let their sons date until they determine that the young lady is tall/skinny/pretty enough for them. But that's just not me. Let my son decide if he finds a girl attractive or not. He needs a wife, not a trophy that I can show off to all my friends.

Anyway, it turned out that this wasn't what the rebbetzin had in mind at all. "Oh, no no no," she said when I protested her suggestion. "That's not what I'm talking about. You see, this young lady has all the wonderful characteristics I told you about, but I'll be honest with you — she also has a slight physical imperfection. There's a pretty obvious scar on her face. I think it happened when she fell as a baby. I don't think you should go into this *shidduch* until you see it for yourself."

I was stunned. It hadn't occurred to me that this was what the rebbetzin meant. I scribbled down the name of the *chasunah* hall where the *simchah* would be held, thanked the rebbetzin with all my heart and hung up the phone.

Frankly, I was ready to drop the whole thing right then and there. As far as I was concerned, Ari was still a boy. What did I need this for? On the other hand, I had promised the rebbetzin that I would make the effort, so at the very least, I had to go. "I'll roam around for a few minutes and then I'll leave," I told myself. "No one will be the wiser."

At 10 p.m. I showed up at Ateres Chaya, a stranger at a *chasunah* I wasn't invited to. In my basic black suit I fit in with the rest of the crowd, and the timing was perfect. The girls were dancing, the ladies were milling about, and nobody paid much attention to me. I figured that while I was there, I may as well do my civic duty. I asked a young married woman if she knew who this girl was, and she smiled as if these kinds of inquiries came up all the time. "That's her," she told me, "in the black-and-white dress."

My spying mission began. I stood back and watched Miss Black-and-White-Dress in action. I saw her dancing gracefully in the circle with the rest of the girls. As far as I could see, there was nothing particularly unusual about that. The sarcasm was starting to bubble up inside me. "Okay," I said to myself, "so she knows how to dance. Big deal. Is that going to make her a good wife and mother?"

A couple of minutes later, things started getting more interest-

The Perfect Girl for My Son / 173

ing. I noticed Miss B.A.W.D. walking away from the rest of the circle. She came over to a girl who was sitting at a corner-table by herself, watching the others. The young lady in question was very overweight, seemed a little reserved and, apparently, was too embarrassed to join the dancing. I watched as Miss B.A.W.D. started chatting with her. With a warm smile, she held out her hand and led her toward the circle of dancers. Before the other girl could protest, she was dancing with everyone else. She was definitely awkward, it was true, and she lacked the natural grace of the others. But there was no mistaking the genuine smile on her face.

Wow. I was floored by this amazing act of kindness. Miss B.A.W.D. was suddenly my hero. How in the world did she even realize that this girl was so miserably lonely? I have daughters. I know how the girls get so caught up in dancing and enjoying a *simchah*. How incredibly special this girl was to take a few moments to include someone else in that same joy. And, most of all, how amazing it was that Hashem had brought me to this place at this exact moment, so that I could watch this drama unfold.

Imperfection? What imperfection? Yes, it's true that her look was a little bit "different." But at that moment I can honestly tell you I had no idea what the rebbetzin was talking about. All I saw was a young woman with outstanding *middos*, who was gentle and kind and giving. All this spoke volumes to me. Nothing else really mattered.

I suppose you can guess how the rest of the story goes. The very next morning I called Duvie and told him I was ready to proceed. Several weeks later we were celebrating the engagement of Ari and Suri.

Today Ari and Suri are the proud parents of a beautiful, growing family. Ari is still learning and Suri is working part-time. In the meantime, I've married off several other children and, *baruch Hashem*, we are exceptionally happy with all of our dear sons- and daughters-in-law. But to me, Suri will always be special.

Sometimes I remind Suri about the wedding and ask her if she remembers the overweight girl, or perhaps the snoopy lady who was staring at her that night. She vaguely remembers the former and says she totally did not notice the latter (thank G-d!). In fact, she finds the entire story more amusing than anything else. And as for Ari, he just rolls his eyes every time I bring it up.

Of course, there are no coincidences in life. On the one hand, it seems to me that the entire incident unfolded as a clear sign from Heaven that this *shidduch* was meant to happen. It kind of makes me feel a little like Eliezer, who, when searching for a proper *shidduch* for Yitzchak Avinu, was shown a similar sign. Rifka's act of kindness was the catalyst that spurred Eliezer to select her as the perfect match for Yitzchak and thus continue to build the very foundation of *Klal Yisrael* that Avraham Avinu began.

Suri's act of kindness was the catalyst that made me jump into this *shidduch* for my Ari, despite my initial reluctance. All it took was a small act of kindness to make the difference. I gave the green light, the kids got married, and their lives are changed forever. By all accounts, they are, *baruch Hashem*, living happily ever after.

THE POTENTIAL IN EACH MOMENT

By Yonoson Rosenblum

Every one of us has infinite potential; our ability to influence the people we meet in positive ways cannot be dismissed.

If we fully appreciated the immense potential that lies within our every action, we would conduct our lives very differently. The magnitude of that potential was brought home to me a few years back by a guest at our Shabbos table. At the time he was studying in our neighborhood at a yeshivah for *baalei teshuvah*, and I asked him what had led him to the yeshivah.

He told me that he had been on the fast track to success as a screenwriter in Hollywood; before the age of 30 he had already sold two screenplays. One Shabbos morning he was eating brunch with a Jewish friend across the street from the Los Angeles *kollel*, at the Revival Café. (A tobacconist's store two doors down the block featured a sign, "If there are no cigars in heaven, who wants to go?") As they sat there, an Orthodox family walked by after Shabbos morning davening.

Something about the family caught my friend's attention. As he explained, he had grown up in Palm Beach, Florida, one of America's most affluent areas. "We didn't just have two-car families," he told me. "We had two-car teenagers." Materially, he had lacked nothing. But there was a fly in the ointment. "The one thing I had never seen was a proud, intact Jewish family," he explained. (When he was growing up there were at least five country clubs in Palm Beach that barred Jews.)

His friend took one look at the passing family and commented, "Boy, do I feel sorry for those kids."

He looked at his friend, who sported a new tattoo that read "tattoo," and replied, "As sorry as you feel for them, they feel a lot sorrier for you."

Shortly after that encounter my friend flew back to Palm Beach for Rosh Hashanah. Services were conducted in a church, and the blanket kept falling off of a crucifix. On his way back to Los Angeles, the plane made an emergency landing.

Perhaps it was the incongruity of Rosh Hashanah services in the presence of a crucifix; perhaps it was the brush with death. But that Shabbos he decided to find the shul from which he thought that family had come.

When he entered the Jewish Learning Exchange, he did not find the family in question. But the first people who greeted him turned out to be Hollywood writers just like him — except that they had been religious for years. And, as he found out when he joined one of them for lunch, they had wives and families, something not then on his radar screen.

Within a year of noticing that passing family he was learning full-time in Jerusalem. Two years after that he had married a *baalas teshuvah* from England and was learning in Hager's Kollel in London. Eventually they returned to Jerusalem so he could learn for a few more years in the Mirrer Yeshivah. Today he is the outreach direc-

The Potential in Each Moment / 177

tor on one of the most heavily Jewish Ivy League campuses, he and his wife have (at last count) five children, and his wife is a widely sought-after lecturer in *kollel* circles on child-rearing issues.

Nor does the story end with my friend and his family. He convinced three of his closest friends in the film industry to join him in Jerusalem. One of those friends later learned in Yeshivas Ner Yisrael and, after his marriage, in the Ner Yisrael *kollel*. Another learned for several years in the Mirrer Yeshivah. Today all three are married with children of their own.

My friend has two younger brothers. They too followed him to Jerusalem, where they live today with their families. One is learning and counseling; the other is a *mashgiach* in a yeshivah for *baalei teshuvah*.

The fleeting impression a family made leaving shul led to seven young Jews becoming full *bnei Torah*. That impact will continue to multiply — not just in the more than twenty offspring (so far) of those seven young men, but in all the generations to come.

Yet the members of that family have no inkling of the cosmic explosion they triggered as they passed by a sidewalk cafe one Shabbos morning, or of the ramifications of the fleeting impression their appearance made. They will never know until they arrive in *Shamayim* and find a totally unexpected A+ on their "report cards."

But imagine if, at the very moment they passed by that café, unaware that they were being watched, the father had spoken unpleasantly to his wife, or had been giving one of his children a *potch*, even if fully justified. Seven Jewish *neshamos*, and all those who will come from them, might have been lost. In the blink of an eye the opportunity of a lifetime could have been missed. The line between opportunities realized and opportunities lost is a very thin one indeed.

JUST A LITTLE LEKACH

As great as is the potential for good in every single moment, the potential for causing great damage is equally great. I once related the incident about the screenwriter in the Bais Yaakov High School in Los Angeles, just a few blocks from where it occurred. After my speech I sat down to talk with Rabbi Yoel Bursztyn, the principal of the school, and he shared with me a story from his *kollel* days in Lakewood.

Among his neighbors in his apartment building in Lakewood was a retired engineer, whom everyone called "Doc." Doc was not in any way observant, so Rabbi Bursztyn was surprised one day to see him coming out of a *minyan* wearing *tallis* and *tefillin*. Doc told him that he had been needed as a tenth man and that this was the first time in seventy years that he had davened with a *minyan*.

He then proceeded to share the story of the last *minyan* he had attended. His mother had passed away in Europe, and shortly thereafter his father, his sister, and he had come to Philadelphia. They were very poor; he and his sister walked miles back and forth to school every day because they did not have the nickel for the trolley fare.

On the day of his mother's *yahrtzeit* he went to shul to say *Kaddish* for her. After *Shacharis* an older man in shul, who had heard him reciting *Kaddish*, asked him, "*Boychikel*, do you have a *yahrtzeit* today?" When he said that it was his mother's *yahrtzeit*, the older man asked him, "Nu, so where's the *lekach*?" When the old man saw that none was forthcoming, he spat out with disgust, "*Phooee*, you call that a *yahrtzeit*?"

The young boy ran home, devastated. His father found him sobbing on his bed. When his father asked him what had happened, the only thing the boy would tell him was, "Ta, I will never set foot in a shul again." And for the next seventy years he did not.

So deep was the pain of that one offhanded remark that as Doc told Rabbi Bursztyn the story he began to weep.

BROADCASTING THE REAL THING

We are all broadcasting on a continual basis, and the messages we transmit are not only about us; they are about what it means to be a Jew shaped by the dictates of the Torah. A radio sends out sound waves over a particular radius, but only those with the proper vessel for receiving its signals (i.e., a radio) can receive its message. In the same way, we have no idea who, at any given moment, has the tools to receive the messages we are broadcasting and will be affected. But we must keep in mind at all times that there may be somebody out there with a "radio."

That particular insight was brought home to me by a real radio show. For about two years I did a weekly live interview from my home in Jerusalem with a small station on the North Side of Chicago. That involved my staying up until 2 a.m. so that the show could run live in the Chicago area, and there were many times when I asked myself why I was depriving myself of sleep just to offer some observations about life in Israel.

Over time, through my participation in the show, I became very friendly with the interviewer, Rabbi Eli Sanbar, even though we had never met in person. When he was appointed principal of a high school in Chicago and could no longer conduct the interviews, I found that my enthusiasm for staying up during those early-morning hours waned, and eventually I dropped the broadcast.

A few years later I was in Chicago to deliver a speech, and a mutual friend introduced me to Rabbi Sanbar in person. I asked him whether there had ever been any positive results from our show. Had we ever touched anyone with our broadcast? He replied with a story.

One day a Jew from the Chicago suburb of Oak Park was driving on the expressway on the city's South Side and decided to turn on the Chicago White Sox game to catch the score. Apparently, the North Side radio station was close to the White Sox games on the dial, and he picked up the station briefly. At that very moment a well-known rabbi was exhorting his listeners to insist that their rabbis teach them Torah, not just offer straight political commentary. Something about the message intrigued him, and when he arrived home he convinced his wife to listen to the station with him. They started listening regularly, and one night they were tuned in as Rabbi Sanbar intoned, "Well, Jonathan, what's new in Jerusalem?"

I launched into a description of something that had happened to me that day. I had gone to visit a new religious school in a community near Netanya. After touring a number of classrooms, all comprised of girls from newly religious families, the principal invited me to meet the father of some students in the school.

The father began by asking me whether I had ever heard of Tzoran, a nearby community. I told him that I had and, a couple of years earlier, had even written a number of op-ed pieces about the battles that had erupted when a *chareidi* class for about twenty-five first-graders opened up in Tzoran. The children found themselves confronted with screaming demonstrators every morning for a month. They had to learn with the windows closed because of rocks pelting the building housing the one-room school, and the building and playground were repeatedly vandalized and covered with graffiti.

The next year the school reopened, not in Tzoran but in nearby Kadima, but instead of twenty-five students it had one hundred. By the third year, when I went to visit, it had three hundred students.

The father with whom I spoke now explained why he had asked whether I had ever heard of Tzoran: He had led the demonstrations against the school. One day, however, as he watched the 19-or 20-year-old Bais Yaakov teachers from Bnei Brak leading the children past the screaming mob, he had asked himself what kind of people would he like to serve as models for his children. His answer was — teachers just like those young women from Bnei Brak.

At the time when we spoke he already had three children in the school.

As I related this story to Rabbi Sanbar on the air, I told him, "Eli, when he told me that, I started crying." And in Oak Park, a Chicago suburb with no observant Jews, a woman turned to her husband and also started crying. "That's fine for the children in Tzoran," she said, "but what about our children?" Shortly thereafter, that couple moved from Oak Park to Rogers Park, the most heavily Orthodox neighborhood of Chicago, so they could place their children in religious schools.

That night, after I finished speaking, a husband and wife

The Potential in Each Moment / 181

approached me and said, "We are the couple Rabbi Sanbar told you about." Then I had the answer to my question of why I had stayed up until 2 a.m. to do that show, as well as the perfect metaphor for the broadcasting that we are doing all the time, when we have no idea who is listening or watching.

JUST A SMILE AND A WAVE

From The Jewish Women's Project for Ahavas Yisrael

No one can do everything, but just doing what we can do, no matter how modest, is enough.

One day when I walked into the local bank I saw a new teller. She was sweet and accommodating, yet very professional. And there was something else I noticed about her: Around her neck she wore a silver Jewish star. I saw her touch it a few times, as if she were seeking acknowledgment of the fact that she, too, was Jewish in this heavily populated Orthodox area.

I took care of my transactions quickly and, as I passed her desk, gave a smile and a wave, acknowledging on a very basic level that we were connected by our spiritual roots.

I've often heard stories about people who met nonreligious Jews in shopping malls or at the gym and ended up introducing them to true Judaism, but I didn't believe this was part of my destiny. It's not that I object to reaching out to other Jews; it's just that I'm a bit of an introvert. I don't get excited about the potential for *kiruv* in every encounter because I'm clueless when it comes to what to say in those first crucial moments.

In the bank, having quickly assessed my own capabilities in this situation and my responsibility as a religious woman, I knew I could manage giving a smile and a light wave with my hand. I left it at that and felt I had done my part. Every time I entered the bank I would follow this friendly routine, and the Jewish teller always smiled back.

One day during my lunch break I was walking down a busy street in the neighborhood when I saw a familiar face.

"Hi!" she said. "It's me, Karen — the new teller at the bank. Do you have a second? I just wanted to share something with you."

"Sure!" I said, wondering what she had in mind.

"I just moved to this area a few months ago, and I started my job at the bank soon after I arrived. When I accepted the position I had no idea the neighborhood was so religious. At first I was slightly intimidated by the fact that all my clients were religious. I'm Jewish too, but I grew up less traditional. When I first saw you at the bank, you waved and smiled at me. It made me feel so good. I know this may sound funny, but somehow, until that point I felt as if I was always being judged because I wasn't religious. Every time you passed my desk and smiled, as crazy as this may sound, it made me feel like you considered me like one of you!"

Whoa! Was I blown away! That was not what I was expecting!

"I...I...don't know what to say. I'm so happy to have the chance to meet you officially."

"It's nice to meet you too! I just wanted to let you know that your small acknowledgment really was appreciated, and I wanted to say thanks. See you later!" She practically skipped down the street, obviously delighted with the realization that she had also done a "good deed" by giving me her message.

If I were really brave I would have continued the conversation and asked for her phone number to invite her for Shabbos or something. I didn't do that, but I learned never to underestimate a pure, simple smile. It costs nothing, takes no time, and is easy to do — even though in my case it was a bit of a stretch. I now see the tremendous impact I can have on another person. Now, I try to smile at everyone I see, because I realize how powerful it can be. Best of all, this experience has transformed me into a more outgoing person — it's truly a win-win situation.

They say, "An apple a day keeps the doctor away." I'd like to add another line to that jingle: "And a smile a day, please don't delay!"

But the story doesn't end there. Eventually I did summon the courage to invite Karen for Shabbos. She and her sister are now learning with a rebbetzin. And to think it all started with a smile and a wave!

JUST ONE BRIEF QUESTION

By Arel Mishory

Finding meaning in the briefest response...

Recently, I tried an experiment. When I was in the grocery store I said "Hello" to the checkout person and asked her how she was. The young woman responded, "Oh, I'm good." I asked her to describe the "good" for me, and she said, "Well, I'm not *really* good. Actually, I'm pretty depressed."

We went on to have a fairly meaningful conversation right there at the grocery-store checkout. I was so surprised, because I had drawn certain conclusions about this person based on how she looked. I learned very quickly that my conclusions were not accurate at all. I realized that I had truly interacted with a real person and not a robot standing there to serve me.

I continued doing this throughout the day, and it had a profound effect on me. It was a pleasure to actually invite people to share their true feelings. I was amazed at how people responded to the question of "Describe *good*," as the almost universal answer to the question of "How are you?" was, "I'm good," or, "I'm okay." In the end, not all of them were good or okay at all. Because I took the time to ask them one more question, I was able to empathize with those who weren't so good and rejoice with those who were.

A STORY OF KINDNESS AND KIDDUSH HASHEM

By Sherry E. Waldman

*To experience kindness is a gift;
to remember it years later is a blessing.*

It's been five years since my mother, *a"h*, died. It was on a Monday in August. The events related in this account took place two days before that, on Shabbos.

For the last eight months of her life my mother battled pancreatic cancer. It was a tough fight, but my mother was a tough lady with an even tougher oncologist. By June of that year crises were becoming more frequent; it seemed I drove my mother from her home on Long Island to the emergency room in her Manhattan hospital every other week or so. These were bad trips, so much worse than the trips for her scheduled chemo infusions: the hours lingering in ER cubicles — or even hallways, when the cubicles were all occupied — waiting for Mom to be admitted; the sounds and sights of illness, trauma and sometimes death, accompanied by groans and sobs from patients' family or friends — all of it raw and bleak. A sick feeling was growing inside me that these ER trips were way too terrible for Mom and, yes, for me, too.

But I was up for anything the oncologist told me to do to prolong Mom's life. The ER doctors all disagreed; they urged me to discontinue the rigorous and painful chemotherapy regimen the oncologist had ordered. They reminded me, unmercifully, even brutally, that pancreatic cancer is still out of our league, has no cure, and cannot be curbed. For an older woman to be subjected to the torments of treatment without hope, they said, was too cruel. I was glad Mom's oncologist was *frum*; I regarded him as an angel walking the earth. I longed to believe, as he told me, that every moment of life was precious, bringing with it the possibility of *yeshuas Hashem*.

But the sight of Mom's pain-wracked body was draining me of what little hope I'd been clinging to. After a crisis-trip to the ER a week before she passed away, the oncologist agreed to adjust Mom's chemo regimen to one that was better tolerated. He was sad, too, and his sadness scared me more than anything else ever had.

As it turned out, there was no time to try the new improved chemo cocktail. That Friday Mom's blood pressure took a steep dive and she lost consciousness. Her regular physician lived across the street from her home and rushed over to check her. He was able to stabilize her and left instructions for the aide and me to follow over the weekend, as he would be away until Monday. To this day I wonder whether at that time he felt that it might be my mother's last weekend on earth. Some questions are too painful to articulate, some answers too painful to hear.

All day Friday my mother lay in her bed, eyes closed, taking only intermittent, shallow breaths. I lit candles in her bedroom, made *Kiddush* using her face as my *siddur*, ate a bit and sang all the *zemiros* and songs I knew. My parents were musical and cherished the sound of anyone singing, but particularly their children. As I sang, Mom shifted in her bed at times and seemed to want to smile. I saw tears and thought they were hers but they were mine. I did my best to keep them out of my voice; I could not mar what I hoped was pleasurable to her with evidence of my grief. Someday, I thought, I hope to know that my singing provided some comfort for her that night.

But then, by some miraculous force of will or love, Mom opened her eyes. She smiled that sweet, Mommy-only smile of hers, and in her Hungarian-inflected, oddly quiet Mommy-voice she said, "I could listen to you sing for the rest of my life." I might have dreamed it, so unlikely it seemed.

The effort to speak had taken too much breath; she closed her eyes again and resumed her former weak breathing and unconscious-like sleep. But I knew the moment for what it was. It was no dream. Mom had given me the precious gift of those few words to replay and cherish in my heart forever.

◆ ◆ ◆

I spent Friday night in a chair near her bed watching her, nodding off from time to time. Early Shabbos morning I awoke from a short nap to hear my mother gasping for air. The aide called 911 (there was no Hatzolah in our town) while I tried to follow her doctor's instructions. EMS arrived, stabilized her somewhat with oxygen but determined that stronger equipment than their mobile machines were needed. They called for a better-equipped ambulance and began to prepare Mom for transit to the local hospital.

I stood outside the house, ostensibly watching for the ambulance to arrive but — truth be told — preparing for the wave of terribleness I felt was about to wash over me. In a daze, I tried to think of things to do but there was too much blur. Suddenly a woman's voice seeped into my brain, asking a question. I did not recognize the woman but tried to give her some attention.

"I came over when I saw the emergency vehicle," she said. "I once met a nice Jewish man who lived in this house. He was a portly, distinguished-looking man with a white beard. I think he passed away. Did you know him?"

"That was my father, Isadore Waldman," I answered. "And, yes, he passed away three years ago."

"I thought so, but I didn't know if he had any family that stayed on in the house," she said.

"Just my mother," I told her. "And now she's very ill and has to go to the hospital. The ambulance should be here any minute."

The woman told me her name and expressed sympathy for my mother's plight. Then she asked if she could tell me the story of her one and only meeting with my father. I was probably feeling a bit impatient at first, wanting to get back to my reverie or perform some other purposeless function for my mother. But then I thought it seemed a kind of *hashgachah* that my father, *a"h*, would become part of this awesome moment in my mother's and my life via a neighbor's tale. I nodded for her to go on.

"I was in my house one Monday — I live a few houses up the block. It was late afternoon. The doorbell rang, and I opened the door to find this man I didn't know standing there. Since he was using a cane I figured he wasn't selling anything, so I asked what I could do for him. He said he had come to tell me something about my son.

"Now, my son was 9 or 10 at that time. We thought of him as a good boy but certainly capable of mischief, like maybe breaking a car window while playing ball. I dreaded what your father was about to tell me. He must have seen the look on my face and reassured me that my boy had done nothing wrong. Quite the opposite, he said. He told me that he had been walking to synagogue on Saturday morning and was having a hard time because of his arthritis. He was leaning on the gate next door to our house when he heard a boy ask if he needed help. Your father assured him that he was all right, just had to walk slowly and carefully.

"My son noticed that one of your Dad's shoelaces was loose. He asked if he could tighten the lace, because it could be dangerous to walk that way. Your father then described how my son bent down, worked hard to tie the open lace and then retied the other lace. Your father thanked him, asked where he lived, and sent my boy off with more thanks. Well, my son never told me the story — I would never have known it happened except your father felt that I should know what a fine young man I was raising. He said that as a father and grandfather he knew how often we worry about our children and that we need to hear the good things to balance out the unpleasant things."

As the woman finished her story the ambulance arrived. She wished good things for my mother, then left. But the chain of *chessed* — her son helping my father with his shoe, my father making the effort to give a stranger good news about her child, and the woman remembering all of this years later and taking the time to share it with me — somehow lent a refreshing air to that musty, frightening day.

THE REAL KADDISH

By Rabbi Nachman Seltzer
As heard from Rabbi David Herskowitz,
who related the story he had heard from a friend

*He didn't want to go; he didn't want to stay.
In the end, all he did was something small,
but it was enough...*

I didn't want to go, but I could imagine the outrage in their voices, the disdain in their eyes, if I didn't show up. "The kid becomes religious and he won't even bother coming to the funeral!" they'd say. And besides, my uncle had been a really nice guy, one of those idealists who had built the land, who'd been happy to settle on a kibbutz and toil away creating an agricultural paradise out of a rocky desert.

Attending his funeral wasn't too much to ask. After all, I'd be representing the American side of the family at this farewell ceremony. It was a small gesture that would mean a lot to everyone, *and* they would see that a religious person could still be a good person. That was important to me.

There wouldn't be much I could do to greet the family when I got there — this was no time for a jovial family reunion; but just the fact that I, whom they would surely consider to be ultra-religious, had arrived at this isolated kibbutz, would serve as a greeting more powerful than the most effusive *hello*.

It was a long bus ride. I distracted myself by conversing with the guy sitting next to me — a scientist from Haifa — and we were just getting into the finer points of desalination when he reached his stop. I was on my own for the rest of the ride, and I tried to prepare myself.

Uncle Yishai and I used to love hanging out together. When I first arrived in the country I used to visit his family whenever I had free time. They were a really cool bunch; fun, warm, athletic…and extremely uninterested in, at times downright hostile toward, a religious way of life. They just wanted their freedom. Today I knew that I was freer than they would ever be, but what they remembered was that first time I'd shown up at their doorstep, long hair blowing in the wind, eyes shaded by a giant pair of Gucci sunglasses, trendy camping pack on my back, genuine Indian moccasins on my feet.

I got off the bus at the entrance to the kibbutz and followed the little yellow arrows leading to my cousin's house. It was a big, sprawling house with tall, leafy trees in the front yard. A tire swing hung from a lower branch of one of the trees. A shaggy dog lay stretched out on his stomach, lost in a siesta on the flagstone path. I could smell the lunch someone had prepared, and I hurried through the yard, past well-tended shrubs and symmetrical flower beds. As I raised my hand to knock on the door, someone inside the house shouted to me to come inside.

I walked in, and I admit that a part of me wanted to stay there forever. The memories and impressions rushed back to me. It had been years earlier when I first met the family. Uncle Yishai was always kind of laconic; he would just sit back enjoying his family, and he wanted everyone to be happy…one of his sons was into growing things, and he had plans to travel abroad to further his education…my aunt was a great cook…I played Ping Pong with them that first night as golden oldies blasted out of the radio…the backyard was lit up with bulbs inside large paper globes hanging from lines strung across the yard, casting a magical glow over the ground.

Now, everything was different. Most of the kids had moved away. The brother who'd been so into his plants had become a field biologist and gained recognition as an expert in his field. He was living in some remote African village, where he was instructing the natives. Now he had returned because the grim reaper had come acallin'.

He'd been the nicest guy, My Uncle Yishai, his cup of malt beer in one hand, an Israeli newspaper in the other, and now he was gone. And here I was, arriving on the very bus I'd taken all those years before, but this time I was wearing a black jacket and hat, and the strings of my *tzitzis* hung down at the sides of my pants. My Gucci shades were long gone, and on my feet were sensible black loafers. They weren't the only ones who had changed. Nothing was the same anymore.

❖❖❖

As I walked toward the kibbutz's small cemetery, where the funeral was to take place, I was wishing that my hairline were as close to my eyes as it had once been. But almost ten years had passed, and all the while that hairline had been receding. Didn't all Orthodox men go bald after a while, the family would think, because they were always stuffing their heads into those hats that didn't allow their scalps to breathe? I chided myself for being so cynical, but I wouldn't allow myself the luxury of harboring any hopes this time around. I had so wanted our relationship to survive my becoming *frum*, but in retrospect I realized that was too much to wish for. I was here for Uncle Yishai's *levayah*, and after I'd done what I had come here to do, I'd head right back to the bus stop and on to Yerushalayim, my home.

I reached up to wipe my brow in the heat. My feet carried me past the playground and the grocery store, past the kibbutz's "shul" (it hadn't been used in years and years), past the nursery and the ambulance garage. I walked under the slowly swaying leaves of the giant palm trees and past an orchard of orange trees. The afternoon sun made everything hazy; it was hard to see anything through the burning light.

Finally, we arrived at the cemetery. I could see a group of people entering a light-blue building, where, I assumed, the eulogies were to be delivered. People stared at me curiously, wondering what a *chareidi* guy like me was doing here. It took a lot of courage for me to stand there, especially since I had once been just like them and I knew how they thought and exactly what they felt about me.

These people had no clue about appropriate garb for a religious ceremony. The fact that this was a *levayah* meant nothing to them when it came to anything like a dress code. They might as well have been out for a day at the beach. I stuck out like the sorest of thumbs. The *chevra kadisha* might have been a *chevra*, judging by the camaraderie of the group, but *kadisha* it definitely wasn't. There wasn't a *kippah* in sight.

I spotted my cousins right away, though I hadn't seen them in years. They were sobbing uncontrollably, and the field biologist was sitting in the corner of the room, shoulders hunched, chest heaving.

Suddenly the years fell away. I thought about how much I had liked these cousins, and I felt so bad for them, but I was hesitant to approach them, because I wasn't sure whether they would care to talk to me now. Today I was at the totally opposite end of the spectrum from where they were.

The ceremony began, and some guy from the *chevra kadisha* delivered his own style of *hesped* about my cousin and his connection to the land and the animals in the kibbutz and how he had helped to build the country. He'd been a hero in the wars and a model father and husband. A few others spoke, and it struck me hard that no one mentioned Hashem at all. Then the *chevra kadisha* decided it was time to recite the *Kaddish*, and I had never heard a *Kaddish* like this before.

Yisgadal veyiskadash shemei ha'adam, they began. "Let the name of man be glorified and made great!" They had lifted Hashem's Name right out of that sacred prayer! I wanted to leave, but I knew it would look really bad if I walked out in the middle of the ceremony. I told myself that this was a small thing to do for my cousin, but this "*Kaddish*" and those eulogies were bothering me something fierce.

I waited until the funeral was over, and I figured I would help them lower the body of the *niftar* into the ground, but just then the members of the *chevra kadisha* went into a huddle with my cousins, and there was the nature guy in the thick of things, gesturing and speaking earnestly. Strangely enough, they kept glancing at me as if I had something to do with whatever they were discussing. Did I feel out of place!

Having very few options, I just stood there minding my own business, waiting to leave, when the head of the *chevra kadisha* pulled himself away from the huddle and came over to me.

"You're Steve," he said, "right?"

"I go by Shalom now," I replied, "but, yes, my cousins know me as Steve."

"I'm Roni," he said, shaking my hand and staring at me with large gray eyes that peered out at the world from under thick eyebrows. "Your cousins were wondering if you could help us out with something."

"Sure," I said, curiosity overcoming my sheepishness.

"For some reason," Roni went on, speaking a little self-consciously, "your cousins weren't comfortable with the *Kaddish* we said for their father. They said they'd like something else from you. [*Of course they weren't happy with your Kaddish*, I was thinking. *Their souls wanted to know that their father was buried like a Jew.*] They asked if you'd recite the traditional *Kaddish* and a few chapters of *Tehillim* in his memory."

"It'll be my pleasure," I said. "How many chapters do you want?"

And it really was my pleasure. I had loved the old man. I recited the *Kaddish* with genuine sincerity and emotion, and the crowd answered Amen loudly. For a second I forgot where I was and felt I was back in the *shtiebel* again. I said the *Tehillim* slowly, enunciating every word.

And then it was all over, and I was saying good-bye to all my

The Real Kaddish / 197

cousins, and they were telling me how good I looked and how nice it was to see me again and would I come visit in happier times, and so on.

I returned all their good wishes, but I knew that I probably wasn't returning to this kibbutz any time soon.

Half an hour later I was on the bus on my way back to Jerusalem, and the funeral was already becoming fuzzy in my mind (must have been that strong sun). I was reading a book I had brought along, then I fell asleep, and the next thing I knew we were back in the city and there was honking all around and the funeral was like a dream that had come and gone.

●●●

It must have been about a week after the funeral that my phone rang. I looked down at the caller ID and was surprised to see the area code of the kibbutz on the display. I wondered what could have happened now.

I recognized my cousin's voice the second she began to speak.

"Steve," she said.

"Hi, Rina," I replied. "What's up?"

"You're never going to believe what happened here after you left," she said emphatically, and I was thinking, "What could have happened already?"

"It was the craziest thing," she said, "and pretty scary, too." Some intangible element in her voice told me that she had something incredible to share.

"Three days after the funeral," she continued, "we were all sitting around the kitchen table rehashing what an emotional event it had been for us, when my brother Shuki [the field biologist] spoke up.

"Now, Steve," she went on, "you know that Shuki was never a big talker even back when you knew him, and the older he got the quieter he got. I guess he got everything he needed just from being around his plants. But suddenly he piped up and started to say how touched he had been by your *Kaddish*, of all things. He said that he really hadn't been in touch with his spiritual side, but that *Kaddish* and the *Tehillim* you recited at the funeral moved him in a very deep way.

"He was in a really introspective mood, and he said, 'You know something, guys? When I became bar mitzvah Abba bought me a *tallis* and a pair of *tefillin*. I haven't seen them in years, but I just realized something: For as long as I can remember I've been telling myself that when it was my time to go I wanted to be cremated. I felt that was the easiest way. Just slip me into the fire and it's all done. But now, after hearing that *Kaddish* of Steve's, I realize that I was wrong. I want someone to say a *Kaddish* like that at my funeral. None of that fake-*Kaddish* garbage that the kibbutz people were saying. I want the real thing!'

"We were all pretty dazed," Rina went on. "I mean, Shuki was never into religion. It was always *nature* and *the way of the world* and *everything has a reason*, but suddenly, here was Shuki getting all religious on us, and it gave me the chills!

"Anyway," she said, "the next day we were all sitting around the house (nobody was in a rush to leave the home where we'd grown up), and we started talking about the funeral again. Everyone had something to say, and all of a sudden, out of the blue, Shuki pipes up — talking in that nostalgic, contemplative tone he'd used the day before.

" 'You know, guys,' he said, 'I'm sure Mom never threw out my *tallis*. I'm sure it's still around here somewhere.' His voice had grown excited. 'I need to find that *tallis*. I don't know why, but that *tallis* is pulling me. I wonder where Mom hid it all these years? I just want to make sure that I have that *tallis*...for whenever I need it!' And Shuki started searching for that old *tallis*. He dug through all the closets, then he went down into the basement and went through everything down there until it looked like a hurricane had ripped through the house, and still he searched while we watched him anxiously, wondering if maybe the funeral had set off something weird in him.

"And then," she went on, "we heard a yelp of victory when he finally discovered the *tallis*, folded into a small square, hidden away in one of our mother's extra linen closets." Her voice had grown teary now, and I couldn't figure out why.

"Steve," she said, "Shuki walked back into the living room clutching that *tallis* in his hand, the one our father had bought him for his bar mitzvah, and he unfolded it and held it like it was some precious item. And then…" for a moment her voice broke, but she collected herself and went on. "And then, he spread that *tallis* over himself and took a seat on one of the couches in the living room. There was a big, peaceful smile on his face as he sat with that *tallis*.

"And then," she said, crying openly now, "then my brother Shuki…died! He died wearing that *tallis* and smiling like a little kid. It was as if he'd found all the answers in that *Kaddish* you said, and it was enough for him — enough for him to leave this world in the right way."

4

LIFESAVERS AND LIFE CHANGERS

THE DOCTOR

By David Kanner

Just a quick, breezy "hello," and a life is saved!

When I was in yeshivah in Eretz Yisrael, I was sharing an apartment in Meah Shearim with several other *bachurim*. One Friday afternoon one of my apartment mates saw a man parking an ambulance on our block. My *chaver* was quite a social boy by nature, and he went over to the driver to say hello. The man was dressed in typical *Yerushalmi* garb, right down to the white yarmulke. My friend asked him if he was the new Shabbos ambulance driver for the neighborhood.

The man introduced himself as Sholom Wallace and said that he'd been there for years and was the local doctor for minor ailments and injuries, that he was a trained paramedic, and that he lived a few houses down.

"If you ever need anything," he said, "come to my house."

Thus were planted the seeds of my *yeshuah*.

Two weeks later...

It was Shabbos morning, and the abdominal pains that I'd been trying to convince myself were only symptoms of the flu were growing steadily worse. The night before, it was all I could do to eat just one *kezayis* of the Shabbos *seudah*, and by now the pain was unbearable. I thought it might be more comfortable to go outside and sit in the sun, but that only made me dizzy, and when I got up I felt faint.

The only *bachur* with me in the apartment at the time was that boy who had spoken to Wallace. I didn't know anything about that conversation they'd had two weeks earlier. In fact, I didn't have a clue how or where he would even find a doctor, but, I told him, I needed one.

Now.

I sat on a bed with a cup of ice-cold water in my hands, and I wet my face every few seconds to keep myself from fainting. Sounds were fading out of my range of hearing while the world spun. The other *bachur* told me he would be back in three minutes. He was. Wallace followed him into the room, smiling.

"Good Shabbos," he said cheerily. I tried smiling back. I couldn't. The pain was excruciating.

When I saw his face I recognized it from an article I had once read about the doctor of Meah Shearim. I'd read about how, from overseas, he had diagnosed a small child with a broken clavicle just by hearing a description of the child's body movements.

"*Oder yuh oder nein* — either yes or no," I had thought to myself at the time. Being that Meah Shearim isn't exactly the home of world-class professionals, I figured that once the *frum* media got their hands on that needle-in-a-haystack-professional-wannabe, they'd transform him into the best thing since sliced bread.

I was wrong. I don't think it took him even 15 seconds to diagnose appendicitis. Next thing I knew, he was on the phone ordering an ambulance.

Who works in an ambulance in Yerushalayim on Shabbos morning? Students. Twenty-year-old students.

Wallace stole the show. He took my blood pressure, pulse, temperature and more while they watched him. Apparently, it was the first time they were seeing someone dressed like that making a medical assessment of a patient.

At the hospital I was put into a little room. Soon a surgeon walked in. Big and burly with a cold expression on has face, his presence didn't set me at ease. He probably thought Wallace was my father. He asked him to leave the room. Wallace didn't like the idea, especially since doctors don't usually ask parents to leave when they examine a patient, and the appearance of this particular doctor did nothing to inspire his peace of mind. Nevertheless, with trained professionalism, Wallace left the room. When the surgeon had gone Wallace came back and asked me for a full report of everything he had done. When I told him, Wallace decided that this surgeon would not be operating. Period.

Wallace knew of a surgeon with a good reputation by the name of Dr. Dagan. He looked him up and entered his office. Wallace explained that he did not want Surgeon X to operate; could Dagan perhaps do him a favor and do the surgery instead?

"Listen," Dagan said, "today is Shabbos, and my shift ends very soon. And besides, Surgeon X is director of all the surgeons in the hospital this Shabbos. How can I tell him not to do the surgery?

"And," he continued, "even if you do manage to get me permission to do the surgery, you'd have to hire me privately, since I'd be doing it on my own time."

"If you want money," Wallace replied, "we can arrange it — after Shabbos."

At this, Dr. Dagan hinted at a respectable sum. Wallace responded with confidence. "I will not discuss money on Shabbos. It will be arranged after Shabbos."

Wallace felt he had no choice. He found Surgeon X and told him directly that he didn't want him to operate, that he wanted Dr. Dagan to operate instead. Surgeon X didn't take it as a compliment. At all.

But Surgeon X agreed. Although he would be overseeing the procedure, Dagan would operate.

There I was, a young boy lying ill in a foreign country, listening

The Doctor / 205

in while someone he never met before tries to persuade a surgeon *he* never met before to do surgery — all on a Shabbos afternoon. He has children at home eating a Shabbos meal without their father, because he's busy trying to persuade a doctor to do surgery — on a stranger.

I told Wallace to go home to his family, but he wouldn't hear of it. "*Ich gei dir lozen in a hefker velt? Ich zog eich, dih menchen duh zenen nisht intresirt in kayn menchen* — Do you think I would leave you alone in a jungle? I'm telling you, the people here are not interested in people."

His assurance made me feel safe. When I was finally wheeled into the operating room I didn't even think it was something to be nervous about. Everything was so spotlessly clean. There were beautiful emerald-green tiles all around. Nice. The thought haunts me to this day.

Most of the time, and especially during the week when the regular weekday director is in, well-placed connections enable Wallace to be let in to the operating room. On this particular Shabbos, however, when Surgeon X was in charge, as Wallace was about to enter the operating room, this director saw a grand opportunity for revenge on the man who had insulted him and he closed the door in Wallace's face. Fifteen minutes into the surgery Surgeon X walked out. As Dagan said later, "He felt unwanted and left. There was nothing for him to do there."

By the time I woke up from the anesthesia it was Motza'ei Shabbos. Wallace was still there. So were a few *bachurim* who had walked over on Shabbos. They came in and, for the first time, I smiled.

Very early the next morning Wallace was back. I was davening *Shacharis* when he came in. We looked at each other but did not speak.

There were no words.

Before he left he gave me his cell-phone number and warned me not to hesitate to call. "If you need something — anything — call. If a nurse doesn't respond to the bell, call." Then he was gone. He cares for many patients, *Rachmana litzlan*, in various hospitals.

❖❖❖

I stayed in the hospital for five days, and Wallace was there to visit me often. He once came to see me straight from a 3-hour drive from Rambam Hospital in Haifa.

His line of work notwithstanding, his smile is forever.

"Are your parents coming?" he asked me. "Tell me when — I'll pick them up from the airport."

Every day I spent in the hospital a group of five doctors came to see me. My surgeon, Dr. Dagan, was among them. Also among them was Surgeon X — now "fondly" nicknamed "The Butcher." The nickname wasn't my idea, but it definitely fit the bill. The man would have made Stalin proud. There are things I learned about him that I choose not to write. When he showed up with the other doctors he stood in the back. He was not wanted there and he knew it.

Dr. Dagan never said a word about money — not to me, not to Wallace.

When I left the hospital Wallace drove me in his ambulance. He pulled out of the emergency parking lot with balloons all over and a *chassidishe niggun* playing in the background. *Baruch Rofei cholim.*

"Reb Shulem," as I have come to call him, is today my best friend, despite the 30-odd-year age difference between us. He called me to invite me to his grandson's shalom zachor. I walk past his house six times a day. From my porch I see his tzitzis swaying on a clothesline — ve'anochi lo yadati....

The Doctor / 207

THE INSCRIPTION
Rabbi David Kaplan

Socially and culturally there may have been a barrier, but the heart understands when the truth hits.

As the plane touched down Kenny smiled. People were already unbuckling their seatbelts and standing up in anticipation of getting off. *You fools*, he thought to himself. *Even after the plane comes to a complete stop you're all gonna wait another 20 minutes before goin' anywhere. You're all so "conventional." This is what everyone else does, so you do it too. Fools!*

Kenny, on the other hand, was just the ultimate in cool — certainly to his own mind. And sure enough, the impatient people crowding the isles waited close to half an hour before deplaning, much to Kenny's sardonic amusement. He stayed in his seat listening to music, making a move to get off only when the isles were completely clear. He met his parents and siblings in the line at the customs desk and smiled his standard "told you so" smile. *You rushed to get off and all it got you was a longer wait in the customs line,* his twinkling eyes practically shouted. And as always, his final clarion-call thought followed: *You're so conventional.*

At 20 years old, Kenny Gelman was anything but conventional. Always fun-loving and irresponsible, he had made it through his modern-Orthodox yeshivah high-school years doing almost no learning. Popular, charismatic, and a great athlete, he was always the center of attention and the class leader. He'd had no plans and no ambitions. His friends would always talk about the various careers and fields they planned on entering; Kenny couldn't understand them.

How could anyone think of anything other than having fun? he'd always wonder during these discussions. And as to Torah learning, he had no interest whatsoever. He'd had absolutely no connection with any of his rebbeim during his school years, nor had he any interest in developing such connections. For their part, his rebbeim perceived him as totally unmotivated (which he was) and didn't have the time or energy it would have taken to get through to him. He wasn't a troublemaker. He would merely sit in the back of the room in any *shiur* he was in and make up basketball teams or schmooze with other disinterested students sitting in the vicinity, as he counted the minutes until *shiur* would end.

After high school he didn't even go to Israel for the year, as almost all his friends did; he just didn't see any point in wasting time overseas. If he didn't enjoy Torah learning all through high school, why would he enjoy it somewhere else? Instead, he went to work in a repair shop, and after a year he borrowed money and opened a kosher ice-cream parlor, which was doing much better than anyone except for Kenny had ever expected. He was earning more than each of his parents and was way ahead of any of his friends financially, as they were all in college working toward degrees.

Kenny bought a sports car and treated himself to all the good things in life, much to the chagrin of his parents, who were always nudging him to save. He only laughed and told them their thinking was so conventional. The prophets of doom had all said his business venture would fail, yet here he was laughing his way to the bank, so he was sure that the future would work out too. He was having fun and enjoying life, so why worry? When it came to religion, he always kept Shabbos and kashrus, put on *tefillin* and wore a *kippah*, so overall his parents were relatively pleased with him.

Kenny's older brother Yossi had "*frumed* out" several years earlier and spent the last four years in yeshivah in Eretz Yisrael. He was now engaged to a young lady from a Yiddish-speaking *chareidi* family from Belgium, and it was to his wedding in Bnei Brak that Kenny's family was headed. Kenny loved and admired his brother, but he viewed *chareidi* people in general as nerdy, out of touch, and oh-so-conventional. That's what his rebbeim had been like in high school (in his expert opinion), and he wasn't looking forward to spending a week in the *frumest* city in the world, surrounded by people who were devoid of personality.

His sister-in-law, whom he had met for the first time when they arrived in Bnei Brak, was surprisingly "with-it" for a *frum*, sheltered girl. Kenny was beginning to think that maybe the blackies were okay after all. But then they arrived at the wedding hall two nights later and he met her family. Each person he met was more religious than the last. She had a number of brothers and brothers-in-law, and although they were friendly, they always seemed to be looking into one *sefer* or another and talking about halachah.

What a boring existence, Kenny thought to himself more times than he could count. With his nearly shoulder-length hair, Kenny projected exactly the image he wanted — the cool, carefree, truly alive person they were not. A couple of times he even noticed his sister-in-law's sisters talking about him and he actually enjoyed the attention. *Get a good look at a real person,* he mused.

The wedding was fun and the dancing was great. At one point someone put a black hat on Kenny's head and grabbed his crocheted yarmulke. Everyone had a good laugh, and Kenny really hammed it up, all the while thinking, *Get this on film, 'cause you're never gonna see it live again.*

The week of *sheva berachos,* on the other hand, was oppressive.

The evenings were spent in crowded little Bnei Brak apartments with bearded rabbis making boring speeches. After the third one Kenny told his parents he'd had enough, and they understood. He informed them that he'd return to Bnei Brak for the very last *sheva berachos*, and he left for Yerushalayim to spend time with friends he hadn't seen in a while.

● ● ●

Meir was one of his brother's new brothers-in-law, and it was in his matchbox of an apartment that the last *sheva berachos* were to take place. In a room full of narrow-minded, lifeless people, Meir struck Kenny as the most narrow-minded and lifeless of them all. Other than a couple of *hellos* at the various events, they'd said nothing to each other.

That was about to change. Meir Milner, a soft-spoken, serious *talmid chacham* and father of eight was a person completely involved in *avodas Hashem*. Part of that *avodah*, he'd always felt, was helping other Jews, and if ever there was a Jew who was crying out for help, it was Kenny! The moment he first saw Kenny at the wedding, Meir had him figured out.

He's a sweet guy, just like his brother, Meir thought to himself. *He obviously feels empty inside and loves attention. He also thinks that nobody here understands him. I'd really love to help him, but how?* Meir realized that there was a language barrier, so a long conversation involving a heart-to-heart talk was out of the question. He could attempt a little learning, but there was still the language problem. Meir was also perceptive enough to realize that Kenny might feel he was trying to influence him, which would automatically cause him to back away. But Meir wasn't willing to give up without trying at all. *If his brother became a ben Torah,* he thought to himself, *then he could become one too.*

Meir thought and thought and finally came up with an idea.

It wasn't anything big or dramatic, but at least it was something. He figured that with the wedding and all the accompanying attention being focused on the *chassan* and *kallah* and their parents, Kenny probably felt just a little left out. So Meir decided to buy Kenny a little gift as a friendly gesture.

Well, Hashem works in funny ways. This little gesture was going to prove instrumental in Kenny's life.

The last of the *sheva berachos* was uneventful and, once again, Kenny was thoroughly bored. When the festivities finally ended, everyone said their good-byes to Kenny's parents. Kenny stood off to the side waiting to leave and was quite surprised when Meir walked up to him.

"I'd like to give you this," Meir said in broken English, handing Kenny a brand-new *sefer*.

Kenny was shocked speechless.

And genuinely touched.

He looked down at the *sefer* and saw that it was a *Kitzur Shulchan Aruch*. The last time he'd seen one of those was back in seventh grade. When he opened it he saw an inscription written on the inside of the front cover: "A little gift in recognition of the nobility of your lofty *neshamah*. May *Hakadosh Baruch Hu* help you find the spiritual satisfaction you long for and deserve. Your friend always, Meir."

Kenny's eyes felt watery and there was a lump in his throat. When he looked up, Meir gave him a warm smile, and they shook hands.

Meir had no idea what a bull's eye he had hit. Kenny was indeed hurting at not being the center of attention as he always was back home, and getting noticed like this was just what the Doctor ordered.

Back in America, Kenny reread the inscription quite a few times. It was the first time he could recall anything positive being suggested about his spiritual side. He'd certainly never heard anything like that in high school. "Do I really have a lofty *neshamah*?" he'd caught himself wondering.

When he had said good-bye to his brother and showed him the *sefer*, his brother, who almost never told others what to do, sensed that a small opening had presented itself. He suggested that Kenny learn from the *kitzur* for just 5 minutes a day. "Don't take on too much," his brother had said. "Make a commitment to an amount of time you're sure you can stick to. And then make sure you really stick to it! Even if you've already gotten into bed at night, pull yourself out and do your 5 minutes."

"It's the least I can do," Kenny had thought to himself.

It was the first learning he had done in who-knows-how-long, and he actually enjoyed it. There were indeed a few times he'd had to get out of bed to keep his commitment, but afterward he felt great for doing it. And the learning led him to realize what a spiritual vacuum he was living in, and to a fresh yearning to do something concrete about it. It wasn't long before Kenny sold his business and went to Eretz Yisrael to give learning another chance.

Well, he really got into it. One year led to another, and eventually Kenny married and spent several years in *kollel*.

Today Kalman — no one's called him Kenny in years — is a rebbi in a yeshivah for boys who need to get motivated, and he proudly counts himself and his family as members of the *chareidi* community. He has found the spiritual satisfaction he was missing…and all as a result of one little gesture that was anything but conventional.

THE GIVER

Mirish Kiszner

A small donation; something anyone could do. You just never know...

As Levi Segal waited for his blue Mazda to warm up, he gazed through the windshield at the gray globs left over from last week's snow. It was Sunday, and the quiet streets were empty save for a few snowmen gracing a front lawn here and there. Montrealers were enjoying a day off, and Levi knew that his kids were expecting him to take them on an exciting outing, as he did every Sunday.

But today he had little patience for snow-tubing or skiing or sledding. Levi stepped on the gas. Today he needed to be away from it all, to take refuge in the private haven of his car. He drove aimlessly, his back hunched, his hands draped languidly over the steering wheel. Fifty thousand dollars...how? Where could he get hold of such a sum?

This wasn't the first time he had overdrawn his account. That was his regular course of business. With his home as collateral, his overdraft was protected, but his latest investment had failed and the bank had placed a lien on his account.

Levi turned off the heater and started the wipers going, but the fog that coated his windshield was on the inside. He stopped the car. As he leaned toward the glove compartment to retrieve a rag, he felt the cell phone in his pocket vibrating. He considered ignoring it but reckoned it wouldn't do him any good to annoy his wife now.

"Levi?"

The booming, Israeli-accented voice didn't sound anything like Esther.

"Hello? Levi? You there?"

Levi Segal cleared his throat. "Uh, who, may I ask, is calling?"

"This is Levi ben Leah, no?" asked the caller.

Segal pulled a face. Levi ben Leah? How did this mysterious man know his mother's name?

"Do I know you?" he asked.

"Yes, yes. We met. On Thursday, you and I met at the corner of Bernard and Hutchison, remember?"

Segal tried to recall Thursday's events. He couldn't remember meeting anyone. "I'm afraid you're mistaken, sir," he said, fingering the "off" button on his dial pad.

"No, I'm not," the caller shot back. "We met at the ATM machine right inside the bank."

From the murky recesses of Levi's mind a hazy memory teased him, as though a thin strand of hair he was trying to grasp was evading him.

"You gave me a 20."

That was it. The image of the caller was now vivid in his mind. *It's him — that middle-aged fellow with the gray beard and grizzled eyebrows that didn't hide the sad eyes.* He felt a sudden tightening in his throat. This man was an expert at bad timing. Levi found himself wishing it had been his wife on the line.

"Listen," he said, annoyed at the gruff way his voice had emerged, "I have your number here on my ID; I'll get back to you."

"That's fine; I just wanted to tell you that..."

Levi slumped back in his seat. *It's no use; this guy will just go on and on.*

"...Yosef HaTzaddik recognized the hand of *hashgachah* that sent the *sar hamashkim* to prison at the same time that he, Yosef, was there..."

Levi closed his mouth and took a deep breath through his nose. Was there no stopping the man? He'd had enough on Thursday.

Thursday. Was it only three days ago that he'd met with the bank manager? How despair can make time stand still! It was at that meeting that he had come to understand that he was perched on the brink of financial collapse. He had stumbled out of the manager's office. At a counter near the ATM machine he had opened up his attaché case and tried to make order of his bank statements, tried to make order of his life.

And then the grey beard had come into view. "Shalom! Let me have some of it too." Levi heard the words before he saw the face. Annoyed, he raised an angry pair of eyes and found himself staring into the smiling face of a *shnorrer*.

I should have ignored him, Levi couldn't help thinking. But how could he have known that with this first glance he would be hijacked for a good 15 minutes listening to the *shnorrer's* witty *vertlach* and anecdotes?

"...So Yosef knew that he would eventually get out of prison...." Levi realized with a start that he was still holding the phone and that the man was deeply immersed in talk. He was speaking in the singsong tones of Gemara-learning and was clearly enjoying himself. "Rav Chaim explains that Yosef told the chief butler, 'Do you know why we're in this jail cell together? It is all *ki im zechartani* — so that you should remember me to Pharaoh and help me get out of here.' Yosef wasn't asking the *sar hamashkim* to remember him; he was only pointing out that this was part of G-d's master plan."

Yeah, yeah; Levi shook his head. This was just what he needed now — more suave talk, further entreaties. Sure, he was all for donating a tenth of his earnings, but this wasn't the time. Now he had too many financial problems of his own. Why in the world had he given this *shnorrer* his phone number in the first place?

Levi was seething. He cleared his throat loudly as he struggled to contain his anger.

"Uh, yeah…I was just getting to the point…"

And you've been awfully long about it.

"*Ki im zechartani*," he said, still singing his Gemara-tune. "I told you I'll remember you, I'll pray for you, Levi ben Leah, and I remembered. Did you?"

"Did I?" Levi rubbed his head with his yarmulka. *Did I promise him something in return?* He couldn't remember.

"Look, I told you I can't give you more, that I can't even withdraw any money from the ban—"

"Who's talking about withdrawing money?" was the ebullient response. "How about depositing some of it *into* your account?"

This was too much for Levi. *Doesn't this man have better things to do with his time?* Levi thought. *Why is he making me crazy?* He shut the phone with more force than necessary.

Moments later, his phone rang again. He ignored it. Soon, though, out of curiosity, he listened to the message:

"Go to Tzvi Saperstein. He's waiting for you."

Tzvi Saperstein? Montreal's business magnate was waiting for him? It made no sense. Levi tapped his fingers on the steering wheel absentmindedly. He'd had some business dealings with Saperstein over the years, but not recently. And he certainly had no personal connections with this entrepreneur.

Then a thought struck him. Perhaps he could indeed meet with Saperstein. He would explain his predicament and ask for some good old-fashioned business advice. Saperstein, for all his prominence and wealth, was an amiable fellow.

He rolled down the window. The wind rushed in and slapped his face. Maybe…maybe he'd even venture to ask the tycoon for a short-term loan.

● ● ●

With the air of a man who is unsure of whether he is entering a palace or a minefield, Levi walked up the steps to the brown oak door. A Portuguese maid ushered him in to an opulent living room where several men were waiting their turn to enter Mr. Saperstein's home office.

Suddenly, Mr. Saperstein stuck his head out of his office. His eyes traversed the room, and when his gaze fell on Levi his face broke into a smile.

"Morning, Segal," he called out as he crossed the room with quick strides and extended his hand in greeting. "Good to see you." Saperstein was pumping his arm as though he were meeting a long-lost relative.

"Yeah, um…good to see you too," Levi stammered, too shocked to speak in a more coherent manner.

"I've been waiting for you," he said, placing a hand on Levi's shoulder and leading him into his office. "Thanks for coming."

Levi opened his mouth to say something, but in his state of confusion he could barely formulate his thoughts, much less turn them into words. In any case, he wouldn't have gotten a word in edgewise even if he had tried. Saperstein was keeping up a steady monologue, repeating over and over how happy he was to see him.

When Saperstein finally loosened his embrace it was to open a drawer and pull out an envelope. "Here's the money," he said. "Fifty thousand dollars in cash. Just send me an IOU by mail. Sorry to rush, but you saw all those people waiting for me. Sundays are long days for me. So take care, Segal…have a nice day."

Levi stood outside of the Saperstein mansion staring straight ahead, vaguely aware that his mouth was hanging open. If he had just landed on the moon he wouldn't have been more bewildered. He wasn't hallucinating; the envelope in his hand proved that much. But how could he explain what had just occurred?

From the corner of his eye Levi discerned a little boy in a light-blue snowsuit looking up from the tunnel he was busy forming out of a mound of snow. The shovel in his hand fell noiselessly onto the snow-packed ground as he turned to regard Levi with unabashed curiosity.

"Hey," said the child, his face red from cold and exertion. "Are you lost or something?"

Levi waved to him as he entered his car. A million questions were circling his mind. As he buckled his seat belt he noticed his cell phone lying on the passenger seat. He picked up the phone, scrolled down the list of phone numbers of recent callers and dialed a number.

"This is Levi," he said. "You called me before?"

"Levi ben Leah," the loud voice boomed through the phone. "You went?"

Levi ignored the question and responded with a question of his own.

"What's this all about?"

"Don't be angry with me. Mr. Segal. I want to tell you something. You must learn from us *Yisraelim*. Have a bit of *savlanut*. Patience. I want to tell you a *maaseh*, a story."

"I have patience, but first tell—"

"Whoa! I told you, Levi, patience. I'm telling you…"

Levi banged his fist on the driving wheel in frustration, which set off his horn, startling a man who was pulling a sled as he crossed the avenue. Levi ignored the pedestrian's angry look, but this *Yerushalmi* who sang instead of talked was grating on his nerves.

"It's like this," said the man as he began his story. "Friday afternoon. It's almost Shabbos. Shaya Levinson the *shnorrer* — that's me — feels horrible. He's in Montreal running around from door to door with an outstretched hand, hoping that people will open their hearts and pockets. Some people answer the door. Some, you know, those who have these fancy-shmancy video intercoms, they make believe they're not home. *Nu*, is that a good feeling for a man?"

Levi felt like screaming, but he controlled himself and set his cell-phone on speaker mode so he could drive while he listened. He put the car in reverse, backed up, then took off.

"Do you think Shaya likes to be a beggar?" Shaya went on. "But this is my fate. I have a wife, she's sick. I have to marry off my son…"

Yeah, right, Levi feels like saying. *I know your story by heart. I've heard it hundreds of times. So what's it got to do with Saperstein?*

"...so I walk down the streets in my torn galoshes, my socks wet from the snow that seeps in, and I imagine myself that I'm an important person, a VIP, they say in English. I have lots of money and I give huge donations, *b'simchah*. I'm the giver, not the taker.

"In Yerushalayim of old, when someone asked for a favor, he would say, '*Zechei bi.*' That means, 'May you gain a *zechus* through me.' Today it's the other way around. The *balebos* thinks he's giving and the *shnorrer* feels he's taking. That's the way it is. So I'm walking and thinking, and there at the corner, what's the name of the street? Bernard and...the other one? Hutchison? There I see Levi Segal at the ATM machine. He's busy with papers and notes and envelopes. And I think, *He must be making a nice deposit.* So I greet him with a little joke and I say, 'Let me have some of it too.' You remember that? So you put your hand into your pocket, you give me a crumpled $20 bill, and you say, 'This is what I have.'

"I know that line — everybody says that. I say, 'You're a businessman. This is all you could give?' But then I look at you more closely. I see that your face is tense, your hands are clenched, and I think, maybe this guy is saying the truth. And I say, 'Something happened?' And you say, 'Be happy with $20. Do you know how much money I have to come up with by Monday?' And I say, 'No.' How should I know?"

Levi sucked in his breath. He suddenly remembered that he did indeed blurt out to this man that he needed $50,000. Why did this Shaya have to relate his story in such excruciating detail? Couldn't he get to the point?

"So you tell me you need $50,000. That's a lot of money. But then you say, 'I have to run now.' And you get into your car, but I catch you by the sleeve and I ask you your name and your mother's name. Remember?"

Levi didn't bother to reply, but Shaya forged right on.

"I want to pray for you. So I get your name, and when I write it down you quickly bang the door shut and turn on the engine. But Shaya doesn't get fazed. I want to be the giver for a change. It's a sweet thing to give, you know? It's a happy thing. I want to find a way to help you. *G-t vet helfen*. I stick my head to the window and you roll it down. I say, 'But give me your cell phone number.' And you give it to me. Just like that. You don't have a very big choice. I'm not letting you drive.

"Sunday morning, it's the day when Saperstein is not busy in his downtown office. I go to his house. I wait, with *savlanut*, and then it's my turn to go inside his room. I tell him my story. He starts to write a check, and then all of a sudden the phone rings. Saperstein gets up from his chair and goes to his inside room, and I wait again. Shaya is used to waiting."

Levi's car skidded across a sliver of ice, but his snow tires handled it well. As for himself, he was still struggling to remain calm and not to interrupt.

"I wait, 5 minutes, 10 minutes, and then Saperstein comes back. He has a big — very big — smile on his face, and he says, 'That was my broker on the line.' Then Saperstein pours me a glass of wine. He's all excited. He made a big profit that he didn't expect. *Nu*, unexpected money.... So he gives me $600 and he says, 'It's a *zechus* to give money to a *Yerushalmi* Jew. Can the *Yerushalmi Yid* give me a blessing?'

"I say, 'A *berachah*? That will cost you more money.'

"He says, 'How much?'

"I say, 'A *berachah* will cost you a loan of $50,000.'

"I tell him everything. I tell him that I met a very *chashuveh* person. It looks like he fell on hard times. We have to get him back on to his feet. And what do you think? He agrees with me. *Nu*? Isn't that some story? And as they say in your country, 'The rest is history.'"

THE RIGHT WORDS AT THE RIGHT TIME

Chani Mishell

A message from the heart will hit home, even without professional training.

It was August, 1973. Two months later Israel would be caught by a surprise attack from her Arab neighbors that would launch the Yom Kippur War.

But that was the furthest thought from anyone's mind as people enjoyed those balmy, pre-global warming, summery Jerusalem days. And the question that had literally taken over my mind at that time was whether or not to become a *baalas teshuvah*, and if so, where to go to get answers to my myriad questions and fill in the void in my oh-so-meager Jewish education.

The pickings were slim; there just weren't many options. "*Kiruv*" had not yet become a popular career choice, and it was very challenging for the average FFB (*frum* from birth)-person to enter the world of the *baal teshuvah* or would-be *baal teshuvah*. And there were almost no English translations of *sifrei kodesh*, so all one could do was learn in a class and be dependent on what the teacher chose or didn't choose to teach.

I don't know if it's possible for anyone in today's *frum* world to understand what it was like back then. Nowadays the Torah seeks you out over the Internet, in any language you choose. And if you want to learn in a program, the only problem is deciding which program from among the vast array of choices best suits you.

This was not the case back then. I narrowed my possibilities down to a certain seminary for *baalos teshuvah*. I went to check it out and came back in complete culture shock. In high-school history class I had learned about something called the Dark Ages. Although I've never lived during that period of time, I was convinced that I had just gone back there.

I was a loyal child of the 60's, in search of profound religious experience bordering on the mystical. But in this new world of religious Jews I encountered regular people living in regular houses, not at all unconcerned with their material needs. This was all too reminiscent of the bourgeois middle-class Jewish world I had rejected. But to just run off to Europe or India without giving the religion I was born into a fighting chance seemed risky. What if Judaism turned out to be the *truth*, while I might be spending years pursuing some other path…?

I remember standing on a hillside in Jerusalem and having a conversation with Hashem that went like this: "G-d, I believe that You exist and that You put me in this world for a purpose. I have no idea what You want me to do here or how to serve You…I just have one question to ask. 'G-d, are You Jewish?'"

I "wisely" decided that I would go somewhere, learn about Judaism for a few weeks, and then decide what I believed in. And if Judaism wasn't IT, then I could freely skip off to new vistas.

It could be if I was a guy and Aish HaTorah had picked me up at the Kotel, I would have been given the opportunity to thrash through weighty philosophical concepts. But I was a 24-year-old "older girl" (how times have changed).

I had come in search of intellectual guidance. What I got was something altogether different. "Don't think — *we'll* tell you what to think. Change your mode of dress — don't wear a short skirt, but don't wear a long skirt either. Your old friends are off-limits. And you'd better start eating white bread — if you insist on being a health nut and eating whole-wheat bread you'll never get a normal *shidduch*. And you must realize that this is the main thing: you need to get married." *Help!!*

Needless to say, I was on the verge of a full-scale panic attack. I didn't rule out this seminary completely, but since I like to breathe, I continued my investigations. Then someone told me about a more modern kind of institution. The place — let's call it "Medrasha" (not its real name) — was open and easy-going, and I would be free to learn anything I wanted in depth there. At the time the fact that it was Conservative — or Conservadox — didn't mean anything to me.

I went down for an interview and was impressed. I found myself relaxing and once again breathing fully at ease as the rabbi told me about the program. He was so open and accepting. The way I was, was simply OK. He gave me an application form to fill out.

One of the sections on this form required me to write about myself and what I was looking for in terms of Judaism. As I wrote I became more aware of what was bothering me. I told them that once I had made the decision to stay in Israel and learn about Judaism, I thought I had solved my dilemma. But no, it only opened up a new string of confusing issues. Everyone I met felt that his or her particular affiliation was the only way and that any other way was not OK. I didn't see how I was going to even begin to find my *truth*.

So it seemed that Medrasha was the best place for me to learn. It would allow me to pursue my explorations without any pressure, without anyone telling me what to do. I was so relieved to have finally made a decision.

But it's so obvious that Hashem runs the world.

That evening someone told me about a class in Chassidus that was open to everyone. I tried it. When the class was over people hung around talking and getting to know one another.

There was a Bais Yaakov girl at the class who must have been around 18 or 19 years old. She greeted me warmly, although we had never seen each other before that day. She went out of her way to treat a stranger with affection and kindness. I was impressed by her demeanor and the mature way in which she spoke. I never asked her what she was doing in Israel. All I remember is that she was there for the summer. We ended up walking outside together and I shared with her what was happening in my life and that I had decided to learn at Medrasha.

I don't know how she knew about Medrasha, but her reaction was quick and decisive. "You can't go there. Even if you do learn there, you won't get the full taste of authentic Judaism."

I wasn't at a point where I could appreciate what she was saying, but I explained my difficulties and my need to be able to learn on an intellectual level and sort things out for myself.

In response, she told me that there was no way a person could understand the Torah without keeping mitzvos. If I wanted the Torah to reveal itself to me, then I needed to eat kosher and keep Shabbos and other mitzvos. Without this basis, I could learn and learn on an intellectual level and never connect to the essence of Torah. And most of all, someone who keeps mitzvos can get understanding and insight into the Torah without ever learning intellectually. Because the mitzvos have a power of their own.

This young Bais Yaakov girl had never gone to a seminar in *kiruv*. No one ever taught her what you're supposed to say to a nonreligious friend. But words that come from the heart can penetrate a heart. And words that come from the soul can reach a soul.

I never saw this Bais Yaakov girl again after that night, and I don't know if I even knew her name. But it's clear that my decision to learn in the Orthodox seminary for *baalos teshuvah* was a direct result of our conversation. And even if there were times when I couldn't take a deep breath, I know I made the right decision.

Writing this account is my way of thanking that Bais Yaakov girl for being such a clear vessel for Hashem's words to reach me.

We should never underestimate the power of the right words at the right time.

A PROUD LEGACY

By Miriam Lea Rosenberg

A moment of caring offers a lifetime of hope and, ultimately, success.

It was my nephew's *sheva berachos* — the first one following the wedding.

The wedding, complete with *mitzvah tantz*, had ended at 5:30 a.m., so I suppose I can't be blamed for not having listened to that particular speaker — or to any of the many speakers at the *sheva berachos*. In any case, not only did the *mechitzah* block my view of the speakers, but we on the women's side could hardly hear them, and besides, there was wonderful company at my table.

Out of the corner of my eye I spotted my sister glaring at me several times, trying to shush me up, but — no way! I was enjoying the company too much, exchanging news with cousins and friends whom I see far too seldom.

When the *sheva berachos* were over and I had managed to ignore another few speeches, my sister came over to me in a huff, reprimanding me as she had always done in the good old days.

"Miriam Lea, you really missed a good one!"

"Huh?" What was she complaining about, anyway?

She introduced me to one of the speakers — a fine-looking young chassidic man.

I looked to the right and to the left in a futile search for a way out; but I was stuck. He was right in front of me, and I had my back to the wall. I would have to hear this one out, I admitted to myself reluctantly.

"You probably didn't manage to hear what I was saying through the *mechitzah*," he said graciously.

Hmm. What could I say to that? "So be so kind," I responded, "and tell it to me again in short."

*In **very** short*, I hoped.

He gave me a sharp glance and sighed. Then there was a faraway look in his eyes as he traveled back in history and began his story. He spoke haltingly; he had to stop several times, breathing deeply in order to keep his emotions under control.

●●●

When I was a small boy my father passed away.

I was the oldest of several children. It was hard for my mother — really hard. She did the best she could, but everything was always lacking. She was under constant pressure to come up with money to pay the rent; we would never have dared to ask for stylish clothing — we had to be thankful for any secondhand offerings that came our way.

The time came for me to help out. I was 16, and I was feeling quite desperate as I set out to bring in some cash.

I went around collecting money. I tried going to shuls — *shtieblech*, where I didn't feel so very alone. I also went to private homes, but it was very difficult. People would look at me suspiciously. I was dead-embarrassed. I always wanted to run away after knocking on a door. People who were nice gave me a couple of dollars, but it was just *so uncomfortable*.

At least I was helping my mother a bit, and I knew it meant a lot to her that she didn't have to handle the situation all alone.

One day I was waiting despondently in an unfamiliar shul for the *tefillah* to start, for the men to come in, hoping that this day I would be lucky. It was an old, musty-smelling shul, but it was in a better neighborhood, so I was somewhat hopeful.

There was one other man in shul. He had an aristocratic look about him, and he seemed totally absorbed in saying *Tehillim*. I was surprised that he even noticed me. He looked up, and he must have seen the sadness and worry on my face.

"Young man," he said, "come here. Tell me about yourself."

Something about the way he spoke gave me confidence. I took a deep breath. At first I was reluctant to have to tell my whole story yet again, but soon enough I started talking. Then I found myself pouring my heart out to him; I was just happy that someone was listening.

And listen he did, with the kindest expression on his face. He encouraged me and seemed to understand me. He had all the patience in the world, and I could feel how much he cared about me. I don't remember whether I cried, but I know that I had hit rock-bottom.

He asked me my name.

"Yosef," I told him.

"Hmm…Yosef," he repeated. "That is a very *chashuveh* name. Like Yosef HaTzaddik."

For a short while he seemed lost in thought. Then he shared with me a *d'var Torah* that I have never forgotten.

Looking at me in a way that reflected both intensity and kindness, he said, "A person's name shows something about him; it is a kind of tailor-made *mussar* from which he should learn.

"Your name is Yosef, like Yosef HaTzaddik's name. Yosef HaTzaddik had a very hard life. He lost his mother; he was hated by his brothers; he was made fun of; he was thrown into a pit; he was sold into slavery; he went through many trials and tribulations in Potiphar's house, in jail, and in many other painful challenges.

"But the Torah calls Yosef HaTzaddik an *'ish matzliach* — a successful person.' No one else in the whole Torah was given such an accolade. How did he earn this title?

"He earned it because of the hard time he had; all that he went through, and the fact that he *did* pull through, made him a successful person.

"At each step along the way he could have said, 'Poor me'; he could have felt sorry for himself and given up, but he didn't. He looked upon each situation as a *nisayon*, a challenge, recognizing that if *Hakadosh Baruch Hu* had sent this to him, he could surely handle it — and handle it he did, and very successfully so. With his *bitachon* and his determination to make the best of every situation, he rose to the highest position in all of Egypt."

This man looked deep into my eyes — he had the darkest brown eyes, and his look was so intense. It was a look meant to fill me with the will to overcome all difficulties, and the strength and confidence to know that I could do it.

He gave me a nice sum of money; but more than that, he gave me a role model. If Yosef HaTzaddik could rise above all the many *nisyonos* he faced, then how could I doubt myself? I just needed to have *bitachon* that I would succeed, with Hashem's help. He took away my self-pity and gave me courage.

I walked away standing straighter and more confident, with the feeling that just as Yosef HaTzaddik had been able to handle his *nisyonos*, so would I be able to handle anything that would come my way.

I learned that his name was Aryeh Leib — Aryeh Leib ben Yitzchak. I stayed in touch with him, and he always had time to listen to me, to encourage me, to help me, and to help me help myself.

I have never forgotten him and I never will. Ever since I learned that he passed away several few years ago, I have been learning *Mishnayos* daily for Reb Aryeh Leib, and I say *Kaddish* for him on his *yahrtzeit*. When I have problems, I daven to Hashem to help me in his *zechus* — and He does, just about always.

Yes, this was your father, to whom I am forever grateful. You have a lot to be proud of...and, actually, you have a lot to live up to.

◆◆◆

It was several minutes before I found my ability to speak. Feeling guilty and small, I thanked him for this beautiful story, which I had never known.

FRINGE BENEFITS

By Rabbi Menachem Nissel

In many situations, some people have far more to lose than others.

Danny was an outsider in the overbearingly parochial environment of the Memphis Hebrew Academy day school. A South African immigrant, he was out of place and out of context. It was bad enough getting used to a new country, a new school, and the colorful idiosyncrasies of Southern-style living. But what truly overwhelmed him was his desperate attempt to keep all the new religious laws that the school had thrust upon him.

He was new at religion, and being a normal, healthy 13-year-old, he was taking the stringencies slowly. Wearing *tzitzis* was certainly not one of his priorities, and the muggy Memphis weather didn't lend itself to inspiring enthusiasm over wearing an extra layer of clothing. So when the whispered rumors circled around the Hebrew Academy that today was "*Tzitzis* Check Day," Danny felt angry. Really, really angry.

"*Tzitzis* Check Day" meant that boys were being pulled in to the office and asked to show their *tzitzis*. Those who could not produce the evidence were reprimanded and sent home. There was only a certain number of times you could be sent home before you were expelled, and Danny wasn't interested in waiting to be expelled from a school he so resented. He made a fateful decision: If he got called in and sent home, he would never set foot in that school again. He would go to White Station Public School. In public school his adjustments to the South would not have to be compounded with adjustments to meaningless religious standards.

Dovid Brown came from the quintessential Memphis-insiders family. His parents were *machers* in the community and had been involved in the school from day one. Dad was on the board and Mum was involved in fund-raising. You couldn't get more "in" than the Browns.

And Dovid was no dummy. One look at Danny's irate, tormented expression told Dovid what Danny was thinking.

Without hesitating, Dovid took Danny aside, took off his own pair of *tzitzis* and gave them to Danny. "Don't worry," he assured him, "the son of Larry and Lorraine Brown is not going to be expelled from the Hebrew Academy...."

Seven years later tragedy hit when Dovid Brown was killed in a car accident while studying in Baltimore's Ner Yisrael yeshivah. His parents received a *shivah* call from a young yeshivah student with a South African accent whom they vaguely recognized.

"Dovid was a true friend in every sense of the word," Danny explained. He proceeded to relate the story of the *tzitzis* and how Dovid's little act of gallantry saved him from switching to public school and formally ending his Jewish education.

"Without question, I would not be religious today if it wasn't for Dovid's intervention. He didn't just help me out; he inspired me and showed me through his actions that I had a future in a Torah world."

I write this story in honor of the *bris* of my grandson, Aaron Dovid Talesnik. He is named after his great-uncle, who is my wife's brother, the late Dovid Brown of Memphis, *z"l*, who died over twenty years ago. The "Aaron" was added, as it is our *minhag* to add a name when naming after someone who died young and tragically.

As I write I have on my desk an invitation to a fund-raising dinner on behalf of the yeshivah where I teach. The special guest speaker is a world-famous *talmid chacham* who has inspired countless *neshamos* and brought them closer to their Father in Heaven. He is a dynamic senior lecturer for an East Coast *kiruv* organization.

He is formerly from South Africa; he came to New York, where he lives today, by way of Memphis, Tennessee.

ONE KIND WORD

Rosally Saltsman

One word, one smile…

I was teaching an English course for students who were trying to pass their matriculation exams. Classes were held once a week over the course of several months. The only other adult contact I had in the building was with the janitor, who was supposed to make sure that the classroom was open and that I had chalk.

This janitor was the stereotypical grumpy, gloomy Gus. He was such a caricature of a grumpy old man that it would have been funny, except for the fact that I needed chalk and he had the key to the storeroom. Every week I would come and ask for the chalk, and he would growl softly at me and open the door if it was locked. I really resented being in this position every week, and I sought a solution.

At the time I was reading a self-help book on getting along with people, and with nothing to lose I decided to try one of the strategies in the book, which was to make the other person feel important, valued, and appreciated. How do you make a grumpy janitor whom you know nothing about feel important?

"You know," I said gingerly to his belligerent back, "I'll bet this school couldn't run without you. You're responsible for everything that goes on here." He turned around, wide-eyed. A big smile began to split his face like a fault line in an earthquake, creating caverns of smile lines in his wrinkles. He was transformed.

"You're right," he told me, beaming. And then he began to regale me with stories of everything he did and had done at the school during his decades-long career. He told me about his life, his family; he wanted me to come home and meet the wife. He wanted to have me over for dinner, to meet the grandchildren — an offer I politely declined.

For the rest of the time I was teaching the class, not only did I have long pieces of clean chalk waiting for me on the board, but the classroom had been cleaned, the desks arranged, and Mr. Janitor — nay, School Superintendent — was waiting with a big smile and his chest puffed out, ready to prove himself worthy of my accolades.

And while this man had been transformed right before my eyes, it was most transformational for me, because I had learned the incredible power of a kind word. Whenever I speak on the subject of the power of words, I find this story to be most illustrative of what just one kind word can do and how famished we all are for a bit of recognition and appreciation. I don't know how much English those kids learned from me, but I know I learned a valuable lesson from one appreciative old man.

THE MAGIC WORDS
A True Story by Nachman Seltzer

It was an awkward time to stop, but he didn't want to miss the chance.

The boys know I love them. They feel it inside their bones, in a place that tells them whether it's genuine or forced. I've been doing the same thing for years — dispensing Torah and words of *chizuk* along with *cholent* and *kugel*. They're hungry for both.

I've watched them grow; I've seen them leave yeshivah — some return and some don't make it back. It's a process I've been involved in for about twenty years. Countless stories have materialized over that time, happy and sad, predictable and unexpected. But one of the most remarkable incidents is one that I found out about only years later; and that's when I came to understand the power of a few words. At the time I was clueless, but now I know…boy do I know.

Back then Friday night was a big night. In the yeshivah where I taught, many of the guys rarely showed up for classes, but they wouldn't miss a Friday night meal at my house. What was so special about Friday nights? I'm not really sure, and I certainly never got a clear answer from any of them, but there was a certain glow, an intangible substance in the air that turned my simple home into a magical kingdom where everyone was welcome and everyone was a prince.

The food was served in abundance, and we tried to prepare a varied menu. The boys appreciated our efforts. Maybe they didn't say anything, maybe they didn't even say thank-you half the time, but I knew how much they enjoyed being there, how much it meant to them.

Many times it wasn't just the boys from my *shiur* who ended up at my house for those meals that lasted way into the night. My boys had friends who were learning in other yeshivos as well, and sometimes they visited for Shabbos and arrived at Chez Friedman's unannounced, together with my *talmidim*, for a meal or two. They sat at our Shabbos table in their funky T-shirts and baggy jeans, and we gave them the love they had been missing for so many years.

One Friday night, Yitz and Reindeer (nobody knew why he was called Reindeer) came by with a few friends. One of them was a sweet boy named Simcha, whom everyone called Smurf. Why they would call him Smurf was anyone's guess. It didn't matter to me. Reindeer, Smurf…they were all welcome in our home.

In my work there are times when everything goes really well, but then there are many times when things don't go well at all, and you feel like maybe you're in the wrong job, maybe you should just quit and go into business, maybe all of your efforts are wasted on these kids who can't appreciate anything anyway. But this was one Friday night meal when everything was just so incredibly amazing and everyone hit it off so well that I was simply at a loss for words. Even the Johnny Walker Red tasted like Black!

Smurf and I got to talking…for about 4 hours, and when we finally parted we were the best of friends. I told him that I fully expected — no, demanded — that he return in the future. I wanted to see him again, even though he wasn't part of my *shiur* and we'd never known each other before, because a conversation like the one we had was worth its weight in gold. He said he planned on coming back to my yeshivah for another Shabbos sometime down the line, and we agreed that when he was back in town he'd be swinging by for some more great food and great conversation.

We were both looking forward to meeting again.

● ● ●

I had Smurf on my mind for months, hoping to see him again over some nice, steaming soup, but even on those few occasions when he did turn up in town, he didn't spend much time at my house, and we never got the chance to continue that ripper conversation that we started. At some point I kind of gave up on catching him for another good schmooze, and he began to slip out of my mind. I lead a very busy life, I had many other *talmidim*, he wasn't even part my yeshivah, and he almost never came back. All things considered, it was pretty impressive that I still remembered who he was!

● ● ●

Then, one Shabbos afternoon, my wife went into labor. Somehow we were able to wait it out until Shabbos was over, but then it was clearly time to go, so we headed off to the hospital. We arrived with time to spare. Actually, we arrived with quite a bit of time to spare, because the baby didn't seem to be in any serious hurry. When the real labor began, it culminated in the birth of our new baby boy. Starry-eyed and so excited, we looked at our son in silent wonder, overwhelmed by the magnificent handiwork of Hashem, time after time.

Soon enough, I had to go home to take care of our other children, who were waiting impatiently for me, anxious to hear all the details. So I bade my wife good-bye and was on my way.

I walked out into the hospital's parking lot and found my car. I was still on a high. New baby. Wonderful. What a *simchah*! How lucky we were! What a *zechus*!

Still in a daze, I turned on the ignition and began driving out of the lot, then hooked a right, intent on reaching the main city arteries, which would lead me to the highway and my hometown. There was a bus stop on my right, set inconspicuously off to the side. As I drove past I noticed some teenagers sitting there in the stop. Part of me wasn't paying the slightest bit of attention to them, but another part of me, the part that had worked with kids like these for so many years, was checking them out.

Smurf — my friend from that Friday night so long ago — was sitting in that bus stop! I screeched to a halt, bringing my car right up to the stop.

"Smurf," I called out. "How's the Smurf-man? It's so great to see you, brother. It's been too long, way too long!"

He got up from the stop and walked over to my car.

"Oh, Rabbi Friedman!" he said. A tinge of some strange emotion that I couldn't place was coming through his voice. "So nice to see you. Yes, we definitely should get together more often." We stayed there shooting the breeze for a few minutes, then I told him I had to go. We parted with promises to see each other more. As I drove off I realized that I hadn't even mentioned my brand-new baby to him. The conversation had been completely about Smurf and what was going on in his life.

Then I went home and cared for my children.

It was years later that I learned the other side of the story. I met Smurf again, but this time there was no longer any resemblance to the Smurf I had known. Gone were the long, unruly hair, the vacant look in his eyes, the apathy, the unhappiness, the sullen glare. In their place was a sweet, joy-filled *yungerman* who enjoyed his learning and his life.

He had sought me out. Said he had something to tell me.

I wondered what it could be — we hadn't seen each other in years. But I was so happy for him, so proud of the way he'd turned out, even though I hadn't had anything to do with that. He'd been at a different yeshivah. We'd shared one good conversation, but that had been the extent of our relationship.

He sat down on my bench, took off his hat and placed it on the table.

"I want to tell you something," he said again.

"I'm listening."

"That night that we met at the bus stop...you remember?"

I nodded my head in sudden recollection.

"You have to understand something," he went on. "That night... I'd hit rock-bottom. I was so depressed. I didn't care about anything anymore. I felt like nobody cared about me at all, like nobody gave a darn whether I lived or died. It was Motza'ei Shabbos, and I was planning to leave the yeshivah, head out to town, and blow all my money on the kinds of things that would have hurt me really badly. Basically, I didn't care what happened to my body that night. I was in such pain that it just seemed easier to leave this world. I was open to that. I wanted to die.

"I left my yeshivah and walked to the bus stop, self-destructive thoughts filling every corner of my mind.

"Nobody cared about me, nobody wanted me.... As I waited for the bus the thought entered my mind that I was so worthless that no *frum* person would even want to speak to me, no one who saw me would want to say hello to me. I was nothing...less then nothing. I was garbage. Nobody would ever want to talk to me....

"And then a car drove by, and suddenly it came to a squealing stop, and this rabbi was calling my name. I squinted over and saw that it was you sitting in the car. And then you greeted me, started to speak to me, showed me how happy you were to see me. And I could tell that you really were happy to see me, that it wasn't just an act.

"And then I knew that I had been wrong — that there was something worthwhile inside me after all, that I had something to live for. And after we spoke and you drove away, I left that bus stop and walked back to my yeshivah, all self-destructive thoughts tossed away and forgotten. I was going to live and become successful, and it was all thanks to you and the fact that you had stopped and spoken to me.

"Just a few words, a few magic words. But they saved my life.

"Thanks, Rebbi. Thank you for everything. I'll never forget what you did for me."

ALL THE WAY HOME

Sarah Shapiro

A gentle but urgent directive toward the path of life.

"You have to honor your parents."

These words were delivered in a thick foreign accent by the rabbi — a diminutive, olive-skinned, white-bearded stranger dressed in black suit and hat — in a kosher luncheonette on 47th Street. If I had to pinpoint one event, aside from being born, that divided my life into *before* and *after*, those six words could serve as the turning point.

I'd met the rabbi 10 minutes earlier, while waiting on line for a phone booth outside the New York Public Library. Something about his appearance (I'd seen pictures somewhere of religious Jews — maybe National Geographic?) had vaguely rung a bell, and I'd turned to say, "You're Jewish, aren't you."

He stared, taken aback. "*You* a Jewish?"

So that's how my life began, and now he was introducing me to my religion over a slice of poppy-seed cake. (*Poppy-seed cake?*)

In memory, all this occurred around a thousand years ago.

The so-called "dairy" restaurant was on an upstairs balcony inside the Diamond Exchange in midtown Manhattan, and the Diamond Exchange was the huge room down below on the ground floor, full of busy men in black and white who all looked like him, and shining glass jewelry cases beneath bright lights, and talkative women in silver and gold trying on necklaces and diamond rings. In nearly two decades on earth I'd never seen anything like it. Who were these people? If these were Jews, what relation could they possibly bear to me, whose childhood was spent on the fringe of a genteel WASP suburb, gazing in hopelessly at sedately well-mannered country clubs and community carol sings on the snowy village green?

Across the Formica tabletop the rabbi had taken a ballpoint pen from a black briefcase and was laboriously spelling out something in capital letters on a paper napkin (the ABCs were not his strong suit, that was obvious), mouthing out the words as he went along. He announced that these lines were what Jews say in Hebrew before eating various foods. (*What they say? You mean, like grace?*) He'd already told me to transfer to college in New York, live with my parents (*you must be kidding!*) and work for my father at his office. (*Ha! For my father? An office job?!*)

"Yes. Days, you work. The nights, night school. Will be very good. Your father," he said, "will be *so* happy."

"Yeah, but I—"

"You have to honor your parents. You come to us for Shabbat."

"What?" I'd never heard that word.

"You will meet my wife. You will be friends. You see them?" I followed his glance to the right. At the lunch counter were seated two annoyingly pretty girls around my own age, giggling and chitchatting in typical teenage fashion. They were in long-sleeved, calf-length dresses, their glossy hair pulled back smoothly into ponytails. "Those girls, see? They are Orthodox."

Something in me recoiled with distaste, scorn, bafflement, and — unbeknownst to my own self — an envy in the marrow of my bones. Those girls — examples, supposedly, of my own people — were card-carrying members in a universe as weirdly inscrutable to me as China, a club even more off-limits to someone like me than… my own hometown. Who did they think they were! *Holier than thou!* What made this man think he could just come up and pontificate to me like this? It was ridiculous; such quaint, old-fashioned ideas! I should get up and walk out! *Get up and walk out!* But…it was interesting, too, in a way, being bombarded by all this 19th-century stuff (and on some strange level, it was striking a deeply resonant chord, familiar and unfamiliar at the same time). To go work for Daddy — as if I needed my father's approval! — that would be exactly the opposite direction from where I had to go in life. The whole point was to become independent. That was the most important thing — to think for yourself. My whole way of seeing things was totally different from my parents'. They were middle-aged! I had to find my own way in life — even they would agree with that.

And anyway, who said that Daddy would even want me there, in his office?

What would I wear?

He'd be embarrassed.

And I couldn't touch-type, or do shorthand.

The rabbi glanced nervously at his watch a few times and signaled the waitress for the bill. So I gulped down my coffee and, with a mental nod to my diet (*I won't have lunch*) finished off the cake. He pointed to the napkin he'd written on and gestured for me to take it. "Remember, before you eat. *Le'at, le'at.* Will be a blessing for you."

Outside again in the muggy heat, amidst the rushing lunch-hour crowds of midtown Manhattan, he stopped a few moments now on the sidewalk to give me directions to his home on the East Side. On Friday night, he said, his wife would be lighting at seven. I should get there by quarter of.

Lighting?

"And now you go, tell your father. Maybe you start tomorrow."

With quick, determined steps he scurried toward 47th and 6th, and for lack of anything better to do, I guessed I would walk over to my father's office, a few blocks uptown. Waiting on the corner for the light to change, I was standing beside the rabbi (he couldn't have been more than five-foot-two), whose mind now was obviously on other things, when my eyes crossed the street and alighted on a fat, squat grandmotherly type on the opposite curb. Long sleeves, buttoned collar. Some sort of round little hat atop her head. With a small flicker of satisfaction I recognized the whole getup — I was an expert already — and gestured in her direction. "She's Orthodox too, right?"

"Yes," the rabbi replied curtly. Then, as the light turned green: "One day *you* will be Orthodox."

"Ha!" I shot back with a tart laugh. The warning bells were going crazy. "Never!"

●●●

So for $100 a week I got a job in the classified ads department of my father's magazine, a position that required knowledge of the ABCs and how to open and close a filing cabinet. I signed up for night classes to finish my degree, moved back in with my parents, and spent the weekends with them at home in Connecticut.

And an amazing thing happened: my mother and father were so happy about all of this. So, so happy. I hadn't known they would feel this way.

Even more amazing, *I* was happy. Happy to be making them happy. I didn't have to think my way into it, this happiness, it just sprouted by itself, like grass, or wildflowers.

Happy like the rain, as natural as the relationship between earth and sky.

Not since I was a little kid in elementary school, or maybe even kindergarten, had this kind of happiness, plain and simple, been mine, day after day. It didn't go away. Every once in a while, I'd turn around to see what I'd left behind, and there, stretching into the distance, was a huge, convoluted grey maze drifting away into the past. I realized now that I'd been wandering around in there for what seemed like centuries. Until a pint-size stranger had appeared out of the blue, pointing to the exit and ordering: "Thaddaway!"

I could have just ignored him — it would have made sense to ignore him; I came very close to ignoring him. Instead, I found myself in a landscape, green and hilly, fed by streams of water and light from some long-ago era. As if I'd entered a garden that had been right outside my door all along, but which I hadn't visited since the beginning of time, and had then noticed that my name — in Hebrew letters — was inscribed on the gate.

A door had opened before me to another dimension…larger than myself, a vast…something or other, and it belonged to me. I recognized it.

● ● ●

One morning about eight years ago, I was hanging laundry out on our porch when my eye was caught by the sight of a little man down below, with a white beard and black hat, coming our way along the sidewalk.

Could it be? I was astonished. I'd always wondered what had happened to him.

But as the man came closer, I saw it wasn't he.

The next day on my way to the neighborhood supermarket, it happened again. Wasn't that he, crossing the grass? I almost ran to see… but stopped. No, it didn't even resemble him.

That afternoon I was at a bus stop in downtown Jerusalem, waiting for the 22. I glanced to the left to see which number was arriving and saw, from the side, a tiny olive-skinned man with a white beard and a black hat.

Just then he turned to look too.

"Rabbi R—!" I cried. "Is that you?"

He looked perplexed. He was bent over and shrunken, as frail as a dried leaf. "Who? You — are?"

"Sarah Cousins!" I exclaimed. "From New York City! How are you?"

"Oh!" His face, wreathed in wrinkles, smiled. "You are here? In Israel?"

I nodded happily.

"At gara po? [You live here?]"

"Ken!"

"At nesuah? [You are married?]"

"Ken!"

"Yesh lach yeledim? [You have children?]"

"Ken! Venechadim! [And grandchildren!]"

He laughed.

"Rabbi R—, tamid ratziti lehagid lecha [I've always wanted to tell you]…todah! Thank you! Todah rabbah!"

"Ein be'ad mah [You're welcome]," he replied. "Ah! Autobus sheli! [My bus!] Shalom!"

And with that he disappeared.

JUST A FEW LINES

By Brachah Stern

A few words on paper save a generation.

The Rosh Yeshivah didn't recognize the middle-aged man who walked in to his office, but it was clear that the man knew the Rosh Yeshivah. He greeted the Rosh Yeshivah with humble deference. Then he said, "Rebbi, I am what I am today only because of you." From his pocket he produced an old, yellowed paper, which he held as he related his story.

"When I was a *bachur* in your yeshivah, the pressure was getting to be too much for me. I felt that I just wasn't cut out for learning all day. I convinced myself that one could be a good Jew in any setting, and I left the yeshivah.

"Well, perhaps it *is* possible to be a good Jew in any setting, but I didn't succeed. I did not manage to surround myself with good influences, and I was headed down a road of steady spiritual decline.

"One day, a letter for me arrived in the mail — it was from the Rosh Yeshivah. It was a short letter, but it contained all the caring in the world. 'How are you doing?' it said. 'I'm thinking about you and am interested in hearing about your progress.'

"That letter weighed heavily on my mind. How could I respond to it? How was I doing? Well, I knew that I was going downhill fast. *The Rosh Yeshivah cares about me*, I thought. *What will he think when he sees me?*

"Those few lines motivated me to pull myself together. I started working on myself, and to this day, I haven't stopped. I keep the letter with me always — here it is, in my hand! *Baruch Hashem*, I've accomplished a lot. I have a wonderful family now.

"My oldest son is to enter yeshivah next year, and I've come to ask if you would accept him in your yeshivah — I believe that I've learned over the years what it means to show a *bachur* love and caring, and as a result, I know that my son truly appreciates Torah learning. He'll fit right in!"

WITH FAITH BACK INTO LIFE

As told to Chani Wagschall

How far can a little caring take a person in life...

Our father's sudden death changed every aspect of our lives. My mother, a widow at the age of 33, had to plunge into the working world in order to provide us with our basic needs. As caterer and waitress, her hours were long and exhausting. Our paths crossed for fleeting moments as each of us rushed on to the next assignment.

At the age of 11 I had to make my own contributions of time and energy in performing supportive tasks. There was little opportunity for me to express the pain and fear that followed the loss of my beloved, sympathetic father. I missed him every moment of the day and night, but I had to mask the tears and sorrow for my mother's sake. She had enough on her shoulders, so I felt it wouldn't be fair for me to add to her grief by sharing my sense of loss.

Since Mother worked late into the night, she was asleep when I began my school day. I can still feel the chill as I moved quietly from bedroom to bathroom to kitchen. There was always a note waiting from her with a coin I could use to buy my lunch at school.

Junior high school began at 8:30 a.m., but my day began at 5:30. It was a long walk to school, and before I went each morning, I would walk to *Shacharis*, to Mishkan Tefillah Shul, which was halfway to school. Every morning I would join the morning service and, as an only child, would recite the *Kaddish*. It was my tribute to my father and, as I realized later, a major aid in dealing with the devastating loss. There was no one else to recite *Kaddish*, so the doting and protective members of the shul overlooked the fact that I was not yet bar mitzvah.

After the first week of this schedule, Mr. Feuerstein, the shul's *shamash*, appeared at my front door each morning just as I was leaving the house for my trek to shul. He was not a young man, and during the first week, before he began showing up at my house, I had noticed that he arrived for *minyan* in a car driven by another shul member. Now, each morning he seemed to be passing my home just as I began my walk to shul. "Your home is on my way to shul," he explained. "I have to go this way anyway, and I thought it might be fun to have some company. That way I don't have to walk alone."

Every morning without fail he was there. We trekked through snow, through the pelting rain, and through the stifling humidity of summer. We walked and he taught. Each morning he had another story about the Jewish people, the *siddur*, or answers to questions of faith. He listened to my expressions of grief and quietly reflected the tradition that deals with sorrow as with joy. He held my hand as we crossed busy intersections, and after some weeks he held my hand throughout our walk. I sat next to him in shul, and he listened and taught and hugged…and he moved into a void that was tearing at my heart and soul.

Years went by, and we were in touch by phone and by mail. I

had entered yeshivah, and the day of my ordination some years later was my gift to him.

Mr. Feuerstein was well into his 90's when I visited Boston with my wife and 6-month-old child. I wanted him to see my baby, so I phoned and asked him if he could come to the home he had passed so often. He agreed, asking if I could pick him up by car because it was impossible for him to walk. I realized that I had never known where he lived, so I asked for directions and set out to bring him.

The trip was long and complicated. His home was a full 20 minutes away by car. I drove in tears as I realized what he had done. He had walked for an hour to my home so that I would not have to be alone each morning. My home was not on his way to shul; it was completely *out* of his way. He had made me feel that I was helping him with companionship, when in fact the opposite was true. He knew my loneliness and he did not want my day to begin without him.

He met my son and held him. Members of the family stood by watching, and there was not a dry eye. Each one knew our story, and no words were necessary to accompany the sight of the next generation nestled in the arms of a beloved teacher and friend. It is a scene that is forever etched in my heart. When I took Mr. Feuerstein back to his own home we wept and embraced. We both knew it would be the last time we would see and hug each other.

My life has been blessed with personal and professional success, thank G-d. Yet wherever I have been, in gentle moments and in moments of exultant triumph, Mr. Feuerstein was holding my hand.

Simply by caring, he took a frightened child by the hand and led him, with confidence and with faith, back into life.

EMBRACING A STREET KID

By Sara Yoheved Rigler

A few words of greeting and a little friendship end up influencing the world of Torah study, with everlasting effects.

At the age of 14 Leonard Kaplan was what you'd call in modern parlance a "street kid." Too smart for his own good, he had been bored in his Bronx public school and had begun to act out. That got him expelled. His home wasn't "home" anymore after his mother's recent death. In 1948, with a father who couldn't cope with raising him and his two younger sisters, Len took to roaming the streets of the Bronx.

The Kaplan family had little connection to Jewish practice, but somebody told Len that he really should say *Kaddish* for his mother. He was directed to a house in the neighborhood where a private *minyan* met every day. The bevy of elderly men there barely noticed

Len. But the *baal korei*, Shloimie Katz, who was paid $3 a week to come and read the Torah, was an Orthodox boy in his teens. Shloimie convinced Len that he should say *Kaddish* in a proper shul and brought him to his own shul in the East Bronx.

On Len's first day there, 14-year-old Henoch Rosenberg eyed the strange boy. Len didn't have *tefillin*, and he didn't even open a *siddur*. He wasn't dressed at all like the Rosenberg boys, who were Klausenberger chassidim. His yarmulke clearly spent more time folded up in his pocket than on his head. The stranger didn't daven, Henoch noticed, but when the time came for the mourner's *Kaddish*, he jumped up and recited it by heart.

Henoch Rosenberg could have made fun of this *Yid* whose ignorance may as well have been a bright-red sign stuck to his back declaring: "I DON'T KNOW ANYTHING." Or Henoch could have ignored him; after all, he had his three brothers to play with, so he had no more need for this stranger than he'd have had for a fifth cup of wine at the Seder. But Henoch approached the strange kid and became his friend.

It turned out that Len didn't open the *siddur* because he didn't know how to read the *aleph-beis*.

This is a story of "could haves": Henoch Rosenberg could have given Len what most of us so magnanimously donate — free advice. Taking a page from Rabbi Akiva's biography, Henoch could have referred the 14-year-old to a *cheder*, where he could have sat among children half his age to learn the *aleph-beis*, but then, Rabbi Akiva didn't have the vulnerable ego of a teenaged orphan. Instead, Henoch and his brothers undertook to teach Len themselves.

The new kid learned fast — amazingly fast. (No one knew at that point that Len had a genius I.Q.) Within days the Rosenberg boys were teaching Len *Chumash*. At the end of three weeks Len knew how to learn a *blatt Gemara*.

The Rosenbergs lived right next door to the shul, so the boys invited their new friend home. Mr. and Mrs. Rosenberg, staunch chassidim of the Klausenberger Rebbe, could have taken one look at this unkempt "street kid" and decided that they didn't want their sons' pure *Yiddisheh neshamos* tainted by his influence. They could have forbidden their sons to play with Len. They could have explained to their sons that boys who go to movie matinees and hang out watching the local wrestlers were not appropriate friends for *frum* boys. Instead, Mr. and Mrs. Rosenberg welcomed Len into their home and their hearts. They invited him for Shabbos — every Shabbos. They made him their *ben bayis*. They gave him a home full of warmth and love such as he hadn't known since his mother's death.

Len responded by wanting what the Rosenbergs had. He started to grow his *peyos*, and he decided to go back to school — at the Klausenberg yeshivah. As Henoch Rosenberg would recall six decades later, "Within a year he was a *talmid chacham*."

Around that time Len became gravely ill with rheumatic fever and was hospitalized for several months. Not only did the Rosenberg boys take the trolley to visit him on weekdays, but even on Saturdays they walked more than an hour each way to bring Shabbos to Len in the hospital.

A successful contemporary *kiruv* rabbi says that no one becomes *frum* because he or she is convinced by the intellectual arguments in favor of Hashem and Torah. Rather, people become *frum* because they are impressed by the kindness and caring of *frum* Jews they meet. The aggregate effect of the Rosenbergs' kindness and caring was that Len Kaplan decided to devote his life to Torah. When he was discharged from the hospital, the former street kid started learning at the Mir and subsequently at Torah Vodaas. Eventually, he received three *smichos*.

Leonard Kaplan went on to become the great Rabbi Aryeh Kaplan, author of over fifty books on all facets of Judaism. Rabbi Kaplan translated more than forty volumes of *Me'am Loez* from Ladino to English. He made concepts such as Shabbos, *tefillin*, *tzitzis*, and *mikveh* profoundly meaningful to a generation of Jews.

The Living Torah, his translation of the Torah into English, is a widely used, scholarly (and user-friendly) tome, with a detailed index, extensive footnotes including maps and diagrams, and references to research on Israel's fauna, flora, and geography. Rabbi

Kaplan's *Handbook of Jewish Thought* is a systematic, encyclopedic treatment of all the basic beliefs of Judaism. He wrote groundbreaking books on Jewish meditation that attracted a host of spiritually searching Jews back from the East. He made dozens of Jewish classics intelligible to modern readers. He wrote Jewish responses to missionary propaganda that left missionaries stuttering. His works on Chassidus in general and the teachings of Rebbi Nachman of Breslov in particular made that avenue accessible to Jews who could not speak Yiddish.

His works have been translated into Czech, French, Hungarian, Modern Hebrew, Portuguese, Russian, and Spanish. Rabbi Kaplan's sheer brilliance and acuity in diverse fields such as physics, philosophy, and botany impressed college-educated Jews with the intellectual cogency of Judaism. And, in a feat almost unimaginable to those of us who have ever tried to author a book, all of Rabbi Kaplan's books were written within an eleven-year period.

He impacted many thousands of Jews by the spiritual depth and wisdom of his books and his live teaching. By the time he was taken from this world, felled by a heart attack at the age of 48, Rabbi Aryeh Kaplan had become one of the Jewish world's most important voices.

And here the "could-have-beens" turn into a horrifying possible "would have been": It's staggering to think what would have been lost to the Jewish world had the Rosenberg family not embraced one lonely street kid.

5
FATEFUL ENCOUNTERS

A NATURAL CHOICE

Sara Chava Mizrahi

A series of small actions in the lives of a religious couple can be the catalyst for change in an entire community.

The concrete was strangling them. City life in Eretz Yisrael was chipping away at their vitality, and they longed for a quieter haven, for fresh air and greenery that stretched farther than the three-foot mini-plots that were hewn out of the asphalt to house fragile, recently planted trees. A walk through the woods, a drive in the country, or a late-afternoon trip to the shoreline was grand — a taste of heaven, actually — but an undersized taste, not nearly enough to sustain them through a long week or month of choking their way through an assortment of temperature-controlled environments.

"Why don't we just move?" Naomi would ask her husband Yossi.

"It would be such a simple step — a step in the right direction!"

Her question never failed to pull at Yossi's heartstrings, but they had their priorities. "How can we know that it would really be a step in the right direction?"

Jewish life abounded and inspiration was everywhere, theirs for the taking. A shul on every block, a *beis medrash* wherever one turned, fine schools and wonderful teachers, and babysitters aplenty for their bright young children, a loving extended family to provide emotional and practical support — how could they dare to complain? And yet...

"I know," Naomi persisted, "that my davening isn't what it should be — I just don't feel the spirituality in this very spiritual city!"

In this wonderful city, all the potential of G-d's world — of grass and flowers and trees and the smell and taste of life and growth — was masked by brick and mortar and the choking exhaust of countless vehicles that held in their bellies hundreds of thousands of human souls, so many of them content to be exactly where they were.

"It would be so simple to just let the car keep on driving," Naomi couldn't help commenting.

And Yossi couldn't help but agree. So simple to just forget to turn the corner when they reached their neighborhood; just drive on, leaving the city and all its amenities behind...

Weeks melted into months and months piled up into years and life was almost pleasant in a world that became theirs simply by their long trek through it, dominated by routine. But when they hit the open roads and the fresh breeze would lash their clothing and tickle their nostrils they would laugh, and when they felt the invisible grit of loose soil tripping across their cheeks they almost cried with longing, for a life close to the earth beckoned to them and would not let them forget that it was there.

Then one day Yossi saw an ad from a *kiruv* organization inviting adventurous young families to move to kibbutzim and moshavim where there wasn't much of a religious presence. All they had to do was live there and let things develop on their own. Yossi was intrigued. "Why," he asked, "do we always feel like we'd be leaving our safe cocoon behind? If Hashem planted within us a love for rural life, maybe our job is to create our cocoon elsewhere. Maybe we can enrich the lives of others simply by living what we consider to be the ideal life."

That was the first seed they sowed; there were many more to come, for change is never easy, even a change that one has always wanted. They proceeded with a great deal of caution, much discussion, and many consultations with family, rabbanim, and mentors. But, they decided at last, it could be done, and it would be done.

Yossi and Naomi packed up their humble collection of belongings and moved to a lovely, endlessly green farming moshav in central Eretz Yisrael. It was a short distance away from a religious village with an exceptional network of Torah schools for their children, and close enough to larger cities that offered opportunities aplenty for work and Torah learning.

Their modest new home was what they had always felt a home should be. Surrounded by greenery that was now theirs to sculpt as they chose, filled with fresh air scented by the flowers and trees that grew freely everywhere, they felt a contentment they could hardly describe. Their children never had to go beyond their own fenced-in yard to keep happily busy, and Naomi's davening felt to her truly sincere at last. Such a simple step had brought about such a change — why had it taken them so long?

● ● ●

The reactions of the people at shul were something they hadn't anticipated. It was a sweet, sturdy, well-built shul that looked welcoming enough, but when Yossi walked into the building on their first Shabbos, dressed as always in a neat dark suit, white shirt, tasteful tie and black hat, the few men in attendance stared, and almost without exception the stares were accompanied by frowns, or by expressions so cold it seemed they would make a warm oven ice over.

For this shul had been standing for fifty years and never yet had a rabbi. No one sought a rabbi because no one felt the need. What's a shul anyway, other than a place to which those with a little faith could come to pray together? So what business had this bearded, rabbinic-looking character in their territory?

Yossi tried hard not to squirm as he waded through his mind, searching for the most efficacious way to present himself. How could he make a *kiddush Hashem* among this most unaccepting crowd he had ever met?

Swallowing his sheepish hesitation, he turned to his neighbor, smiled broadly, and offered his hand in greeting. The fellow in the next seat, dressed casually in clean blue-jeans and a loose plaid shirt, was not a boor after all, and he touched Yossi's hand and gave a slight nod.

Yossi davened with the small group, and as he had been blessed with a sweet voice, a man named Moshe, who sat two rows back, asked him to lead the *Mussaf* service.

A small victory it was, but simply by davening he had planted a seed, and back home he reported it to Naomi in as cheerful a tone as he could muster. But now a germ of disappointment and even dread had planted itself in his heart; for even after he had given them his best, liveliest *Mussaf*, he stepped down to find no more warmth than he had experienced earlier. A few nods of acknowlegment were all they offered to his outstretched hand.

● ● ●

Apparently, word of the "new kid on the block" got around, and a few more curious faces turned up in shul the next Shabbos. This time, the same Moshe who had asked Yossi to daven *Mussaf* asked him to read the Torah as well, and no one protested. "So," thought Yossi, "it seems this Moshe is in charge of the services here." This was a man it would be worth getting to know, and sooner better than later.

Yossi read the Torah and did a fine job of it, but that was the last time he could get away with *leining* without putting in extra time during the week to prepare it properly, as catching his few subtle errors soon became entertaining sport for those who assembled week after week. "At least it keeps them focused on the *parashah*," he thought wryly. And he had another seed planted.

● ● ●

Arguing between *Minchah* and *Maariv*, whether over moshav life or politics, seemed to be a sacred tradition in this homey shul. Yossi made sure to leave a *sefer* in the building to keep himself productively occupied during that time, as he knew he had nothing to gain by protesting their choice of diversion. "No reason to alienate them any more than I already have by my very presence here," he told himself. He only hoped that minding his own business would not make a bad impression on them. He made sure to smile at his fellow congregants whenever they glanced his way; the last thing he wanted was for them to view religious people as snobs.

But his sitting there with his *sefer* made them feel uncomfortable. They began to lower their tones when they spoke, and before long some of them started finding other ways to pass that time. Some of the men were frustrated to see that the atmosphere was somehow changed, but they could find nothing concrete to complain about.

Finally the one named Moshe rose and walked over to him. "What's that book you're reading?" he asked just a little too gruffly.

Yossi smiled warmly. "Oh, it's a collection of insights on the *parashah*. I always find it fascinating," he said cheerily, hoping that he might be able to plant yet another seed here.

"Well," Moshe said, "if it's so interesting, why don't you just get up there before it's time for the next prayer service and tell us about some of those things you're reading."

Thus began the first *shiur* Yossi gave on the moshav, and more curious visitors began showing up in shul in the weeks that followed.

To be sure, there were those who considered Yossi's 20-minute *shiur* nothing more than an annoyance, but Yossi chose to ignore the growing circle of his detractors. He tried to keep the negativity from Naomi, who spent her late afternoons with her children, blissfully planting flowers and vegetables in their garden and pursuing simple landscaping projects of her own design, gradually transforming their yard into a place of beauty.

She even made a few friends among her neighbors. The scowls of the naysayers hardly reached her.

Still, she knew that plenty of their fellow moshavniks would have liked to see them gone, and she did her best to mollify them. One of their most vehement opponents lived nearby. When Naomi learned that the woman sculpted eyebrows in her home for a small fee, she made an appointment to have her eyebrows done. The two women became fast friends, and a potential problem was defused. Naomi was planting more than flowers.

● ● ●

A few of the men were genuinely attracted to Yossi and his intellectual bent. Perhaps he could find the time, they asked, to give them an hour each week to share a little more of his rare expertise — and a weekly shiur in *Ein Yaakov* was begun.

● ● ●

There was a lawyer on the moshav who wanted nothing to do with shul and, in fact, nothing to do with anything religious. But he had a great deal of professional ambition — so much ambition, in fact, that he sought out Yossi on his own.

"Hello there, Rabbi," he told Yossi. "My name's Shimon. I wonder if I could have a word with you."

"Sure!" Yossi said with a grin.

"You must have heard of the well-known Judge Cheshin. He's not at all religious, but he's a scholar, and often, when he hands down his rulings on complicated issues, he cites the Talmud to back up his logic. It's most impressive, I must say."

"Yes, I've heard about that judge. He's earned himself quite a reputation."

"Well, a couple of us professionals were saying how we wished we had a little Talmud under our belts too — you know, to help us advance in our respective careers.... I was wondering how you'd feel about teaching me a little Talmud — maybe just an hour a week when the two of us could get together..."

Yossi was just a bit too enthusiastic in his response. "I'd love to! Nothing would give me more pleasure. You'll find it opens up a whole new world for you!" Then he caught himself, cleared his throat and asked, in a more subdued tone, "When would be a convenient time for you?"

"Some evening in the early part of the week, if you can make it then," Shimon said. "But," he warned, his eyes narrowing, "this is purely a matter of professional interest. I'm not looking to make any changes in my life — none!"

"I understand," Yossi said warily.

"We'll discuss no philosophy of Jewish life," said Shimon, "and there will be no talk of my incorporating anything we learn into my own life. This is strictly business. If you say one word about *teshuvah*, or about making my home more Jewish in any way — our study partnership will end right there!"

"Of course," Yossi agreed, wondering what he was getting himself into. But, he told himself, it's always worthwhile to teach Torah. All he could do was try to plant seeds any way he could.

So another *shiur* was under way. They began to meet in Shimon's home, and Yossi kept his word. The Gemara he taught was purely an intellectual exercise. At first it was just the two of them, but one by one, others joined — a high-level commander in the police force, a stockbroker, a handful of other bright academics — none of whom ever went to shul. They formed a comfortable little clan, and Yossi never broke his promise; he never made any attempt to change anyone. Yossi's relationship with Shimon began and ended with their weekly class.

Almost a year after that first *shiur*, Yossi's phone rang. Shimon was on the line. "That's surprising," Yossi thought.

"Hello, Rabbi. I have one of these countertop hot/cold filtered water dispensers in my kitchen at home," Shimon began. "Do you happen to know if I'm allowed to use it on Shabbos?"

Yossi nearly whooped with joy, but he managed to contain himself and responded to the question as if it were the most natural thing in the world for Shimon to be asking about such matters.

● ● ●

Then there were the bar mitzvah lessons. Yossi taught one boy, who thoroughly enjoyed the lessons; that boy's friends' parents wanted their sons to perform as well as that first boy had, and soon Yossi found himself teaching almost all the bar mitzvah-aged boys in his moshav and in the neighboring moshavim. When parents came to pick up their sons, they would catch the last 5 minutes of the lesson. Within a few weeks they'd begin joining their sons for the entire lesson. Yossi's spiritual garden grew and blossomed.

● ● ●

Yossi and Naomi took that simple step of making their home on the moshav, and by the end of the year, Yossi was delivering at least one *shiur* of some sort every night of the week, and a number of *shiurim* throughout the day on Shabbos. They brought small platoons of *bachurim* to stay with them on *Yamim Tovim* — so that Yom Tov would feel like Yom Tov. And when the moshavniks were trying to cope with major events in their lives, whether happy events or sad, they'd turn to Yossi and Naomi to see them through their challenges.

"The first time I took my children to the park to play," Naomi told her mother one day, "all the other mothers stood up and pulled their children out of the park. Within seconds the park was empty. Today people beg me to bring my children over to their homes to play with their children, because they love how respectful *frum* kids are, and they want their children to benefit from the good influence. I don't send my children to play in other people's homes if I can't supervise them myself, but I make it a point to visit these families and take the children along, and the parents are thrilled."

The first time Yossi stepped into that shul, everyone there had a whole long bench to himself, and there were plenty of benches to spare. Today, thanks to Yossi's determined patience, there are few empty seats to be found. Yossi has a set of blueprints he had an architect draw up for a new, much larger shul to comfortably house all the many new attendees. He is working hard to raise enough money for the building project to begin.

For fifty years no one sought a rabbi for this community because they never felt the need. Nor are they seeking a rabbi today — for the same reason: no one feels the need. The difference is that now they have Yossi to turn to for spiritual and emotional guidance.

For Yossi and Naomi, life is far more complex than it was before they moved to their beloved moshav, but they are more content than they ever imagined they could be. They are living close to the land, the way they'd always dreamed of living. Naomi keeps planting more seeds in her garden, gently setting in one seed after another, and Yossi does the same.

And the seeds that they plant, the natural greenery, and the beauty of G-d's world that they sought, in both *ruchniyus* and *gashmiyus*, grow ever more lush and lovely.

SHAB*BUS*

By Yitzchak Kornblau

The opportunity of a lifetime may be just a few footsteps and a few words away.

Little did they know what lay ahead on the fateful bus ride they took that day some ten years ago. A busload of middle-aged, blue-collar Tel Avivians decided to take a tour of one of the fastest-growing parts of the country, setting their sights on the Modiin region, which included our comfy little outpost of Kiryat Sefer. As it happened, they arrived in Kiryat Sefer on Shabbos, which set the stage for an unexpected change of plans.

Back then the Modiin region wasn't yet graced with areas like Brachfeld, Ganei Modiin, Lapid, Menorah or, for that matter, even Modiin — all vibrant populated centers today. So their tour through miles of desolate construction must have been pretty devoid of life, except for some foreign construction workers and the few small villages they skirted. So when they arrived at Kiryat Sefer's city gate they were more than anxious to see some of the natives — probably almost as anxious as the residents of Kiryat Sefer were to see a busload of people pull up smack in the middle of their family Shabbos stroll.

Now at this juncture, anyone malnourished on a diet of whatever the secular Israeli media serves might be conjuring up images of throngs of *chareidim* armed to the teeth with rocks, converging on a bus sitting there defenseless as a beached whale...but we'll leave that scenario to the fertile imaginations of our ever-doting Israeli journalists.

What *happened* painted quite a different picture. The busload of secular tourists disembarked amid the Kiryat Sefer residents in their finest Shabbos apparel, and the first sparks of fusion between the two groups took hold. Nothing common seemed to exist between them other than their shared heritage, which provided the impetus for what happened next.

Slowly, unrehearsed — though it seemed to come almost naturally — the residents and visitors connected and bonded in ways that only Jewish "complete strangers" can.

"*Shalom aleichem!* Welcome to our little community! Maybe you would come over to our house to taste a real Shabbos meal and sample a little bit of what we look forward to every week!"

"You have the whole afternoon off? Well, why don't you come over and spend the time with us? I can guarantee you an experience you'll never forget!"

"*Well, my Saba, alav hashalom, kept Shabbat, and to tell the truth, I'd love to hear some of the zemirot he used to sing.*"

"*You know, this is the first time we've really ever spoken to a chareidi couple. We appreciate dialogue. Maybe we can talk a little bit. I don't think the guide has anything more engaging on the schedule anyway.*"

And so it went, to the dismay of the bus driver and, in the backdrop, to the vocal ire of the tour guide. One by one the entire busload of tourists gingerly slipped away into the welcoming crowd and was enveloped in the love of their compatriots and the aura of Shabbos.

Their bus might have left empty, but the tourists left that Motza'ei Shabbos fulfilled. Many of them were so inspired that they decided to keep up with their Shabbos hosts who rekindled the spark and unified them with their heritage forever.

THE NAMES IN THE FLAP

By Rabbi Nachman Seltzer

A rabbi who goes out of his way with a few words; two sets of grandparents who went out of their way with a simple gift…with world-changing results.

Some communities have lots of shul-going Jews; in others you'd be hard-pressed to find yourself a *minyan* on any day other than Rosh Hashanah or Yom Kippur. I grew up in the second kind of community: affluent; suburban; materialistic. My parents were members of Beth Shalom, the local Conservative temple, but we didn't attend services any more than was strictly necessary.

Sports was my thing…and making money; definitely not going to shul for hours at a time. I couldn't think of a more boring way to spend a Saturday morning, and I was fairly vocal about my feelings. All my friends knew that I cared little for the whole religion thing, and after the year of bar mitzvahs had passed, for a very long time nobody talked to me much about being Jewish.

Then I met the rabbi.

I was in the supermarket buying myself some bagels and stuff for Sunday morning brunch (we were still Jewish enough to enjoy that kind of food), and there was this guy standing at the counter holding a carton of Tropicana orange juice in one hand and a plastic encased *tallis* bag (that much I knew) in the other. He had a trim beard and a ready smile, and he turned to me with a warm "Hello." I was a bit surprised at his greeting, considering I didn't even look Jewish, but I suppose the bagels were giving me away.

I felt like I should respond, especially since he was so obviously out of place in my neighborhood, so I said "Hi."

He asked me my name.

"Sandy," I told him.

"I'm Rabbi Josh," he said.

"Whereabouts are you from?" I asked, and he explained that he'd been invited down south for a month as a scholar in residence at the Young Israel across town — a place where I'd never been. He loved the Jewish people and was looking forward to making a difference.

"So what are you doing on this side of town?" I asked him, and he explained how he was visiting some relatives who lived nearby and he hadn't wanted to come empty-handed, so he was bringing them some juice.

"You know what," he said to me, "I'm running this program for youth over at the Young Israel. You're youth, and it would be great to see you at the shul."

On the day before that brief exchange, if you would have asked me if I'd be talking to a rabbi and enjoying the conversation, I'd have told you that the probability of something like that happening was pretty near zero. But the fact is, here I was shmoozing with this rabbi dude, and he was funny and charismatic and I was enjoying his company. And, really, what was the harm in going to shul to hear him speak, or whatever? So I went.

◆◆◆

When I arrived at the shul someone directed me to the main sanctuary, where the services were being held. I entered this oversized room where the acoustics magnified every single sound. I think the echo made people feel better, because they could pretend it wasn't so empty in the shul. I couldn't help wondering why so few people cared enough to come to pray in this immense sanctuary that held row after row of pews but just a few worshipers scattered all over the room. Since it was my first time at the shul, I decided I should find myself a seat alongside someone else, just in case I needed to ask for instructions during the prayers.

I spotted a couple of younger guys sitting together in one section, and I seated myself near them; their easy bantering was a comfortable addition to this first-time shul experience. They were friendly guys and they welcomed me to their group.

"What's your name?" the guy sitting next to me wanted to know.

"Sandy Glenner," I told him.

"Nice to meet you, Sandy," he said. "To what do we owe the honor of your presence in our shul?"

I told them how I had bumped into Rabbi Josh and how I'd decided to stop in for prayers at the Young Israel. They all agreed that Rabbi Josh was the man.

I figured I would need a prayer book; at the back of the room there were shelves and shelves of them, but I noticed an old, worn-out prayer book sitting peacefully in a wooden pocket built into the back of the bench in front of me. I picked it up and began leafing through its wrinkled pages, trying to get a feel for what I was doing here. Then, for no particular reason, I opened the cover of the *siddur* and read what was written there, and my mouth dropped open in shock. There on the flyleaf someone had penned in: "This prayer book was donated by Charles and Karen Glenner, in honor of their dear friends Marvin and Sandra Berman. May they have much success."

Charles and Karen were my grandparents. I would never have imagined that they were the kind of people who would have prayed in an Orthodox shul, or that they had friends who prayed in a shul like this, but here was the evidence, staring me right in the face. They were Orthodox. They cared enough about these friends to spend their money to purchase a prayer book in their honor and donate it to this shul.

Suddenly I felt a connection to this place, and, holding up the *siddur*, I tapped the guy sitting beside me on the shoulder and pointed excitedly at my grandparents' names.

"Look!" I told him. "This prayer book was donated by my grandparents. It says so right here on the flyleaf! I can't believe this! I didn't even have a clue that they were the kind of people who'd ever have prayed in a place like this. I mean, this is the first time I've ever stepped into an Orthodox shul, and this was the last thing I was expecting!"

The guy looked at the inscription, bemused.

"You say this is your first time in our shul?" he asked me.

"That's right," I replied.

"This is really interesting," he said. "The first time you come to this shul you discover your grandparents' *siddur*, and — what do you know — they donated this *siddur* in honor of friends, who, by the way, just happen to be *my* grandparents! How's *that* for a coincidence?"

"Pretty unlikely," I had to admit.

I mentioned it to the rabbi the next time I spoke to him.

"What are you going to do about this?" he asked me, and I, who couldn't help but agree that something should be done, couldn't see myself actually following up on that thought. I mean, great, I had gone to shul once and even managed to make an acquaintance with my grandparents' gift to the shul...but now what? Change my whole life around? C'mon!! Who was he kidding?

● ● ●

This incident took place in August, 2001. Just a few weeks later, terrorists attacked New York's Twin Towers and the Pentagon in Washington DC.

I was sitting in my office at the time of the attack, working on

The Names in the Flap | 273

the computer. The next moment I went into the hall to make myself a cup of coffee, and someone had the radio on, and things would never be the same again.

"...Reporting live from the World Trade Center..." The reporter began stumbling over his words, swallowing them in his haste and shock.

"One of the towers has been rammed into by what appears to be a plane that lost control. There is smoke emerging from the tower. I don't think anything will happen, and I'm sure that there is a rational explanation for this...wait a second, what's going on?... I can't believe this! It looks like there's another plane heading toward the second tower...the smoke is blocking my view...this is much more serious! It's heading straight for the second tower. This is insane. It appears to be a kamikaze pilot. He just flew his plane into the side of the tower!!!! The first tower is on fire...this is like a nightmare! **The second tower is burning now as well!** The smoke is getting thicker. The hysteria is intensifying by the second, and if I'm speaking too quickly and not clearly enough, it's because I have never seen something like this in all my years reporting for the network!..."

I reached out an arm to steady myself on a filing cabinet, and for a second I felt the room swaying. My cup of coffee went crashing to the floor, and I couldn't even call out. I just stared at the floor with a blank look.

I had to go home. Forget about work for today. I wouldn't be able to concentrate. Might as well leave now. It didn't look like it was going to matter anyway, because with Manhattan out of commission, most international businesses were taking a hiatus anyway.

I kind of stumbled down the hall, then I remembered that I had forgotten my jacket in my office. It was a nice, quilted Reefer jacket — navy blue with beige trim around the collar. All I wanted was to snuggle into its warm sleeves, drive home, and go to sleep.

I passed the open doorway of my boss' office. He was on the phone as he sat staring out the window with his back to me. He was gesturing with his hand to some unseen party on the line. "It's all because of the Jews," he was saying.

I paused in the doorway, trying to make sense of that statement I had just overheard. The other person made some kind of response, and my boss said, "Don't be ridiculous! Now the world will unite against the Arabs, just like the Israelis want, and there will be another war! I wouldn't be surprised if the Israelis themselves weren't behind this attack."

I couldn't believe that this otherwise rational human being would say something so insane, but I'd heard him myself. He was delivering his lines with such ease, I had no doubt that he really believed them. No political commentator in the Western world would dare to spout such racist filth, so I knew he hadn't stolen those lines off some talk show. And if he felt this way, then surely there were others as well. All across America they were sitting in front of their computers, pouring their theories out to each other for all the world to share. I felt like I was losing my mind — first the airplane attacks, then, immediately afterward, a different kind of attack altogether. What next?

I was shaking so much I could hardly press the elevator button. I entered the empty elevator cabin and the doors closed behind me with a barely audible *whoosh*. Some banal popular song played over the sound system, and I remember thinking that just that very morning I might have enjoyed the song — might have even sung along. Now the song was nothing but emptiness.

It was a long drive home.

One truth I've discovered is that a fully loaded SUV can't fill you up once the emptiness has come to visit.

● ● ●

The next few days were a haze of suspicion, vulnerability, fear and anxiety over what the future would bring. Would there be a war? If so, who would it be against? Americans like knowing who the bad guy is. The fact that President Bush had promised "to find those responsible and bring them to justice" wasn't making anyone feel any better.

Before I knew it, it was Yom Kippur. I hadn't attended Yom Kippur services for many years, I got in my car and drove to work as I did any other day. But in the office, as I sat at my desk staring blankly at my computer monitor, I realized I wouldn't be able to do this, especially after that last visit I'd made to shul. I realized that I had a little more thinking to do than I'd been doing up until that point. My boss was blaming the Jews for 9/11, for crying out loud, when anyone with half a brain knew that Jews would never, ever do such a thing! But if he and many others felt this way, I decided I might as well be with my people on this very holy day. And if I was finally going to visit a shul for Yom Kippur, it might as well be the shul where my grandparents had donated a *siddur*. It wasn't as if I had any serious ties to any other shul.

Unlike on my previous visit, this time there wasn't an empty seat in the house.

◆◆◆

I wanted to sit in the same place where I had discovered my grandparents' *siddur*, but there were other people sitting there, and I wasn't about to throw them out, especially on Yom Kippur! I looked and looked for somewhere else to sit. Eventually I spotted an available seat on the far side of the room. There were people seated on both sides of the bench, but this particular spot was empty. Maybe the guy who purchased the seat changed his mind about attending services this year. Anyway, I slipped past all the people, and when I finally settled myself in the seat, I realized that I didn't even have a *machzor*.

I really didn't want to climb over the people sitting next to me again, but I needed some sort of prayer book. I glanced around, trying not to be too obvious about my little dilemma, and then I saw this old, tattered *machzor* in the back of the pew in front of me. I reached for it and saw that it was indeed for Yom Kippur. Even if I didn't have a nice ArtScroll *machzor* like all the other people sitting around me, at least I had something to pray from.

I flipped open the cover of the *machzor*, and my jaw dropped.

This was beyond coincidence! On my first visit to this shul, I opened the first *siddur* I saw and it turned out to have been donated by my grandparents. Now, when I opened this tattered *machzor*, I found it had been donated by my great-grandparents! This was uncanny; it was as if my ancestors were sending me messages, as if my grandparents knew that I was there in the shul and had conspired with my great-grandparents to make sure I realized that I was meant to remain where I was. They wanted me to understand that I had roots right here in this shul.

(Actually, the thought crossed my mind that perhaps my family members had donated every prayer book in the shul, so I went back the next day and I checked — boy did I check — and there were no others. I had opened up the only two books that had been donated by family.)

The message got through. If 9/11 could arouse a spark, then those two prayer books could light that spark and turn that little tinder into a roaring flame.

It was only a couple of months after this episode that I landed in Yerushalayim to join a yeshivah there.

My life was changed forever, due to a greeting, a catastrophe, and two gifts — two gifts that were linked to eternity. Rabbi Josh, who greeted me, could never in a million years have orchestrated what came about as a result of his "little" greeting. But his simple "Hello" was the start of it all.

Nowadays, when I come back to visit my hometown and reach across the shelf at shul for a *siddur*, I stand there for a second and wonder, "Will it be from them again or not?" And you know something? It never is. Because I found the only ones there, the only ones that count.

A FEW WORDS THAT BUILT A LIFE

As told to Chani Wagschall

Another few hours and he would have been lost to the world of Torah.

One day, as we were about to begin *Minchah* in our *kollel*, an elderly man entered. I quickly found him a seat for davening, and after *Minchah* I inquired respectfully about his origins. He mentioned a *shtetl* whose name I don't recall, then he related an incident that was etched in his memory — and that has since become etched in mine.

"I learned in Slutzk," he said, "in the yeshivah headed by Harav Isser Zalman Meltzer and Harav Aharon Kotler. I enrolled in the yeshivah as a young *bachur* of 16 and was overwhelmed by the challenge of finding my place there. When I tried to find somewhere to sit, I felt really lost. I wandered around from one spot to another because I had no *shtender*, and wherever I tried to sit I was told that the place had a longtime occupant.

"When it came time to daven *Minchah*, I stood in the aisle on the side and poured out my heart to Hashem. I made up my mind that if I didn't find a place by the end of the day I'd go back home and build my future elsewhere.

"As second *seder* began I was standing in the aisle once again, eyeing my surroundings to find a spot, when a young man came over to me and said with a warm smile, '*Shalom aleichem!* I see you have no *shtender*. I'll give you one.'

"He walked up to the front where the yeshivah's rabbanim sat, took what was obviously his own *shtender*, and placed it in the first row, where the *talmidim* sat. '*Nu*, now you have a place. *Hatzlachah*.'

"I found out later that the young man was Rav Eliezer Menachem Man Shach, a nephew of the Rosh Yeshivah. If not for him, who knows where I would be today?"

A simple act of kindness or even a warm word can mean the difference between life and death.

THE CANDLE LADY

By Rabbi Shimon Finkelman

Such a small thing, done to give a lonely soul a little encouragement, shaped a life.

Rabbi Avraham Pam would cite Avos DeRabbi Nassan: "Even if a person cannot give his friend anything tangible, if he greets him pleasantly it is as if he has given him all the gifts in the world." Rav Pam would add, "A person can do chessed with a smile or a friendly word. With a little time and effort, one can pull a sad person out of his troubled mood."

Rav Pam would also say that sometimes when we do things for others we do not realize the great dividends that we will one day gain from these mitzvos.

●●●

My mother's family lived in Vienna before the Second World War. My grandfather, Reb Moshe Hilsenrath (henceforth "Zeidy"), was a comptroller for the Austrian Railroad System. His gentile coworkers respected him for his soft-spoken manner, his integrity, and his inherent goodness.

But there was a side to Zeidy that his coworkers never saw. Though he was clean-shaven, Zeidy was a chassid, a loyal follower of the Chortkover Rebbe, Rabbi Yisrael Friedman, one of the great Torah leaders of that time. When the Rebbe passed away in 1933 and there was no immediate successor (neither of the Rebbe's two righteous and exceedingly humble sons wanted to assume the mantle of leadership; it took some time for the elder chassidim to convince them to serve as Rebbes side by side), it was a difficult time for Zeidy and his devoted wife Shaindel (henceforth "Bubby").

Not long after the Chortkover Rebbe's passing, Zeidy and Bubby were walking down the street when they saw a woman of strange appearance shouting, "Candles for sale! Buy candles for Shabbos!"

They had never seen this woman before; perhaps she had come from another neighborhood to sell her wares. But she did not seem to be doing well as a saleswoman. Her grotesque features were scaring people away.

Zeidy and Bubby were exceptionally kindhearted people. When they saw how the "candle lady" was being shunned they took pity on her. They had no need for her candles, but they did feel a need to lift this woman's spirits by acknowledging her presence and making a purchase.

My grandmother was a friendly, outgoing person. I can picture her greeting the "candle lady" with a big smile, making conversation and then admiring her wares. Zeidy and Bubby bought a pair of candles from her, and as she handed them their purchase the woman turned to my grandfather and asked, "Do you have a Rebbe?"

It was a strange question, for Zeidy did not have the outward appearance of a chassid, and in any case, what difference did it make to this woman whether or not Zeidy followed a Rebbe?

Zeidy responded truthfully, "Well, I had a Rebbe, but he passed away recently, and no one has succeeded him yet. So I am currently a chassid without a Rebbe."

The woman handed Zeidy a scrap of paper with an address

scrawled on it. "Here," she said. "Go to this address and you will find yourself a Rebbe."

My grandparents thanked the woman and continued on their way.

Who was this woman and what had possessed her to give them this note? These questions remain unanswered, for my grandparents never saw the "candle lady" again.

Either curiosity or a sense that this encounter was a fateful one impelled my grandparents to seek the address on that note. They discovered that it was the home of the Skolye Rebbe, Rabbi Dovid Yitzchok Isaac Rabinowitz, a *gaon* and *tzaddik* of awesome spiritual powers. That initial encounter was the start of a very close relationship between the Rebbe and our family, a relationship that continued until the Rebbe's passing in 1979.

But it was more than a relationship. Zeidy played a key role in the Rebbe's escape from Nazi-occupied Austria. And in later years, Zeidy and Bubby would say that it was the Rebbe's blessing and assurance that earned them the Heavenly assistance they needed to escape to America in the nick of time.

PATHWAYS TO FREEDOM

On March 13, 1938, the Germans marched into Austria. Almost immediately, Zeidy was fired from his job and his family was forced to move out of their comfortable condominium into a small apartment. "Don't think of leaving the country," the authorities told Zeidy. "You had an important job with the railroad system and we may yet need your services. You're staying in Vienna."

Despite the warning he had received, Zeidy was determined to do everything in his power to emigrate with his family.

His first order of business was to visit the American Consulate and register for a visa. America had a strict quota system, and one could not apply for a visa without first being given a registration number, which meant that one was within the quota limits. Zeidy succeeded in registering and was given a number. This was an important first step on the road to obtaining an actual visa.

The Skolye Rebbe and his family also hoped to flee Vienna, but the Rebbe was in hiding, because the Germans were already seeking to round up rabbis for deportation. For the Rebbe or his sons to visit the American Consulate would be extremely dangerous. When Zeidy realized the Rebbe's predicament he immediately gave the Rebbe his own papers and registration number.

Zeidy later returned to the consulate, calmly requested a new number and, miraculously, received it without any problems.

As a government official, Zeidy owned a leather cap and a leather coat. From the time of the *Anschluss* (the political union of Austria with Germany), Zeidy, in his leather attire, accompanied the Rebbe whenever he wanted to immerse in a *mikveh*, which was often. Thus it appeared that the "official" was leading the "rabbi" somewhere, and the Germans left them alone. Zeidy accompanied the Rebbe on his journey to the airport for his flight out of Austria. As they took leave of each other at the airport, the Rebbe told Zeidy, "We will see each other, with the help of Hashem, in America."

●●●

On a hot day in August 1939, just days before war broke out, the Hilsenrath family quietly left their apartment in Vienna for the last time. Because the government had warned Zeidy that he could not leave, it was necessary to take special precautions so as not to arouse suspicion. Zeidy had no choice but to leave with very little money.

When the family arrived safely in Paris, Zeidy scanned the faces of the many people in the train station and decided to approach a particular stranger. After confirming that the man spoke German, Zeidy told him the story of his family's flight from Vienna, explained why he had arrived in Paris almost penniless, and asked that the man help them to complete their journey to Liverpool.

To this day the family does not know this man's identity. What they do know is that he took them immediately to a hotel, booked rooms for them, paid for the rooms and gave Zeidy money for boat tickets to Liverpool. They crossed the English Channel and, a couple of days later, boarded a boat that departed Liverpool.

War erupted while they were at sea, and the trip across the Atlantic was tense. The boat that left ahead of theirs was sunk by the Germans; but with G-d's help, they arrived safely at Ellis Island, where their Uncle Yossel and their son Tovia Zev were waiting to greet them.

WITH THE REBBE ONCE AGAIN

Materially, their new life in America was very difficult. Zeidy went from being a comptroller in a national railroad system to sewing zippers in a sweatshop. They lived in a small apartment on the sixth floor of a building without an elevator.

But Zeidy was always happy. He would come home and tell the children, "You think I am sad to be working so hard and earning so little? At work I dance from machine to machine, delighted that, *baruch Hashem*, we are alive and safe."

Yes, it was very different from their comfortable life in Vienna, but one thing that did not change was their close relationship with the Skolye Rebbe. When the Rebbe moved from the Lower East Side to Willamsburg, Zeidy became the *gabbai* of his shul and Bubby became the cook for whenever the Rebbe conducted a special *seudah* with his chassidim.

Zeidy and Bubby consulted the Rebbe on every important matter. Their second son, Aryeh Leib, had left on a transport from Vienna to Eretz Yisrael in 1939. He fought in the War of Independence in 1948. At some point during that war all contact with him ceased. Concerned, Zeidy and Bobby went to the Rebbe. "Do not worry," the Rebbe said calmly. "Aryeh Leib is alive and well."

On an Erev Shabbos my grandparents received a telegram from Eretz Yisrael: "*Ich leib* [I'm alive], *Aryeh*." At that time the Rebbe was still living on the Lower East Side. Bubby hurried out the door and traversed the Williamsburg Bridge on foot to bring the Rebbe the happy tidings. Hearing the news, the Rebbe smiled and said, "For this you had to come on Erev Shabbos? I *knew* he was alive!"

One day Zeidy developed what seemed to be acute laryngitis, but the doctor had a grimmer prognosis. "Mr. Hilsenrath, I'm sorry to have to tell you this, but your voice is gone forever. You will never speak again."

Zeidy and Bubby went directly to the Rebbe. After Bubby explained the problem, the Rebbe said, "As I recall, back in Vienna Moshe also suffered from this sort of problem."

"Yes," Bubby replied, "but then we went to the renowned specialist, Dr. Grabscheid, and he provided a cure."

"*Nu*," the Rebbe responded, "so go back to Dr. Grabscheid!"

Zeidy and Bubby did not understand. "Go to Dr. Grabscheid?" Bubby asked. "But that was in Vienna, and now we are in New York. And Dr. Grabscheid was Jewish. Who knows if he even survived the war?"

"Look for Dr. Grabscheid," replied the Rebbe, "and you will find him."

Zeidy and Bubby did not need to hear more. As soon as they returned home they began to search through phone directories for the number of Dr. Eugene Grabscheid. Their search took but a few minutes. He had an office in Manhattan.

Dr. Grabscheid declared that the original prognosis was wrong. He provided a regimen of therapy, and within a short time Zeidy's voice returned to its full strength.

❖❖❖

In 1966 Zeidy took ill; he passed away shortly thereafter. When the Rebbe came for *nichum aveilim*, he told Zeidy's children, "You have lost a father; I have lost my best friend."

And it all began by lifting the spirits of a forlorn "candle lady."

❖❖❖

ACCEPT ME AS I AM

From The Jewish Women's Project for Ahavas Yisrael

One kind person can turn a life around.

This story isn't about the particular details of how or why I became disenchanted with Judaism. It's not meant to frighten or disturb you but to inspire you with an account of *why* I decided to return. *Baruch Hashem*, I am totally back on track now, but it's not likely that this would be the case if it weren't for the actions of one very special woman.

In my early teenage years I went through a very hard time. For various reasons I suffered from low self-esteem and, therefore, associated with the wrong type of people. I had no interest in challenging myself to pursue any goal or dream; I just wanted to get by. Every day I experienced sad, negative feelings. There was no one I respected or admired to whom I felt I could talk. The only way I had of expressing my frustration at that time was to rebel.

Gradually, sadly, the life that had been somewhat stable grew further away from my everyday reality. I would often be on the streets just hanging out and thinking about partying. Many times I would meet family members and neighbors. Their reaction to me would be either to totally ignore me and act like I didn't exist, or to condemn me because I was an embarrassment to my family. Somehow people felt that if they ignored me I wouldn't notice and if they rebuked me it would help. Every once in a while I would meet someone who would speak to me in a normal way, but such encounters were few and far between.

I was just having a hard time with life. I didn't need *mussar*; I didn't need to be made to feel guilty; I didn't need to be ignored or embarrassed. What I needed was genuine love, care, and concern. I needed someone to treat me like a person and talk to me like I counted in spite of my different appearance and my peculiar hobbies.

One day, as I sat on a curb in front of a busy shopping area, Mrs. Cohen, the mother of an old friend of mine from elementary school, approached me. She had a big smile on her face and looked genuinely happy to see me. "Hi! Wow!" she said. "What a nice surprise! I haven't seen you in so long! How are things going?"

I wasn't sure how to react, but I felt safe with her. I wasn't accustomed to people speaking to me with such warmth. Today, looking back on that time, I realize that in many ways I had created that situation myself. Through much of my teenage years I assumed that most adults I knew were judging me. Their disappointment showed whenever they'd catch a glimpse of me. I avoided eye contact, I dressed differently, and my hair was unkempt.

Mrs. Cohen stood there for about 10 minutes just to schmooze and discuss what was happening in my life. I think after the first minute she could tell that I wasn't exactly the same person she had known back when I was in elementary school, but it didn't seem to bother her.

We finished our conversation and she walked away. For some reason, for months I hadn't felt as good as I did at that moment. It's not that she had said anything monumental. She just treated me like a regular person. I even felt some respect in her voice. I hadn't remembered feeling respected for a long time. It made me feel a little giddy.

Over the next two weeks, Mrs. Cohen would somehow always be shopping in that area where I had met her the first time. She always made a point of approaching me and discussing with me whatever was on my mind. At one point she realized that I didn't really have a place to sleep on a consistent basis, and she invited me to come for dinner and sleep over for the night. Some nights I accepted her offer, while some nights I needed my space.

I continued with my decadent lifestyle for several more months. I was so filled with confusion that my only comfort was in the freedom I felt in the streets, but her constant positive attention, genuine care and nonjudgmental concern made a deep impression on me. She never gave up on me. I knew that if I needed anything I could call her and she would be there for me. Whether she felt any discomfort about it, she never showed that she was embarrassed to be seen with me, and she never tried to pretend that I was something I wasn't. I felt that her respect for me made up for what I was lacking in myself.

Eventually, I did move in to her family's home, and with her love, care, and concern I was able to turn my life around completely and become the person I am today.

I now know that one of the best gifts you can give someone is absolutely free; it's the gift of honor and respect. When you show that you respect someone else, they in turn come to the realization that they are respectable, and they end up viewing life through totally new lenses. This enables them to see their own value and the unique contribution they can make in the world, and it empowers them to actualize that potential.

I owe my life to Mrs. Cohen. If not for her I might still be sitting on a street curb. Thanks to her kindness I am happy, productive, and willing to grow every day, and I can honestly say that now *I like myself.*

OVERCOMING PAINFUL FEELINGS

By Tzipora Kloc

We are moved by an inspiring story. Perhaps we choke up and our eyes well with tears...but then we move on. At what point are the stories — and the shiurim and all that we've learned and heard and read — put into practice?

When my daughter Bracha was in twelfth grade, we started applying to seminaries. Bracha had her heart set on attending either of two specific seminaries; she would consider no other. When she was not accepted to one I told her not to worry, as I was quite certain that she would have no problem being accepted to the other — I myself had been a student of the Jewish Teachers' Seminary for several years. As a matter of fact, I was fully confident, explaining to Bracha that she was sure to get in — why wouldn't they accept a child of one of their best former students? And in any case, Bracha's reputation could stand on its own — she is bright, kind, friendly and a *baalas chessed* par excellence; in her senior year she had spent most of her free evening hours helping mothers who were ill or overwhelmed with their young broods. She also volunteered for an organization that assists children with illnesses.

But even if that were not the case, I felt I had been one of those students who had helped the Jewish Teachers' Seminary earn its golden reputation. I had been a straight-*aleph* student, president of the student council, and recipient of academic awards, and I had given many *divrei Torah* during my time there. How could anything go wrong for Bracha?

Well…"*A mentch tracht un G-t lacht*" — Bracha was not accepted.

"Not to worry," I thought. "I'll just pick up the phone and pull some strings, and everything will work out."

And that's just what I did: I picked up the phone and…I was rejected! "Bracha is wonderful," Mrs. Solomon, the *menaheles*, told me. "But we are only taking girls with very high marks, and although Bracha's marks were just fine, they didn't measure up to the level the seminary was seeking."

I must admit, *I WAS MAD! You call this chinuch?* I thought. *My child is a paradigm of how we want our bnos Yisrael to be. So what if she's not Harvard material? Boy, oh boy….*

Now, I must tell you that, in all honesty, Mrs. Solomon is a doll of a person, and so I kept my composure and hung up without relaying to her my wrath (read: disgust). Instead, I told myself, "*Gam zu letovah* — everything is for the best. Mrs. Solomon is just a *shaliach*, a messenger to carry out Hashem's Will…something better is surely destined for Bracha." But I must admit that I couldn't help fantasizing about a disaster occurring in the general area where the seminary was located and the joy I would feel at knowing that my daughter was not there…

◆◆◆

Well, life goes on. *Baruch Hashem*, the following year Bracha found herself a rewarding job working with special-needs children, and she began formal study toward certification as a therapist for such children.

Yet even then, when I was pleased with the direction Bracha's life was taking and I had gained much clarity on all that had transpired, I still felt terribly uncomfortable whenever I met Mrs. Solomon on the street. It seemed, too, that the frequency of our chance meetings were inversely proportionate to my desire (or, I should say, lack of desire) to see her. Nevertheless, I would nod and say hello, all the while chanting in my head, "*Lo sisna es achicha belvavecha* — Do not hate your brother in your heart" (*Vayikra* 19:17).

Sometime in the fall, my parents invited my husband and me to join them for Shabbos at a convention of a notable Torah institution; and — you guessed it — not only was Mrs. Solomon there, but her family's table was right next to mine.

That is one moment about which I can say: *I grew up*. You hear a *shiur*, you read inspiring books, you study in the best seminary in the world, and what good is it if you can't implement all that you've learned? Taking a deep breath, I told myself, "No bad feelings anymore. I'm going over to say hello with genuine respect and kindness. If I don't do that, then what was the point of everything I've ever learned?"

I turned toward the next table and wished Mrs. Solomon and all the women at the table a *hartzig gut Shabbos* — without a trace of any sarcasm. And they must have felt that my warm greeting was genuine, because they asked my husband to make *Kiddush* for them (the men in their family were not with them).

While my husband was making *Kiddush* I got a good look around their table and noticed that one of their party was a lovely single girl in her mid-20's. I learned that her name is Shayna.

For me, one of the most disturbing things in the world is the *shidduch* crisis; so when I see a single person in need of a *shidduch*, I do my best to introduce him or her to someone, or to connect the person with someone else who may be in a better position to help.

I stayed in touch with Shayna, and I mentioned to her that we knew a boy named Shaul who was a regular Shabbos guest at our table, whom I thought she might wish to meet.

Shaul was an immigrant whose family was traditional, but he had found his way into the yeshivah system at a young age. He excelled as a *talmid chacham*, and his love of Torah is unparalleled. When I asked him what type of girl I should be on the lookout for, he responded, "First and foremost, a *tzanua* — a modest girl; and secondly, someone who is *mistapek bemu'at* — satisfied with little." Shaul radiated *tzidkus*, and he has a rare combination of fine *middos* and *hashkafos*.

Shayna was from a family that excelled in Torah and *chessed*, and I thought she might make a connection with him.

To Shayna's credit, she looked into the idea thoroughly and got back to me in a timely fashion. The *shidduch* was not suitable for her, she told me, but her aunt, a Mrs. Fine, knew a girl from a background similar to Shaul's.

Not one to be lax in follow-up work for a *shidduch*, I called Shayna's aunt, Mrs. Fine. She told me that, indeed, she knew a girl who sounded perfect for Shaul, but that girl had just begun seeing someone. I touched base with Mrs. Fine a few weeks later and learned that the girl in question had become a *kallah*; but Mrs. Fine directed me to a friend of hers, Mrs. Baum, who had a *bas bayis*, an orphan named Tamara, who was age-appropriate and was looking for a *talmid chacham*. I called Mrs. Baum, and she told me that Tamara was looking for someone who is primarily *mistapek bemu'at*.

Yes! Those words exactly — *mistapek bemu'at*! Fireworks went off in my head.

It took some time to get this *shidduch* going, but I was persistent, and after a little (okay, a *lot* of) nudging, I prevailed upon Mrs. Baum to agree to let Tamara meet Shaul.

Tamara and Shaul got along splendidly, and with guidance from family and *bnei Torah* on both sides, they became engaged a few months later, just around Pesach-time. This happened, I knew, because Hashem had willed it — and it happened through me because I had suggested a *shidduch* for a girl sitting at a table where I went over to greet someone in spite of the petty feelings I had been harboring.

Wait — you were going to ask me about the wedding, weren't you? I can tell you about only one small part of it — the very end, when my family and I arrived. It was gorgeous summer weather and the mood was glorious and radiated with the *simchah* of the new young couple. We arrived quite late because we had a prior engagement that evening — we were at family *sheva berachos*, because two nights before Shaul and Tamara's wedding was our Bracha's wedding.

Chasdei Hashem olam ashirah (*Tehillim* 89:2).

PENETRATING WARMTH

By Tzvi David

A small measure of caring when the opportunity presents itself can change all of eternity.

Roni Macabi's family moved from Iran to the Israeli city of Givatayim when Roni was 3. He grew up in a traditional home; in fact, his grandfather was the *chazzan* in the Ramat Gan Great Synagogue for Iraqi Jews. Roni himself was not religious, but he was a yoga instructor and considered himself a very spiritual person.

His wife Dorit had grown up in Ramat Gan. Her father, who was born in Poland, arrived in Israel at a young age. Her mother had immigrated from Iran as teenager.

Dorit's home was traditional. Every Yom Kippur, she remembers, the family would go to the *beit knesset*, where her father would blow the shofar at the end of the day. When the fast ended, her family invited the entire congregation to their home, where they would supply everyone with cake and light refreshments with which to break the fast.

The Macabis lived in Kfar Saba, an upscale town that is a 12-minute drive from Bnei Brak, though as far as the Macabis were concerned, Bnei Brak could have been on the other side of the ocean. Bnei Brak and its residents had virtually nothing to do with the Macabis' lifestyle and community. The Macabis had never known a *chareidi* person. Their entire exposure to the *chareidi* world consisted of a passing glance on the television screen. There was nothing wrong with *chareidim*, they felt, as long as they stayed a safe distance away.

The Macabis had three children — a girl and two boys, and they were always very family oriented. Friday nights were spent visiting with friends, and Saturday mornings were times to take the family to the beach; their home didn't really see a Shabbos experience.

●●●

In November of 2001, Roni started feeling pains in his back. He visited his local GP, who sent him to the hospital for further tests. The results couldn't have been worse. Roni was diagnosed with terminal cancer.

Roni and Dorit agreed that he wasn't going to go down without a fight. After several meetings with top specialists in the field, they concluded that in this case his best chance for recovery would be in the prestigious National Hospital for Neurology and Neurosurgery in Queen Square, London, which had earned a reputation as the premier place to treat Roni's cancer using the then-new gamma knife to remove the tumor.

It was a Friday afternoon when the Macabis arrived in London, and the day was as dark and overcast as were the people, each of them in his own world. That night would be the first night of Chanukah, but the Macabis could not sense the light and warmth of the day. They knew not a soul in this city that felt so cold and miserable. All they knew was the name of one man who lived there — a Mr.

Kornkraut, who was reputed to know the doctors and who might be able to help them if he could spare some time to speak to them.

Before they left Israel they had booked a room in a London hotel, but when they arrived they found that it resembled more an immigrant absorption center in Beer Sheva than a hotel in London. "No way," Dorit told Roni. "We can't stay in such a dump." But what was there to do at this late hour on a Friday afternoon?

Then Dorit remembered the slip of paper she had tucked away in her wallet, where she had jotted down the name and phone number of Reb Chaim Elya Kornkraut. It couldn't hurt to call him, she decided, to ask if he could recommend a better place for them to stay.

To their surprise, the charming hotel they checked into on his advice was across the street from the hospital where Roni's surgery was to take place.

What the Macabis did not know is that another Jewish patient, Sammy Homburger, was hospitalized in the same ward where Roni would be, and was in close contact with Reb Chaim Elya Kornkraut. When Reb Chaim Elya realized that the Israeli couple was going to be there, he asked that patient and his family to look out for the Israeli couple so that they would experience a little warmth and not feel so alone.

The Macabis checked into the hospital that Sunday morning. While the nurse was registering Roni, Dorit decided to have a look around. Upbeat and outgoing, Dorit knew that they would meet plenty of people in the hospital, and, she felt, she might as well get started on making new friends, as they would be there for at least a few weeks.

Walking along the corridor, Elisheva Homburger spotted the new arrivals immediately and went over to introduce herself and offer to help them in any way she could. Dorit accepted the offer gratefully, telling Elisheva that she would come over to talk as soon as they had settled in somewhat.

A short time later Dorit glanced through the patient list at the nurse's station and spotted the name Homburger on the list. That patient was in the room next to Roni's, so she walked over to room 511 and peeked in.

Dorit recoiled in shock, for there on the small night table lay a round hat with fur all around it. The patient in the room must be one of those *chareidim* who live in places like Bnei Brak!

A closer look revealed a man lying in bed with a big smile on his face. He was mumbling something, but with his hands he made a gesture of greeting. A few minutes later he invited her into the room. He introduced himself as Sammy and apologized for the fact that he hadn't spoken, explaining that he had been davening and couldn't talk.

Sammy and Roni soon discovered that not only were they both suffering from the same illness, they were also both professionals in the same field — real estate assessment.

Sammy was so warm and friendly that even though they knew he was part of the *chareidi* world, the Macabis soon stopped paying attention to the yarmulke on his head. A wonderful relationship developed between them; at the time none of them dreamed how deep and far-reaching this relationship would become.

Sammy's mother-in-law was the late Lady Jakobowitz, widow of the Chief Rabbi of England, Lord Immanuel Jakobowitz. She was one of the best-known and most colorful personalities in London's Jewish community, and it wasn't long before Roni and Dorit were introduced to the extended family and came to know Lady Jakobowitz, as well as numerous other families. The Macabis were being exposed to levels of *chessed* they had never before experienced or even known existed.

Whenever anyone came to visit Sammy in the hospital he would tell the visitor about his new friends. He explained to all his visitors that the Macabis had no family in England, so of course their visits became visits to Roni's room as well. Initially those visits were brief, but soon enough most of the visitors saw that, although they were from different backgrounds, they had much in common with the Macabis. Before long Roni found himself with a whole new group of friends, all of them *chareidim*.

Dorit could not fathom how Mr. Kornkraut found the time to be so intensely involved in all aspects of Roni's medical treatment. One day she told him, "You know you have a large family to support — you ought to go to work! All day long you're here taking care of my husband and other patients; you need to support your family." She had no idea that this man dedicated himself solely to helping sick people with their needs.

A whole new world was opening up to them, little by little. Although the circumstances that had caused this to happen were ever so tragic, so much positive energy was resulting from them.

◆ ◆ ◆

Roni was to be released from the hospital soon, and Sammy realized that Roni would have to remain in England for several weeks for treatment. He knew that the Macabis would have nowhere to stay. Mrs. Homburger contacted her close friends and neighbors, the Berisch family, and arranged for the Macabis to stay at their home upon their release from the hospital.

Overwhelmed by the Berisch's kind offer, the Macabis accepted gratefully. Although they had never in their lives experienced a real Shabbos, the Macabis would now be exposed to a Shabbos they would never forget. *Chareidim* just didn't seem so frightening anymore.

The Homburgers invited the Macabis to enjoy the Friday night *seudah* at their home. There the Macabis saw a family that radiated respect, warmth, and love. The children were polite but friendly, and the atmosphere was nothing less than inspiring. The table, covered with a bright-white tablecloth, was beautifully set, and the food was delicious. Dorit offered to help serve, but everything had been prepared in advance, so there was nothing for her to do but sit back and enjoy the *seudah*.

Sammy discussed the *parashah*, and all the children offered *divrei Torah* of their own. Roni and Dorit were greatly impressed, but what happened at the end of the meal, when it was already quite late, really shocked them. Pinchas, one of the Homburger's sons, rose to leave. "What?" Dorit asked in surprise. "The '*dosim*' [a slang Israeli term for Ashkenazic *chareidim*] spend Friday nights out on the town?"

"No," they were quick to tell her, Pinchas was on his way back to the *beis medrash* to learn Torah.

"To learn Torah? In his spare time, of his own free will? And he's actually happy to do so?"

After the *seudah*, when the Macabis were preparing to return to the Berisches, Dorit wanted to carry her bag but was told that she could not, since there was no *eiruv*. "That's okay," she said, not really understanding what an *eiruv* is. "It's a law for English people, but for us it's permitted; we in Israel can carry on Shabbos. We don't need the *eiruv*!"

That night Dorit slept so well that she wanted to phone Israel to tell her father that she felt as though she were in prewar Poland; but then she realized that in this house she couldn't use the phone on Shabbos.

By Motza'ei Shabbos the Macabis felt, for the first time in their lives, a real feeling of *achdus*, of being connected with all Jews. They began to recognize that not only do their differences not separate them, they actually unite them.

Before the Macabis returned to Israel, Sammy and Elisheva Homburger visited them to say good-bye. Sammy gave Roni a parting gift of the *sefer Shemiras Shabbos Kehilchasah*, authored by Harav Yehoshua Neuwirth, *shlita*. He also arranged for a friend in Israel to learn privately with Roni once a week. The arrangement continued for years.

Back in Israel, Roni started going to shul on Shabbos; Dorit was nervous — was he on his way to becoming *frum*, and if so, where would that lead them?

When Roni began learning about the mitzvah of *netilas yadayim*, the Macabis were in the process of building a new house. Roni asked the architect to make sure to include a *netilas yadayim* sink outside the bathrooms. When the architect explained that the current plans allowed no room for such a sink, Roni had him change all the plans to fit in the sink!

On one occasion some family friends invited the Macabis for a Friday-night barbecue. In the past they would have accepted the invitation happily, but this time Roni would not go; Shabbos meant too much to him. It wasn't long before they were inviting friends to their home for Shabbos, and within a short while Roni was telling his guests that if they came for Shabbos they could not drive back home; their only option was to spend the night and be their guests for the entire Shabbos.

In the year 5770 (2009) Roni passed away in his sleep. At his funeral Dorit stressed that Roni had merited to become religious before he passed away. Although the rest of the family was not fully religious, they kept Shabbos and kashrus; and, Dorit explained, they had gained so much.

Ever since the Macabis had experienced such a warm, friendly Shabbos in London, Roni wanted to create that same sort of atmosphere in his own home. Shabbos and Yom Tov with the Macabis became a special experience; week after week many guests would pile in and stay for the weekend. This ensured that Dorit and her family would always be surrounded by good friends even after Roni was gone. When the week of *shivah* was over, Dorit said, "If not for the Shabbos experience in our home we would be so alone. Look what we've gained from this!"

It all began in a London hospital with a warm smile on a miserable winter day. All it took was a smile of greeting from a total stranger, a British *chareidi*, to a secular Israeli, to change the course of an entire family's life.

TEAR-STAINED PAGES

Tzipy Caton

The smallest gift bourgeons into something truly amazing.

My kitchen was a mess. Pots and pans were littering the stove, cut-up vegetables were in piles on my countertops, and a light dusting of flour was everywhere. I was happily humming off-key, hoping that my husband was sufficiently immersed, as I was, in the bubble of *shanah rishonah* and wouldn't mind very much eating his lunch in this pre-Shabbos wreck.

Nothing could bring down my mood as I determinedly made *kugels* and braided *challahs* in my tiny apartment. A song that I had loved last year in seminary was playing loudly, and I had to make a serious effort not to use a spoon as a makeshift microphone, in case my husband decided to walk in at that moment and see me in all my immaturity.

When the phone rang I almost dropped my pan of *kugel* batter. I quickly closed the oven door, wiped my hands, and tried frantically to remember where I had left the cordless. Triumphantly unearthing it from beneath a load of dirty dishtowels, I glanced at the caller ID and pressed "*Talk.*" And the world stopped.

HOLT, BRIAN. It had been almost two years since I had seen that name on the incoming calls list. But I still knew it.

"Hindy?" said a woman's voice. "Is that you?"

I could barely respond. My heart had stopped beating as soon as I saw that number.

"Who is this?"

"It's Megan. Remember me?"

I forced myself to sound natural. "Megan! Of course! How are you?"

I could picture her face as she said something in reply. I was sure it hadn't changed much since the day I met her, almost four years earlier.

She wasn't tall, but she was intimidating. She was only two or three years older than I was but seemed more mature. It may have been the makeup, or the cool sophistication of her tight jeans and expensive sweater, but I think it was just a natural confidence that seemed to announce to the world that Megan Holt was untouchable. She was just so much better than everyone else around her.

She *was*, literally, much better than anyone else around her. Everyone else with us in the ward at the time was sick. I was there to start chemotherapy; she was there with her sister Riley.

Riley and I hit it off right away. It was her smile that got to me first. In that dreary hospital where all I saw were bald kids and intravenous lines, Riley's bright, welcoming grin called to me from across the room, and I agreed to sit near her when she invited me over with a wave.

She was my age, in her junior year of high school, even though she looked a lot younger. She assured me that once my hair started falling out and after I lost as much weight as she did, I'd look like I was in fifth grade too.

It was the last thing I wanted to hear when I was already so scared and nervous, but the way she said it, with a grin that took over her entire face, made me giggle. We laughed together until we cried, and then she hugged me and held my hand — the hand of a perfect stranger — while the nurse came to insert the line that would give me my very first dose of chemo.

●●●

"You're Jewish," Riley said two hours after we met. It wasn't a question, it was a statement. "I'm Jewish too, but not like you are."

I didn't know what to say, so I kept quiet, trusting that Riley's talkative energy would fill in the blanks that my silences left. I was already feeling nauseous from my treatments, but Riley seemed fine with hers and kept up a steady stream of questions and comments.

"My parents are Jewish, so I know I'm Jewish, but we don't do all the things you do. My parents say that not all of it is necessary for G-d to consider you Jewish, but I'm curious, you know? 'Cause there must be a reason you guys are doing all this stuff, and I always wonder why. 'Cause if you could be Jewish enough and still wear pants and whatever, why would you be wearing skirts?"

Her constant chatter was distracting, and that first day I was grateful for it. It kept me from thinking too much about myself. Her questions about *Yiddishkeit* were simple enough at first, and later, when they became harder, I would beg off to rest. Chemo was catching up with me.

She helped me pull the curtain around my station, and, left alone, I finally let my tears fall, soaking my face and dripping back into my hair, the hair I knew was going to fall out, the hair that would be only a memory to me in just a few weeks. Soon enough I would look like her, another greenish, bald head in the infusion room.

I was facing the almost-certainty of my own death, and yet losing my hair was what I cried about on that first day of chemo. The irony of it all…

"Riley, you're annoying." That must have been her sister, I thought — the older, intimidating girl who had been listening silently to our conversation. "She's not interested in you and your questions. And she's different from us. She has no life. You'll get well and party every night. When *she* gets out of here, it's to get married before she's legally allowed to drink, and then to have ten kids before we even graduate college."

"You're so mean, Megan." Riley said, but I could tell it was still with a smile in her voice. "She's nice, and she's lonely. And I really am interested in all that stuff. I think it's cool that they do whatever they believe in, even when you think they're crazy."

Megan replied, but I had stopped listening. Her voice was so similar to Riley's that after a while I lost track of who was saying what, and I dozed off.

●●●

And now that voice, like a blast from the past, was talking in my ear. It ached how much it reminded me of her sister's, but it also amused me to hear that the sarcasm had never left her tone, even when, as now, she wasn't trying to be condescending.

"Congrats, by the way," Megan was saying. She still had this offhanded way of speaking that made everything sound like it was a passing thought to her. "I know you got married a few months ago. We got the wedding invitation."

I knew they did. Her mother had come.

"So, no avoiding it anymore — you're wearing a *sheitel* for real now, huh?"

I laughed in spite of myself.

Of all the things that worried me most about chemo, losing my hair won hands down. My hair equaled my popularity and status in school. Losing it would destroy me. And yet Riley cheerfully reminded me each time I saw her that it was only a few days away. She was wrong. I never did lose my hair. Not everyone did. It was rare, but I was one of the lucky ones. Oh, it got thinner, and I cut it shorter, but I never went completely bald.

Riley did. She lost her hair very early on. Way before I was even diagnosed or exposed to the world of cancer and chemotherapy.

But Riley never wore a wig. Her spunk wouldn't allow it. Occasionally she would wear colorful bandannas that matched her T-shirts, but more often than not she would flaunt her head in all its bald glory. She jokingly claimed she liked the feel of the breeze in her nonexistent hair.

But she tried to convince me to get a *sheitel*. "Even if you don't lose your hair now, you'll have to cover your hair once you get married anyway, so you might as well get an early start."

Neither one of us ever wanted to talk seriously about the fact that we might never live long enough or be well enough to get married. So we joked. Once, when Riley tried on my mother's *sheitel* for fun, it struck me, as the face of that natural blonde peeked out from my mother's ash-black bangs, that she had once been a healthy, pretty, girl. Maybe even more beautiful than Megan.

"Ooh Hindy! You're going to get like ten different wigs and change your look like every day! You'll just plunk it on your head and... voila!" Riley said, with a dramatic sweep of her hand that almost sent the *sheitel* flying. "Lucky you!"

Megan scoffed at her sister and flipped her thick blond hair over her shoulder. "I would *so* not consider being religious if I had to cover this."

I explained carefully the theory behind married women covering their hair, but Megan only rolled her eyes and left the room.

"Ignore her," Riley said with a sad smile. "She'll come around on her own. But seriously, you should get a *sheitel* now, just for fun. You *know* you'll use it later."

She liked to talk that way about the future, tried to bring it up whenever she could, even though we both knew there was hardly a chance that either of us would have one. At the time of my diagnosis we learned that my case was practically hopeless. There was only a small chance that I would survive the school year. And from what I learned over the first few weeks of chemo, Riley's chances, while somewhat better than mine, were definitely not good.

But that didn't stop her from planning. She was determined to make it as far as she could and live whatever life she had left to the fullest.

◆◆◆

"… and I was going through her room, and I found some things that I thought you might want to have…," Megan was saying. I was listening, but with only half an ear.

I remembered that room, a small one with a sloping ceiling, right under the roof of her house. I recalled the room's transition, from the day I met her until the last time I saw it, during her *shivah*.

Her old posters were replaced with collages of pictures of the two of us. We documented almost every chemo session and every day that we spent together outside of the hospital. There were pictures of us in Disney World and at concerts, and in baggy sweatshirts that used to fit us perfectly before we went on what we called our "Chemo Weight-Loss Program."

There were her shelves, one full of makeup and perfumes, and the one underneath it piled with orange prescription bottles. There was a box of old paperbacks that she had been meaning to give away for a while, and a shelf of some of my favorite Jewish novels. She helped me decipher Charles Dickens for school, and I introduced her to my favorite reads.

I considered asking Megan if the corkboard with all her hospital paraphernalia tacked onto it was still there. She had an impressive collection of bracelets, business cards, deflated balloons, and notes from well-wishers.

The last time I was there, her closet held only the clothes we had shopped for together. We both needed smaller stuff, and Riley chose to buy only skirts and long-sleeved tops with me. When I last visited her in her room I was shocked to find all her old clothing in boxes labeled to go to the Salvation Army. I hadn't known how committed she had been to really changing her way of dress.

"Hindy? You there?" Megan asked, annoyed. I had spaced out again.

"Yeah, Megan. I'm sorry." I blushed deeply. She still intimidated me.

"I was just saying that I found her *siddur* — you know, the one you gave her?"

Of course I knew. How could I forget?

I had spent at least half an hour debating whether to buy it or not. It was a dark-brown ArtScroll *siddur* with English translation. I didn't even know if Riley knew how to read Hebrew, but something kept telling me she'd appreciate it.

And so I bought it in the end, and I wrote her a note on the inside cover.

It took ages for me to actually give it to her. I picked a day when her mother was with her for treatments and Megan wasn't around. Most of what I was afraid of was what Megan's reaction to my gift would be.

Riley loved it and immediately insisted that I teach her to read. We spent mornings on *kriah*, and afternoons we took turns being sick. Riley caught on fast and admitted that she was practicing a lot at home. It wasn't long before she and I were having intense discussions on the meanings of the words she learned to daven every day, and it was shortly after that I noticed she actually cried when she read some of the *tefillos* slowly.

I was shocked that someone as new to davening as she was could feel so strongly about the words, and I was jealous that after being *frum* my whole life, my prayers weren't infused with half the meaning hers were.

Later, when the chemo made things so bad that Riley wasn't able to focus well enough to read from her *siddur* anymore, I would daven out loud near her, and she would still cry and raise a finger, begging me silently to pause for a minute so that she could communicate with Hashem in her mind.

"That *siddur* was very special to her," I told Megan, trying not to let the tears come into my voice. "Be careful with it."

"Yes, I know. I remember," Riley's older sister whispered. "Do you think it's bad if I keep it? Even though I'm not, you know, religious like she was? Do you think G-d would mind?"

I wiped my eyes with a floury hand and assured her that it was fine.

"There are things I really wanted to talk to you about," Megan said slowly, after an unusually long pause. "There were some questions I had…," she trailed off.

I pulled out a kitchen chair and sat down slowly. "Ask away, Megan."

"I know that it's before Shabbos for you, so if it's not a good time, just let me know."

Megan was familiar with Shabbos. She spent many weekends with Riley and me, missing parties with her friends, listening as we sang *zemiros* quietly and watching as we got blood transfusions while eating gefilte fish that my mother snuck into the ward.

There was one time, when Riley already knew she was dying — she couldn't talk much anymore so I was singing for both of us — when Megan, who was normally quiet at times like this, interrupted me, sobbing.

"You're insane! Both of you! Neither of you is ever going to make it to be my age! You'll never go to parties or graduate high school or be old enough to wear heels, and this is what you're going to spend your last days on? You're on a feeding tube, Riley, and all you want to eat is *challah*?"

Then she turned on me. "I hate you, Hindy, you know that? My sister is dying, and you're encouraging her with all this stuff that we don't care about. She should be doing normal things now. She's dying!"

Megan stopped talking and cried, her usually composed face dissolving in a mess of runny mascara and smudged eyeliner.

Riley, with her blue eyes wide open, struggled to sit up in bed and took her sister's hand.

"Megan," she whispered, her whole body straining with the effort, "my body is dying, but I'm living now. This," she said, pointing to our makeshift Shabbos table, "is living for me. I lived like everyone else, but I want to die Jewish, okay?"

"You *are* Jewish, Riley!"

Riley leaned back and closed her eyes. "I want to die Jewish and *frum*."

And then the tears began to roll down her cheeks, and she seemed too tired to even wipe them away. "No, I'm lying." She hiccupped. "I don't want to die at all. I want to be *frum*, but I don't want to die."

She held her other hand out to me, and the three of us cried for the rest of that Shabbos afternoon.

She told me later, after Megan had gone and her mother came for the night shift, that *Yiddishkeit* was her own personal journey and that she was sure one day Megan would see what she saw in it. She was confident that her parents were already becoming more *frum*, and that one day they were going to move to my neighborhood and we were going to be next-door neighbors, and we'd both marry boys who learned in the same *shiur*.

"What do you see in being *frum*?" I asked. I needed to know. Here we were, two girls dying in the pediatric oncology ward, and I needed to know what kept her so strong.

Riley opened her eyes and, with effort, focused her gaze directly on me. "In *Yiddishkeit*, I see…you. And that's all I want. I want to be like you."

I noticed the tears pooling on the kitchen table before I realized I was crying. "It's fine, Megan. I have time to talk now if you want. I'm not especially busy."

It was too late anyway. There was no possible way I could clean up the mess growing on my counters before my husband came home from *kollel* for lunch.

"Anything specific you wanted to ask?"

Megan took a deep breath, "There's lots, but I'm nervous, because I don't want you to laugh if they're silly questions or anything."

"I won't," I promised.

"I'm holding that *siddur* you gave her, and I thought maybe you would know why some pages look like they got wet. Because she was always so careful with her books and stuff, and I know this was important to her and she would never let it get ruined."

I took a deep breath. "Megan, it's hard to explain, but those are pages where Riley cried. She felt those prayers were very meaningful to her, and she used to cry when she said them."

"Oh." There was a long pause, and I was almost sure Megan had hung up.

"Hindy?"

"Yes?"

"Can you tell me what some of those prayers mean?"

"There's a translation on the side," I offered.

"I know that," Megan said quietly. "I meant if you could explain what those prayers meant to her."

My lip quivered as I recalled how she used to cry when she davened for Yerushalayim. Even though we didn't know if I was ever going to be well enough to finish school, I was already applying for seminary in Eretz Yisrael. Riley used to cry knowing she would never visit the holy sites we spoke about in our almost two years together. She wanted the *geulah* more than anyone else I knew. She davened for her own personal *tza'ar* and begged for Moshiach so that she could experience all the beauty of a world and a life she had never known.

I explained all this to her sister.

Shortly after Riley was *niftar* I recovered. It seemed so twisted, that as things were at their worst for my best friend, they only got better for me. She was taken to Eretz Yisrael to be buried, and I was flown there with all of my friends, for the year and experience of our lives.

"You know, I'm sorry about everything," Megan was saying, and I could tell she was finding it hard to talk through her own emotions. "I thought I hated you once, but I think I was just jealous.

"Riley was my little sister and I loved her. I was jealous that she seemed to love you and your way of life more than she loved me. It's been bothering me for years now. I need to know what it is that she saw, and I want to live the kind of life she lived.

"It's so rude of me to do this to you, but please, Hindy, you're the only one I can ask…"

I took a deep breath and wiped my eyes yet again. Riley had been right. Her mother was covering her hair today and her father was learning with mine as a *chavrusa* a few nights a week. Now it was Megan's turn.

I could hear my husband turning his key in the lock. I stood up, determined that he should not see me so torn, and put all the emotions I had raging inside of me into my next words.

"You know what, Meg? How about if you come for Shabbos?"

6

FROM OUR GEDOLIM

Excerpted and adapted, with permission, from Sefer Shalom Rav by Harav Shiloh Ben David

THIRTY DAYS TO DIVORCE

The couple came to *beis din* just a year after their marriage, seeking to arrange a *get*. The *dayanim* asked them a series of questions, concluded that they were serious in their intentions, and then set a date to meet with them again several weeks later.

One of the *dayanim*, Rabbi Refael Levin, son of the *tzaddik* Rav Aryeh Levin, was extremely perturbed by the fact that these two intelligent, sincere people wished to separate and break up a Jewish home. He decided to make his own attempt to patch up their relationship. He stopped the couple as they were leaving the courtroom and asked them to meet him in his home that evening to discuss their issues.

When they arrived, Rabbi Levin asked the couple why they felt they were unable to live in peace together. They replied that although they did not argue or squabble, they seemed to have no common bond. Each of them had different interests and neither was capable of sharing in the other's problems or achievements. Having spent many months in these circumstances, they realized that their marriage was making them both depressed, and they agreed that the best thing for them would be to separate.

Rabbi Levin thought about this for a short time and he came up with a strategy. He suggested that one of them try adding a name. Sometimes, he explained, a person's entire situation can change as a result of assuming a new name. He urged them to try it out for a while to see if it could make a difference for them. They agreed, figuring that even if it would not help, at least it couldn't hurt. They asked the rabbi to choose which of them should have a name added, and he chose the young wife.

Then he addressed the husband, explaining that his brother-in-law, Rabbi Yosef Shalom Elyashiv, is of the opinion that in order for a name-change to be effective it has to be used actively for at least thirty days. In order to accomplish this, Rabbi Levin suggested that the man greet his wife by name every time he enters the house for the next thirty days. In that way they would be giving the new name the maximum opportunity to have effect.

After a couple of weeks the couple returned to Rabbi Levin's home, all smiles. They had followed his instructions, they told him, and their relationship had improved 100 percent, just as he had hoped. The husband's simple act of greeting his wife and wishing her a good morning and a good afternoon day after day had opened up channels of communication between them. They were growing closer and bonding with each other more strongly every day, and they no longer had any interest in pursuing a divorce.

Rabbi Levin was overjoyed with the wonderful results of his approach and thrilled that he had the merit of having saved this beautiful marriage.

ONE GREETING FOR 5,000 SOULS

Yaakov was born to *chareidi* German parents when the Reform movement was in its heyday. His father invested everything in raising Yaakov to be a *ye'rei Shamayim*, but he passed away when the boy was still quite young. Then, bit by bit, the winds of the Enlightenment began to wear away at the youngster until he reached the point that he had very little to do with Torah and mitzvos.

One morning Yaakov awoke with a gnawing suspicion that he had something to do. He grappled with his feelings until he remembered that it was his father's *yahrtzeit*. Before he passed away, his father had extracted a promise from Yaakov that he would never fail to recite *Kaddish* for him on his *yahrtzeit*. Yaakov kept trying to suppress his feelings of guilt and to ignore this calling, but in the end he gave in to his conscience and went out in search of a shul.

Since moving to the city of Wurtzburg, Yaakov had never visited a shul. He didn't even know where to find one. And so he stepped out into the street and began walking, reading the signs, looking at the buildings, and asking passersby for information.

Over an hour after he had left his home he found himself at the entrance of an imposing shul, and he began to have second thoughts. *What will people think of me — a young man who has obviously left his Torah life behind? Surely they will all realize that I have come only to recite Kaddish for my father.*

Yaakov entered stealthily and breathed a sigh of relief when he saw that the congregation was already in the middle of *Minchah* and no one could engage him in conversation. He waited patiently until the end of *Minchah*, then recited a loud, clear *Kaddish*; he tried to make a quick getaway before anyone could ask him any questions.

He almost made it out, until he found his way blocked by an imposing rabbinical figure. "*Shalom aleichem!*" said the rabbi. "My name is Yitzchak Dov Halevi Bamberger, and I am rabbi of this city. Tell me, how are you doing? Are you new in the city? Do you have a job? You know, I really respect you — so many youths just like you have cast away their Judaism, but you have maintained your connection to it. It's really wonderful to see someone like you here in town!"

Yaakov stood immobilized by the sudden friendly attention he was receiving. Any response he might have given was stuck in his throat. His eyes became watery and his vision was blurred. He tried to hold back the tears, but they poured forth suddenly in a torrent, washing away any feelings of antagonism he may have felt toward the shul and the people it served.

When Yaakov stepped out of the shul that afternoon his soul was on fire. It was not long before he was back on track as a fully observant Jew. Two years later, Yaakov stood under the *chuppah* with a devout young lady from a prominent *chareidi* family. Together they chose to build a household of Torah and *yiras Shamayim*.

Yaakov and his wife bore and raised thirteen children, all of whom followed in their footsteps. Today, over 150 years after that *Kaddish*, Yaakov's descendants number over 5,000. All of them are fully observant, and many of them are outstanding *talmidei chachamim*.

One of these descendants, reflecting on his ancestry, commented, "Imagine if Rabbi Bamberger had decided to ignore the young man who showed up that day to recite *Kaddish*. What would have become of him, and where would his descendants be today? Imagine what kind of greeting Rabbi Bamberger would have received in Heaven after his passing. There would have been 5,000 souls accusing him, 'Why didn't you save us? All that would have been necessary were a few words and a smile.'"

TURN RIGHT FOR LIFE

Rav Shmuel Shapira, the *rav* of Prochnik, Poland, in the years before World War II, was in the habit of taking long walks in the forests near his town. Rav Shapira was known for his pleasant demeanor and benevolent disposition. As he walked he gave a warm greeting to everyone he passed, Jew or non-Jew. Every morning as he passed by the farm just outside the city, he would greet its owner: "Good morning, Mr. Mueller." At first the man ignored the rabbi and looked away, but in time, as Rav Shapira greeted him consistently in a friendly manner, the man began to nod his head in recognition. Eventually Mr. Mueller began to tip his cap in response to the rabbi's greeting, and the edges of his mouth would turn up in a wan smile.

All this came to an abrupt stop with the Nazis' lightning-fast blitzkrieg-conquest of Poland. The Jewish residents of the township, including Rav Shapira and his family, were shipped off to concentration camps. Rav Shapira was transferred from one labor camp to another until he was brought to his "final destination" — Auschwitz. He stumbled out of the cattle-car and stood in line for the selection. As the line moved forward he became filled with apprehension — he had a pretty good idea of what the selection meant. Judging by those he saw being sent to each side, he realized that anyone who was sent to the left would be taken immediately to the gas chambers.

There were two people in line in front of Rav Shapira; then there was one; then he stood face-to-face with the officer in whose hands his fate lay. He glanced up at the man's face and their eyes met. Suddenly, Rav Shapira took a step forward and said quietly, "Good morning, Mr. Mueller."

The officer's steely-cold eyes opened wide for a split second. Then he said, "Good morning, rabbi," and waved him to the right.

Rav Shapira survived the war to tell the story.

ONCE-IN-A-LIFETIME OPPORTUNITY

The Alter of Slabodka, Harav Nosson Tzvi Finkel, displayed a special affinity for beggars, especially those who were deformed or whose appearance caused anyone else to avoid contact with them. He always made sure to greet them with a huge smile, and he would offer them his assistance while encouraging them and giving them a few minutes of his full attention.

Harav Avraham Noach Paley was one of the Alter's leading disciples. He related a conversation he had had with his mentor on the eve of a trip he was about to make to see his family.

Rav Nosson Tzvi said, "Tell me, what will you do when you first enter your home and your family members are rushing over to you to embrace you and tell you all about what has happened in your absence — and suddenly a ragged, dirty, repulsive beggar knocks at your front door?"

Without waiting for a reply the Alter continued, "Of course, you will be upset that this fellow has come to disturb you at this time, marring the atmosphere and the high emotions of the family reunion. Nevertheless, you will not hesitate to take a fair sum from your pocket and give it to him, hoping that he will go away and allow you to turn back to your family.

"But that is not what the halachah demands of you. The *pasuk* says, 'Bring the destitute into your home,' and *Chazal* taught us in *Pirkei Avos*, 'Poor people should be your household members.' Even at a moment when you would rather be alone with your own family, this is still your obligation. You must treat these unfortunate individuals as members of your own household. You must greet them with genuine joy. In fact, you must show them greater love and concern than you would your own family. After all, with Hashem's help you will have plenty of opportunities to interact with your family, but who knows if you will ever have another chance to meet this beggar and help him out."

Rav Paley asserted that the Alter practiced what he preached.

SIX SMILES

Harav Eliyahu Baruch Kamai, Chief Rabbi of the city of Mir, told the following story about his close colleague, Harav Yitzchak Elchanan Spector of Kovno:

Being that Kovno was part of the Russian empire, every young man who resided there was required to serve in the Russian army. For Jewish men this service was fraught with danger for both their physical and spiritual well-being. It was nearly impossible to observe even the most basic mitzvos while in the army. Thus, every yeshivah student did his utmost to gain an exemption from service.

Yaakov was one of Rav Yitzchak Elchanan's favorite students. When he and his friends received their draft notices, they, along with their teachers, waited with bated breath to find out whether their requests for exemptions were accepted.

A couple of weeks later Rav Yitzchak Elchanan was sitting with his *beis din*, which included Rav Eliyahu Baruch, when two prominent businessmen came for arbitration regarding a dispute involving a fabulous sum. Each one presented a strong argument for his position, and the atmosphere in the room was very tense.

Suddenly the door was thrown open, and a teenaged yeshivah student came running up to Rav Yitzchak Elchanan. "Rebbi," he exclaimed, "we just found out that Yaakov's draft exemption was granted."

The rabbi's face broke into a wide smile. "May Hashem reward you well for giving me this wonderful news," he replied, adding numerous blessings for the youth. The student then left, thrilled that he had been able to bring joy to his rebbi.

A few minutes later the door again swung open and another student came in announcing, "Rebbi, we just found out that Yaakov is exempt from army service."

Rav Yitzchak Elchanan reacted to this student exactly as he had to the one who preceded him. He thanked him profusely, and the young man left thinking about the great merit he had to be the "one" to bring the good news to his rebbi.

Barely five minutes passed when another student came in. "Has the rebbi heard? Yaakov has received his exemption."

For the third time, Rav Yitzchak Elchanan broke into the widest of smiles. He thanked the student for coming and gave him warm blessings.

This scene repeated itself no less than six times that afternoon. Rav Yitzchak Elchanan did not give even the slightest hint to any of the students that he had already heard the good news. Each time he interrupted the serious business at hand in order to give warm, profuse thanks and blessings to the student who had come to bring him the news. Each time, he reacted as if he had not yet heard the news, so every student who came would think that he was actually the first to inform him.

REMEMBERING WHEN OTHERS HAVE FORGOTTEN

Every Friday evening after davening, Chacham Salman Musaffi would go to the home of an elderly, bedridden *rav*. He greeted him and sat with him for an extended period, telling him *divrei Torah*, catching him up on what was going on in the community, and asking his advice on a number of matters. This went on for many months — on late summer Friday nights, on cold winter Friday nights, and even on Yom Tov nights.

Someone once pointed out to him that every week his family was left waiting to eat their Shabbos meal with him. The person suggested that Chacham Salman change his schedule and make his visits on Saturday nights instead.

Chacham Salman refused, explaining that the *rav* he was visiting had once been a prominent, well-respected individual. "He certainly remembers," he pointed out, "how scores of people used to line up to wish him *Shabbat shalom* every Friday evening, and how he was escorted from the synagogue to his home by a crowd of admirers who drank in every word he spoke. Now, he probably feels like a worthless castaway. I am afraid that he might become depressed because it is Shabbos and no one cares to visit. I am convinced, in light of this, that it is worth it for me and my family to suffer a bit of discomfort in order to see to it that this venerable scholar has a joyful Shabbos."

THIS IS HOW TO GREET A JEW

After World War II, Harav Shraga Feivel Gibraltar was appointed by the Joint [American Jewish Joint Distribution Committee] as a rabbi in southern Italy, and later in northern Italy. In 1948 he visited Eretz Yisrael to investigate the possibility of immigrating.

One day, as he was walking with his son along Zevulun Street in Tel Aviv, a porter passed them. Suddenly, the man set down his heavy load and came running back, calling, "*Shalom aleichem*, Harav Shraga!"

This porter's clothes exuded a strong stench from the salted herring that he carried around all day. Rav Gibraltar, his son knew, was particularly sensitive to such unpleasant odors and avoided them completely, feeling great revulsion. His son was surprised, therefore, to see Rav Gibraltar grasp the porter's outstretched hand enthusiastically and embrace him warmly. The *rav* then began asking him how he was doing and where he was living now that he had moved to Eretz Yisrael.

The man explained that he was working as a porter in the open market. The Immigration Ministry had given him a tent for his family in Yaffo, and since then a baby boy had been born to him. He summed it up by saying that he was content with his lot, as he was not in need of any outside assistance. Rav Gibraltar then accompanied him back to where he had set down his load and blessed him with further success.

After the man left, Rav Gibraltar's son asked his father who the man was. The *rav* replied that he had no idea. "Why, then," his son wondered, "did you act as if he were one of your closest friends?"

"Well," his father answered, "that is how every Jew should be greeted."

DISCOVERING THE GEM AMONG THE RUBBLE

Harav Yisrael Meir HaKohen, author of *sefer Chofetz Chaim*, wandered from town to town to sell his *sefarim*. While making a stop at an inn in Vilna he could not help but notice a huge monster of a man, unkempt and bareheaded, sitting at a table and barking orders at the waitress to bring him a roasted chicken and a pint of vodka, and to bring them quick. Duly served, he set his hands and teeth into the chicken without reciting a *berachah*. Guzzling down the vodka, he hurled a stream of insults and curses at the waitress. Shocked and horrified by the man's behavior, Rav Yisrael Meir decided to speak to him and try to influence him to control himself and act more humanely.

As Rav Yisrael Meir rose and turned toward the man, the innkeeper ran over and blocked his way. "Please stay away from this person, rabbi," he pleaded. "He is a Cantonist, kidnaped from his mother when he was only 7 years old and forced to serve the czar for thirty years in an atmosphere totally devoid of Judaism. He returned bitter, totally uneducated and with nothing but two iron-hard hands, which he wields against anyone who dares challenge his behavior. I am afraid the rabbi is liable to be harmed if he attempts to rebuke him."

Rav Yisrael Meir simply smiled and said, "I know how to deal with a Jew like this. Don't worry about a thing. I'm sure it will turn out just fine."

He walked over to the man, greeted him warmly and asked if he could join him. Seated, he looked up into the man's eyes and said, "You know, I heard that you were kidnaped as a child and forced to serve for thirty years in the czar's army. I was told that you were never given the opportunity to study Torah. You must have been persecuted constantly because you are Jewish. I find it hard to imagine — thirty years of Siberia, of whippings, of hunger, of taunts and danger. They surely forced you to eat pork and to work on Shabbos and even on Yom Kippur.

"But despite all that, you came back home. You didn't give in and convert to another religion. You remained a faithful Jew! How I wish that I had your merits, that I would be able to have a place like yours in the World to Come. Surely your place is among the greatest *tzaddikim* of our history. How many people who ever lived would be able to withstand thirty years of suffering as you did and yet retain their Jewish identity? Why, your trials far surpass that of Chananyah, Mishael and Azaryah!"

All the while the Cantonist stared at him impassively. Suddenly, tears welled up in his eyes as the warm words penetrated his scarred skin and softened the stone that had been his heart. He looked up and asked the innkeeper who this rabbi was.

"This is the Chofetz Chaim," was the reply. Upon hearing this, he burst out crying. He grabbed Rav Yisrael Meir and kissed him repeatedly.

Rav Yisrael Meir continued his speech, saying, "A person like you, who is held in such esteem in Heaven, would be the most fortunate person on earth if you would only begin to observe the mitzvos properly."

From that day on, the Cantonist refused to leave the Chofetz Chaim's presence until he had become a fully observant Jew with genuine *yiras Shamayim*.

A HEALING VISIT

Once, people saw Harav Chaim Chizkiyahu Medini, author of the encyclopedic work *Sdei Chemed*, rushing through the streets in the heat of the day. When they asked him where he was going, he responded that he wished to fulfill the mitzvah of *bikur cholim*, visiting the sick. They asked him who the sick person was, and he told them.

"But that person is known to commit serious *aveiros*," they protested. "He does not deserve a visit from the *rav*!"

"*Chazal* taught us that even a sinner is chock-full of mitzvos as a pomegranate is filled with seeds. Besides, I am going not only to visit this person but also to visit the *Shechinah* that is hovering over his bed."

The *rav* continued on his way, and the people who had questioned him now accompanied him. When they entered the sick man's room the man forced himself to sit up in honor of his esteemed visitor.

A number of days later the sick man was back on his feet and at his business, and from that day on he left his sinful ways.

A MATTER OF PRIORITIES

It was a Saturday evening, only a couple of weeks before he passed away, and Harav Yechezkel Sarna, Rosh Yeshivas Chevron, made his way to the yeshivah for *Maariv*. As he was very weak, the short walk took much longer than anyone had expected, and by the time he and his attendant reached the yeshivah building *Maariv* was almost over.

Nevertheless, Rav Yechezkel started climbing the steps, one by one, to get to the *beis medrash*. His attendant commented to him that he did not understand why he was pushing himself so hard, when davening would certainly be over by the time he arrived in the *beis medrash*.

Rav Yechezkel smiled and looked lovingly at his attendant. "Davening with the congregation is only a mitzvah *mi'd'rabbanan*," he replied, "and that is certainly the case regarding *Maariv*, since it is technically a voluntary prayer. But wishing each of the yeshivah students a *gut voch* is an expression of the important mitzvah of the Torah to love one's fellow Jew as oneself."

ABOUT THE CONTRIBUTORS

BARBARA BENSOUSSAN is a prolific writer for many newspapers and magazines, including *Hamodia* and *Mishpacha*. and the author of the book *A New Song*.

RABBI SHLOMO BORENSTEIN is a yeshivah rebbi and a teacher in a girls' seminary in Yerushalayim. He is an amazing fount of inspiration for the countless students he influences daily. And you can be sure that everyone cleans up at the Borenstein house, because, hey, you just never know!

TZIPI CATON, a talented newcomer on the Jewish writing scene, is the author of the best-selling *Miracle Ride,* in which she describes, with poignancy and humor, her battle against Hodgkin's disease.

CHAVA DUMAS lives in Yerushalayim with her husband and children. Her stories, interviews, and features have appeared in numerous Jewish publications, anthologies, and websites.

YAFFA GANZ is the award-winning author of more than forty books for Jewish children, including the beloved *Savta Simcha* series, the *Mimmy and Simmy* series, *Sand and Stars* — a Jewish history for teens, and many picture and informational books. She has also published several books for adult readers. The Ganzes have been living in Israel for the past forty years and are the grateful grandparents of a growing clan.

BRACHA GOETZ is the author of twelve children's books, including *Aliza in Mitzvahland, What Do You See at Home?* and *The Invisible Book*. To enjoy Bracha's presentations for both women and children, contact bgoetzster@gmail.com.

NANCY HOCHMAN is a certified elementary- and secondary-English teacher, a member of the creative writing staff at USDAN Center for the Performing Arts, and a frequently published journalist and essayist whose credits include *The New York Times, Newsday, Woman's World, Seventeen, Hadassah Magazine, B'nai B'rith Jewish Monthly, Na'amat Woman,* and many other national and regional publications.

GAVRIEL HORAN is a columnist for *Mishpacha* magazine. He writes with an insider's eye, capturing the essence of the conflicts that face all of us.

FAIGIE HOROWITZ, M.S., a veteran community advocate, has spent twenty years in social services management. She serves on several nonprofit boards and is a founder of Rachel's Place, a home for at-risk girls in Brooklyn. A member of the editorial advisory board of *Binah Magazine*, she has started a writing group in her new community of Lawrence, NY, where her husband is the rabbi of Congregation Heichal Dovid and a regular speaker at the Ohel Sarah Amen Group.

BATYA JACOBS is a wife, mum, writer, and narrative therapist who lives with her family in Eretz Yisrael.

HANNAH KAFREE is a writer living in Israel. Currently she is working on a book titled, *Challenged to Grow, the Nine Lives of Hannah Kafree*.

DOVID KANNER is a writer who grew up in Toronto. Today he is married, lives in Yerushalayim, and learns in Yeshivas Mir. His story took place when he was a *bachur* learning in Mir.

RABBI DAVID KAPLAN is the author of *The Kiruv Files*, *Impact!*, *Major Impact!* and a host of articles and books on the subject of Jewish education. A popular international speaker with a terrific sense of humor, he serves as both a rebbi and a *mashgiach*.

MIRISH KISZNER is a Jerusalem-based writer and the author of *Extraordinary Stories About Ordinary People* and *Dear Libby: Real kids raising real issues and Libby's sound advice*.

CHAYA KLEIN is the pen name of a woman who listens to, supports, and interviews people coping with illness and crisis.

RABBI SHMUEL YAAKOV KLEIN is a noted *mechanech*, author, columnist, and popular speaker. Currently he is director of publications and communications of Torah Umesorah, the National Society for Hebrew Day Schools.

RABBI YITZCHOK KORNBLAU is a beloved rebbi and the author of the *Wordwise Adventures of Yisrael and Meir* series for kids, released by the Chofetz Chaim Heritage Foundation and published by ArtScroll Mesorah, as well as a number of other books, which he produced in conjunction with artist Gadi Pollak.

CHANI MISHELL is a pseudonym. The writer grew up in New York and currently resides in Yerushalayim.

AREL MISHORY is a wife, mother and grandmother, an artist, Weight Watchers leader, assistant director of the Mizel Museum Artist Alliance, active in her Jewish community, and a certified life coach. Her husband always told her to write because she "tells stories in such a literary style," and this is her first effort.

SARA CHAVA MIZRAHI is a writer and editor. For a number of years she served as managing editor of *Hamodia Magazine*, and she is the editor of this anthology. She lives in Jerusalem with her family.

RABBI MENACHEM NISSEL is a rebbi and teacher in various yeshivos and seminaries in Yerushalayim. He is the author of many publications, including the highly acclaimed *Rigshei Lev — Women and Tefillah* (Targum / Feldheim 2001). He is a popular public speaker and is NCSY's Rabbinic Resource.

SARA YOHEVED RIGLER is the author of the best sellers *Holy Woman* and *Lights from Jerusalem*, as well as *Battle Plans: How to Fight the Yetzer Hara* (written in conjuction with Rebbetzin Tziporah Heller). She is a regular contributor to *Binah Magazine* and *aish.com*.

MIRIAM LEA ROSENBERG — she's the inspiration behind this book — is new on the writing scene. A grateful mother and grandmother, she is passionate about the concept of creating *shalom* in the world through our "giving *shalom*" and greeting one another.

RABBI YONOSON ROSENBLUM is a columnist for the *Jerusalem Post* and numerous Anglo-Jewish publications, as well as the author of the following biographies: *Reb Yaakov, Reb Chaim of Volozhin, Lieutenant Birnbaum, The Vilna Gaon, They Called Him Mike, Rav Dessler, Reb Shraga Feivel, Rabbi Sherer.*

ROSALLY SALTSMAN is originally from Montreal and now lives in Eretz Yisrael. She is the author of *Finding the Right Words, Parenting by the Book, Soul Journey,* and *A Portion of Kindness*; she has also edited the anthology *The Beauty of the Story.* She recently released a disc of original songs for women, entitled, *Like a Rose Among the Thorns.*

B. SCHREIBER is an English teacher who also enjoys copyediting and writing. Her articles and stories have appeared in *Hamodia Magazine, Mishpacha Junior, The Writer's Journal,* and other publications.

RABBI NACHMAN SELTZER is the author of eight books, including three novels (*The Edge, The Link,* and *The Network*), two memoirs (*Nine Out of Ten* and *Child of War*), and four books of short stories (*In The Blink of an Eye, Stories With a Twist, Moments,* and *It Could Have Been You*). He is a regular writer for *Hamodia Magazine*, and has worked diligently to ensure the success of this anthology.

SARAH SHAPIRO is the author of *Growing With My Children, Don't You Know It's a Perfect World, A Gift Passed Along,* and *Wish I Were Here*. She is also an editor, most recently, of *All of Our Lives: An Anthology of Contemporary Jewish Writing*. Her story, *All the Way Home*, is excerpted from an article that appeared on *aish.com*.

THE JEWISH WOMEN'S PROJECT FOR AHAVAS YISRAEL is an organization of thousands of women around the world who are gathering in small groups to create tremendous merits for *Klal Yisrael* through "stretching" in their mitzvah of *ahavas Yisrael*. To get started, contact Shuli Kleinman at connect@ayproject.com; (301) 237-7306.

SHERRY E. WALDMAN, a psychotherapist in private practice, lives and works in Far Rockaway, NY. Her focus is in helping people understand their pain and learn to live more fully in the wake of — sometimes because of — painful experiences. Says Sherry, "The death of my parents, the ways I learned to speak with them during their final illnesses and about them ever since, has deeply informed the way I practice my craft."

"YOSSI" lives in Israel with his wife and two children. He teaches Torah to many teens from all over the world. His first book, *Straightalk — About Being a Teen from a Teen,* was published while Yossi was serving in a combat unit in the IDF. His second book, *Straightalk —The Next Step,* was published more recently.

TOVA YOUNGER lived with her husband and children in Los Angeles for over twenty years, working in a broad spectrum of positions: candy distributor, teacher, and babysitter, to name a few. To their great joy, their first three children married and settled in Israel, and they decided to join them. There Tova became a freelance writer, while she and her husband continue to raise their family.

GLOSSARY

a"h — contraction of *alav hashalom* or *aleha hashalom*, meaning may he (or she) rest in peace

achdus — unity

ahavas Yisrael — love of fellow Jews

aleph-beis — the Hebrew alphabet; this is also a term for "the basics"

aufruf — celebration marking a *chassan's aliyah* to the Torah on the Shabbos before his wedding

aveirah (pl. *aveiros*) — sin

avodah — religious service

avodas Hashem — serving G-d

avreich (pl. *avreichim*) — member of a *kollel*

baal chessed (fem. form: *baalas chessed*) — a person who performs acts of kindness

baal korei — the person who reads the Torah for the congregation

baal simchah — the person who hosts (or is celebrating) a *simchah* occasion

baal teshuvah (fem. form: *baalas teshuvah*; pl. *baalei teshuvah*; fem. pl. *baalos teshuvah*) — someone who has dedicated him- or herself to a Torah lifestyle although he or she did not grow up religiously observant; the term also applies to a Jew who was a sinner and has since repented

bachur (pl. *bachurim*) — a male youth, usually referring to a yeshivah student

balebusteh — woman of the house; one who cares for the house well

baruch haba — "May the person who has arrived be blessed" — a greeting

baruch Hashem — thank G-d; literally — "may G-d be blessed"

baruch Rofei cholim — blessed is [G-d], the Healer of those who are ill

bas bayis — a regular (female) guest who comes to be considered almost part of the family

bas Yisrael (pl. *bnos Yisrael*) — a Jewish woman

bashert — destined from heaven

bein adam l'chaveiro — mitzvos that apply to the relationships between human beings (as opposed to mitzvos that apply between man and G-d)

beis din — a rabbinical court of Jewish law

Beis Hamikdash — the Holy Temple

beis medrash — study hall where people study Torah

ben bayis — a regular (male) guest who comes to be considered almost part of the family

ben Torah (pl. *bnei Torah*) — someone who acts according to Torah standards; someone engaged in full-time Torah study

berachah (pl. *berachos*) — blessing

b'simchah — happily

bikur cholim — the mitzvah of visiting the sick

birkas halevanah — the blessing recited over the waxing moon

bitachon — trust in G-d

blatt — one folio of of Talmud, consisting of two pages

blech — a metal plate covering a stovetop, on which food is kept warm for Shabbos

boker tov — good morning

chareidi — Orthodox Jew; one who is rigorously observant

chas v'shalom — G-d forbid

chashuveh — important

chassan — groom

chassidishe — chassidic

chasunah — wedding

chaver (pl. *chaveirim*) — friend

chavrusa — Torah-study partner

Chazal — our Sages

chazzan — cantor

chessed — act of kindness

chevra kadisha — a society that takes care of funeral arrangements

chinuch — proper Jewish education

chizuk — offering strength and encouragement

chol hamoed — the five or six days of the festivals of Pesach and Succos, following the first day

cholent — stew eaten on Shabbos day, traditionally made with meat, potatoes, and beans

chozer bit'shuvah — one who accepts upon himself or herself a Torah-observant life after having lived a different lifestyle

chuppah — a marriage canopy

dayan (pl. *dayanim*) — rabbinic judge

daven — to pray

der Tatte in Himmel — "the Father in Heaven" (Yiddish)

d'var Torah (pl. *divrei Torah*) — a Torah thought

ehrlich — honest; also used to refer to a devout person

ehrliche kinderlach — fine Jewish children

eidel — refined

eiruv — a halachic device used to enable carrying on Shabbos

erev — evening; or, the day before an occasion

frum — Torah observant

galus — exile; the Diaspora

gashmiyus — physical and/or materialistic matters

geneivas da'as — fooling someone for one's own gain

geshmak — delicious; charismatic; enjoyable

geulah — redemption (often used to refer to the ultimate redemption with the coming of Mashiach)

Gut Shabbos — a Shabbat greeting, spoken in Yiddish

G-t vet helfen — G-d will help

gut voch — a greeting given after Shabbat is over, blessing people with a good week

hachnassas orchim — hospitality

Hakadosh Baruch Hu — the Holy One, blessed is He

Hashem — G-d

hashkafos — one's outlook or philosophies on life

hartzig gut Shabbos — a heartfelt blessing of "Good Shabbos"

hashgachah — divine directing of events; watching over

hashgachah pratis — divine directing of events for every individual

hatzlachah — a blessing for success

Havdalah — ceremony marking the end of Shabbos

hesped — eulogy

hishtadlus — an effort one makes, usually toward a specific goal

Kabbalas Shabbos — the prayers recited on Friday nights as Shabbat begins

kallah — bride

kavannah — focused intent (in prayer)

kedushah — holiness

kehillah — congregation

kezayis — a portion the size of an olive

kiddush Hashem — sanctification of G-d's Name

kiddush levanah — a ceremony for sanctifying the waxing moon

kippah — yarmulke; head covering for Jewish males

kiruv — activities related to introducing Jews to a Torah way of life

Kitzur — short for *Kitzur Shulchan Aruch*

Kitzur Shulchan Aruch — abridged compendium of religious laws, authored by Rabbi Shlomo Ganzfried

Klal Yisrael — the Jewish nation

kollel — an institution for Torah study for men, most of whom are married

kriah — reading practice

Krias Shema — the recitation of the *Shema* prayers

kugel — a delicacy made of potatoes or noodles, traditionally prepared in honor of Shabbos

l'chaim — a toast, or a celebration of an engagement

leining — chanting the Torah reading

levayah — funeral

lo aleinu — expression meaning, "may it never happen to us"

Maariv — the evening prayers

machzor — a High Holiday prayer book

madrichah — female camp, dormitory, or guidance counselor

mashgiach — one whose job it is to ensure the kashrus of a product or establishment; also, a spiritual director/mentor in a yeshivah

mazal tov — congratulations; good luck

mechitzah — partition, often separating between men and women

mechutan (pl. *mechutanim*) — parent of one's child-in-law

Megillah — lit., scroll; term commonly applied to the Book of Esther

menaheles — female principal

a mentch tracht un G-t lacht — "man plans and G-d laughs" (Yiddish phrase)

meshulachim — messengers sent to raise funds for a charitable institution

mi'd'rabbanan — a rabbinically ordained law

middah (pl. *middos*) — character trait

midda k'neged middah — measure for measure

Minchah — the afternoon prayers

Mishnayos — passages from the Mishnah

mishpachah — family

mitzvah tantz — a series of symbolic dances with the bride at the end of a chassidic wedding

motza'ei Shabbos — Saturday evening, after Shabbos is over

Mussaf — additional prayer recited after *Shacharis* on Shabbos and Yom Tov

mussar — moral and/or ethical lesson

neshamah (pl. *neshamos*) — soul

netilas yadayim — the mitzvah of washing one's hands at specific times to purify oneself

niftar — to pass away

niggun (pl. *niggunim*) — songs of Jewish content and/or melody

nisyonos — trials in life

oheiv Yisrael (pl. *ohavei Yisrael*) — someone who loves Jews and Judaism

olah chadashah (pl. *olot chadashot*) — a new immigrant to Israel, feminine form

peyos — sidelocks

Pirkei Avos — Ethics of the Fathers, a tractate in Mishnah

Poskim — halachic authorities

potch — smack, hit

Rabbosai — a respectful way to address a crowd, equivalent to "Gentlemen"

Rachmana litzlan — may G-d save us

rav — rabbi

Ribono shel Olam — Master of the World; i.e., G-d

rosh kollel — the head or director of a kollel

Rosh Yeshivah — head of a yeshivah

ruchniyus — spiritual matters

sar hamashkim — chief butler (in ancient Egypt)

seder — a learning session

sefer (pl. *sefarim*) — book, usually referring to books of Torah content

seudah — a meal

seudah hamafsekes — the final meal eaten in the afternoon before a 24-hour fast begins

Shabbat shalom — a Shabbos greeting, spoken in Hebrew

Shacharis — the morning prayers

shadchan (fem. form: *shadchanit*) — a matchmaker

Shalom aleichem — "Peace unto you" — a standard greeting among Jews

Shalom Aleichem — hymn sung before the Friday-night meal

shamash — sexton of a shul

Shamayim — Heaven

shanah rishonah — the first year of a marriage

sheitel — wig

shep nachas — to gain spiritual pleasure

sheva berachos — festive meals honoring the bride and groom during the week after their wedding

shidduch (pl. *shidduchim*) — a match suggested as a possibility for marriage

shiur (pl. *shiurim*) — a Torah-study class or private lesson

shlita — contraction of *sheyichyeh le'orech yamim tovim amen* — a blessing to be granted a long and good life; generally, this blessing is said when mentioning the names of Torah scholars

shmuess (pl. *shmuessen*) — Torah lecture

shnorrer — colloquial term used for someone who collects funds for charity (usually derogatory)

shochet (pl. *shochatim*) — ritual slaughterer

shtender — a podium-like stand, used by both individuals and lecturers in Torah study

shtetl — town; village (Yiddish)

shtiebel (pl. *shtieblech*) — a small synagogue

shver — father-in-law (Yiddish)

sifrei kodesh — books of Torah literature

simchah (pl. *simchos*, *simchahs* or *semachos*) — happiness; also, a happy occasion, such as a *bris*, bar mitzvah, wedding, etc.

smichos — certificates of ordination (sing. *smichah*)

taharah — the process of cleaning and purifying a body to prepare it for burial

talmid (pl. *talmidim*) — student; disciple

talmid chacham (pl. *talmidei chachamim*) — a Torah scholar

taryag mitzvos — the 613 mitzvos of the Torah

tatte — father

tefillah (pl. *tefillos*) — prayer

tefillin shel rosh — tefillin worn on the head

Tehillim — Psalms

teshuvah — repenting one's sins; adopting a Torah-observant lifestyle after having lived a non-observant lifestyle

tza'ar — pain

tzedakah — charity

tzenius — modesty

tzidkus — righteousness

ve'anochi lo yadati — and I never knew

vidui — confession of sins

vort (pl. *vertlach*) — Torah thought

yahrtzeit — anniversary of a death

Yamim Nora'im — the High Holidays

ye'rei Shamayim — a person who possesses genuine fear of Heaven

Yerushalmi — adj.: characteristic of Jerusalem; noun: one who lives (or was born) in Jerusalem

yeshuah — salvation

yeshuas Hashem — G-d's salvation

yetzer hara — the evil inclination

Yid (pl. *Yidden*) — Jew

Yiddisheh — Jewish

Yiddishkeit — Judaism

yiras Shamayim — fear of Heaven

Yom Tov (pl. *Yamim Tovim*) — a Jewish holiday

yungerman — a *kollel* student

zechus — merit

zemiros — religious hymns sung during the Shabbos meals

z'man — a structured period of study, usually several months, in a yeshivah

zt"l — contraction of *zecher tzaddik livrachah*, meaning, "the righteous person's memory will be for a blessing"